THREE DAYS IN THE SHENANDOAH

C&C

CAMPAIGNS & COMMANDERS

GREGORY J. W. URWIN, SERIES EDITOR

THREE DAYS IN THE SHENANDOAH

STONEWALL JACKSON AT
FRONT ROYAL AND WINCHESTER

Gary Ecelbarger

University of Oklahoma Press : Norman

ALSO BY GARY ECELBARGER

"We Are In for It!": The First Battle of Kernstown, March 23, 1862
(Shippensburg, Pa., 1997)
Frederick W. Lander: The Great Natural American Soldier (Baton
Rouge, 2000)
Black Jack Logan: An Extraordinary Life in Peace and War (Guilford,
Conn., 2005)

Library of Congress Cataloging-in-Publication Data

Ecelbarger, Gary L., 1962–
    Three days in the Shenandoah : Stonewall Jackson at Front Royal
and Winchester / Gary Ecelbarger.
        p. cm. — (Campaigns and commanders ; v. 14)
    Includes bibliographical references and index.
    ISBN 978-0-8061-3886-2 (hardcover : alk. paper)
    1. Shenandoah Valley Campaign, 1862. 2. Jackson, Stonewall,
1824–1863—Military leadership. 3. Front Royal (Va.)—History,
Military—19th century. 4. Winchester (Va.)—History, Military—19th
century. I. Title.
E473.7.E28 2008
973.7'3092—dc22
2007032540

*Three Days in the Shenandoah: Stonewall Jackson at Front Royal
and Winchester* is Volume 14 in the Campaigns and Commanders
series.

1   2   3   4   5   6   7   8   9   10

TO BOB MAHER

Contents

Illustrations

Preface

Jedediah Hotchkiss was far from satisfied with what he was reading in his Staunton, Virginia, home during the spring of 1895. Earlier he had offered to review several chapters written by Col. G.F.R. Henderson, who was in the midst of writing his ambitious and enduring two-volume biography of Gen. Thomas J. "Stonewall" Jackson. Renowned as Jackson's former cartographer, Hotchkiss carefully read Chapter 8 of the British officer's manuscript, and on May 1, he typed out thirteen pages of comments and suggestions for Henderson to improve his work.[1]

A considerable portion of Hotchkiss's commentary rebutted Henderson's depiction of the pivotal days of the Shenandoah Valley Campaign of 1862. This portion of his manuscript focused on the near-continuous battling from Front Royal on May 23 through Winchester on May 25. With the thirty-third anniversary of these battles fast approaching, Hotchkiss bristled at Henderson's narrative—yet another instance, he thought, of fact being turned into fiction.

By 1895 several embroidered versions of this portion of the Valley Campaign had already appeared in print as magazine articles, chapters in memoirs, and in regimental histories. Hotchkiss was irritated to see their effect on Jackson's biographer. He chided Henderson for permitting the prose of novelist John Esten Cooke to influence his writing. "You have a little too much of Cooke's idealism," warned Hotchkiss, complaining that when he had relayed his campaign observations to Cooke, the novelist "dressed them up in his stories to suit himself." Hotchkiss saw far too much "Cooke" in Henderson's chapter. "I will not comment on your extract from Cooke—simply calling your attention again to the fact that he was a writer of fiction," typed Hotchkiss on the twelfth page of his commentary.[2]

Neither Confederate spy Belle Boyd's version of the action nor Maj. Gen. Richard Taylor's "take" escaped Hotchkiss's pointed criticism when he read their words in Henderson's chapter. "Don't make too much of the Belle Boyd story," he cautioned Henderson. But Hotchkiss appeared more concerned about the popularity of Taylor's sixteen-year-old book, *Destruction and Reconstruction*. When he read Henderson's reliance on Taylor's memoir for much of his description of the action at Front Royal, Hotchkiss corrected him. The former mapmaker was particularly perturbed over Taylor's insistence that Jackson was with him after the Front Royal battle, sitting silent and motionless at a campfire, where he supposedly remained throughout the night. "I am sure Jackson did not spend the night there," Hotchkiss retorted, explaining to Henderson that the general shared a rubber-lined blanket with him in a yard at the corner of the Cedarville crossroads during the night of May 23. Hotchkiss made sure that Henderson understood how unreliable Taylor was:

> You will have to take what Taylor says with a great deal of allowance. He wrote sometime after the war was over and has mixed up what he had read and what he had heard others tell with what he had seen and heard himself, and it is right difficult to distinguish his personal recollections from his imbibed ones. I don't think his statement about Jackson is correct; especially about his sitting for hours "with his eyes fixed on the fire." Under such circumstances he invariably fell asleep in a very short time.[3]

Hotchkiss's adherence to accuracy was admirable, particularly in the postwar era when apocryphal recollections rolled off the presses to influence the Civil War literature then being written. To Henderson's credit, he removed most of the anecdotes to which Hotchkiss objected. Unfortunately, most subsequent historians failed to heed Hotchkiss's savvy advice. Belle Boyd's and Richard Taylor's tall tales (complete with Jackson staring at Taylor's campfire) appear with alarming frequency in twentieth-century descriptions of the action.

Most important for a comprehensive and objective narrative and analysis of a battle and a campaign is a dedication to serve both sides of the fight. For the fourth week of May 1862 in the Shenandoah Valley, the Union perspective has been neither adequately nor accurately represented in Civil War historiography. The result is a lasting void in our understanding of the campaign. This is all the more unfortunate given the archival riches existing from the Northern force, most of which have remained untapped. The same criteria used for analysis of Confederate sources must be equally applied to the U.S. documentation. Unfortunately, the Union perspective has also been muddied by overreliance on suspect accounts. A particular case in point comes from the handling of the writings of George H. Gordon, the lieutenant colonel of the Second Massachusetts Infantry during May 1862 and by far the most prolific Union historian of the heart of the Valley Campaign, having contributed two lengthy books about his regiment. Gordon was a strident critic of Gen. Nathaniel P. Banks, the commander who led the army facing Stonewall Jackson throughout that May. Gordon's opinions of Banks have tainted not only his own perspective of the campaign but also every subsequent version that quotes his account.

A close inspection of Gordon's writings reveals a more disturbing discovery. Gordon insists that Banks was ill prepared and hesitated to evacuate Strasburg on May 24, disregarding the overwhelming evidence of the danger to the Union position. Gordon claimed to receive Banks's evacuation order "between ten and eleven o'clock in the morning" in a dispatch that Gordon retained and published in his books. Banks's order still exists in Gordon's papers, and although there is no specific time designated to it, Gordon carefully wrote below it: "May 24 received a few minutes after the one on following page announcing withdrawal of enemy." The order Gordon referred to on the following page of his papers—based on supporting documents in Banks's papers, the *Official Records*, and the National Archives—can be timed between 7:00 and 7:30 A.M. Thus, Gordon has effectively timed Banks's dispatch to withdraw no later than "a few minutes after" 7:30 A.M.—three hours earlier than he records in his histories of the campaign.[4]

This evidence leads to one of three conclusions: 1) it took three

hours for Gordon to receive this order even though he was within one
mile of Banks's headquarters; 2) Gordon was sloppy in his interpretation; or 3) Gordon deliberately changed the timing of Banks's decisive
order to place his commander in the worst possible light. Ample supporting evidence indicates subordinates of Banks received their dispatches in a timely manner, and that the entire army was marching
northward at 9:00 A.M. This leaves the third option as the strongest
possibility, thus tainting the accuracy of all subsequent accounts of
the campaign that freely cite Gordon as the source of their time line
for Union withdrawal from Strasburg.

The aforementioned Confederate and Union examples demonstrate that too many published histories, laced with hyperbole and
teetering toward fiction, have cloaked these memorable moments of
Jackson's escapades and Banks's downfall in the Valley in a shroud of
lore. Beneath these layers of legend lies a 145-year-old military mys-
tery, one that I believe can be solved by investigating a series of important questions incorporating what is known and accepted as his-
torically accurate about the late-May period of the Valley Campaign:

1.   What effects did the U.S. and Confederate War Departments have
      on the campaign, and vice versa?
2.   Knowing that Jackson's "foot cavalry" marched at dawn with his
      vanguard just ten miles south of Front Royal, why does the attack
      on the town begin so late in the day (after 2:00 P.M.)?
3.   How did the Union force at Front Royal, surprised and vastly out-
      numbered with two rivers behind them, escape across both Shen-
      andoah branches before Jackson's cavalry chased them down on
      May 23?
4.   Why did Jackson maneuver cautiously on the offensive against
      Maj. Gen. Nathaniel P. Banks on May 24 after having successfully
      planted his own overwhelming force on the Union commander's
      flank and rear the day previous?
5.   What was the tactical sequence of events that produced the Con-
      federate victory at Winchester on May 25, 1862?

The answers to these questions exist in both published and un-
published reports, diaries, and recollections. Important information
concealed from the Shenandoah Valley Campaign authors of yester-
year has recently surfaced to reveal a more comprehensive history
of the action than could have been compiled a century ago. These
sources not only narrate a version of this portion of the Valley Campaign that departs from the traditional lore that has spun from it; they

also mock many of the colorful anecdotes that have been retold as fact concerning the engagement.

The most plausible way to reveal this rich source material is to peel away the mythical shrouds that surround it. Doing so forces an entire reconsideration of the narrative and analytic history of the heart of the Shenandoah Valley Campaign of 1862—the May 23–25 portion of the campaign that had the greatest impact on Union and Confederate strategy both in and outside the Valley. This book attempts to do just that.

Acknowledgments

This book is the product of many who contributed their expertise, generosity, and time. Foremost to thank is my wife, Carolyn, who patiently endured the years it took to produce this book, including the necessary trips and prolonged writing sessions that often interrupted family activities.

I also drew huge benefits from my Shenandoah Valley "connections." Thanks are extended to Colonel Joseph Whitehorne of Front Royal for his impeccable knowledge of the War in the Valley and his trained eye for terrain. Sam Riggs proved to be a great asset for me and the historical community of Front Royal because of his dedication to the interpretation of the battle that transpired in his town. I also extend my appreciation to my Winchester friends—Ben Ritter, Rebecca Ebert, and Dr. David Powers—for providing valuable information on the battle of May 25, 1862. Bill Petersen, who lives between the two towns, spent several hours with me exploring Valley roads to test my research findings.

Historians with related interests have been especially generous. Bill Miller of Churchville provided important transcripts from the Hotchkiss collection. Robert K. Krick guided me through the collections held at Fredericksburg National Military Park. John Hennessey shared his trove of soldiers' letters published in newspapers. Robert

E. L. Krick in Richmond was particularly thoughtful in sending primary source material he discovered. Elliott Hoffman in Vermont aided me tremendously by mailing several sources from his collection. Don Pfanz of Fredericksburg not only mentored me about Richard Ewell, but also joined me on a great day up and down the banks of the Shenandoah looking for (and finding) old bridge sites. Dr. Joseph Harsh in Centreville allowed me to pick his brain about Union and Confederate strategy in 1862. Robert G. Tanner in Atlanta became a favorite e-mail sounding board. He offered his time and expertise to critique several chapters of this work.

Thanks are extended to Scott Patchan and Rod Gainer—both good friends and top-notch historians—who shared their company and knowledge with me on several research trips and field studies relating to this book.

I truly appreciate the efforts of everyone associated with the Campaigns and Commanders series at the University of Oklahoma Press. Special thanks to Dr. Gregory Urwin, Jay Dew, and Bob Fullilove for their contributions in editing and producing this work, and to Bill Nelson for contributing the maps. All have helped to make this book the best it could be.

THREE DAYS IN THE SHENANDOAH

Introduction

O n April 14, 1862—one year and one day after the United States
surrendered its Fort Sumter garrison to the Confederate States
of America—six leaders of the Confederate army met in Richmond to
discuss the conduct of the war. At 10:00 A.M. Confederate president
Jefferson Davis greeted his top military advisers and generals in his
executive office on the third floor in the Treasury Building. Maj. Gen.
Joseph Eggleston Johnston, commanding the Army of Northern Virginia, and two of his chief subordinates, Generals James Longstreet
and Gustavus Smith, arrived promptly as did George W. Randolph,
the third and newest secretary of war. Robert E. Lee, the commanding
general of Confederate forces "charged with the conduct of military
operations in the armies of the Confederacy," took his rightful place
in the meeting of top Confederate personnel. (Despite the month-old
responsibilities of General Orders No. 14 that would have Lee function essentially as the general in chief, Lee's actual duties appeared
more those of the president's chief military adviser.)[1]

The Union threat to Richmond precipitated the meeting. Maj.
Gen. George Brinton McClellan, the thirty-five-year-old commander
of the Army of the Potomac—the largest army in the Western Hemi-
sphere at one hundred ten thousand—had transported that Union
force to the tip of the Yorktown Peninsula at Fort Monroe and had

begun to advance within fifty miles of the Confederate capital. Stymied at Yorktown, McClellan had laid siege to an entrenched Confederate line constructed between the seven miles separating the York
and James Rivers. General Johnston inspected the Southern fortifications and believed they were not constructed properly. He also agonized over his flanks, which he considered to be vulnerable to Union
naval attacks. That McClellan outnumbered him nearly two to one
also could not escape his thoughts.[2]

Johnston had met with President Davis earlier on April 14 and
informed him that the Yorktown line could not be held. Johnston
questioned the feasibility of protecting Richmond with the entire
available army. Davis listened with heightened interest at Johnston's
idea to draw McClellan inward toward Richmond and away from his
supply base at Fort Monroe. A Mexican-American War veteran and
former secretary of war in the Franklin Pierce administration, Davis
was well fitted for his role as commander in chief of the Confederate
armies, but he faced increasingly dire circumstances in the early
spring season of 1862. He had 400,000 men mobilized in all theaters
compared to 637,000 for the Union. His western theater was substan-
tially weakened after the Army of the Mississippi lost 10,700 men at
the Battle of Shiloh on April 6–7. The vital railroad junction at Corinth was threatened as well as the valuable port of New Orleans.
South of Richmond fared no better with the loss of Roanoke Island
and New Bern in February and March. Maj. Gen. Ambrose Burnside's
Federal army had been menacing North Carolina since then and
could soon threaten Richmond from the south. With McClellan's
offensive now added to this unsavory mix, Davis was considerably
weighed down; Johnston's proposal for removing a major threat therefore warranted a discussion among other capable and respected military minds.[3]

These circumstances yielded a fourteen-hour conference, one
that began with an audacious proposal from a normally conservative
army commander. General Johnston argued to abandon the Yorktown
Peninsula, leave a garrison force to protect Richmond, then take the
bulk of the available Confederate troops and launch an offensive
against Baltimore and Washington. If successful, the Confederate
army could then penetrate deep into the North and attack Philadelphia and New York. Supported by General Smith in this presentation (Smith wrote a memorandum outlining this northern thrust),

Johnston maintained that McClellan would chase after him, thus relieving the threat to Richmond. A second option, argued Johnston, was to conduct an offensive against McClellan by luring his army closer to Richmond and away from his supply base. Again this option required a concentration of Confederate forces from other states to the capital to initiate this offensive thrust.[4]

It was an eye-opening proposition, and it was vehemently opposed by Secretary Randolph (a naval officer who naturally abhorred evacuating the Norfolk naval yard) and General Lee. Without a field command since 1861, the fifty-five-year-old Lee's major role of presidential military adviser did not go unappreciated by Davis. The president valued Lee's opinions more than anyone present at the meeting. Lee presented his case. He maintained that the Southern army could defeat McClellan on the Yorktown Peninsula, contrary to Johnston's pessimistic claim. Furthermore, Lee believed the Confederate navy and artillery could adequately cover Johnston's flanks. Lee also openly questioned the soundness of Johnston and Smith's strategy of stripping forces from South Carolina and Georgia to embark on the invasion of the North, or to concentrate them at Richmond for an attack against McClellan, for it risked the loss of Charleston and Savannah.

The conference broke for an hour at 6:00 P.M. for dinner, and then the participants reconvened at the executive mansion and instantly picked up where they had left off. Davis's fostering of a free-speaking atmosphere produced lengthy discussions that periodically escalated to heated and contentious debates between disagreeing members of his counsel.[5] As the conversations continued, Davis—in his characteristic style—mostly listened and barely spoke. Sometime during the night, however, he did make an important suggestion, one that he believed could relieve the strain on the beleaguered capital. Davis invoked the name of a commander who had yet to figure in the conference discussion: Maj. Gen. Thomas J. Jackson.

"Stonewall" Jackson had commanded an independent division in the Shenandoah Valley for nearly six months. He earned the command, as well as his catchy *nom de guerre*, for his stellar performance on Henry Hill at the Battle of Bull Run (Manassas) the previous July. Known for his experience, determination, and leadership ability under fire, Jackson had carried much promise when he left from under Johnston's wing at Manassas and based himself at Winchester in

November to head the Valley District in the Department of Northern Virginia.

But Jackson had not been impressive in his half-year tenure as an independent commander. He had suffered through a miserable 1862. He began the year with nearly ten thousand soldiers under his command, but illness, desertions, reassignments, and battle losses diminished his strength to fewer than three thousand by the last week of March. Stonewall's performance in those three months became legendary more for his litigiousness than for his military prowess. He burdened the Confederate War Department with three courts-martial against subordinates (two were immediately dropped), and he had even resigned from the army temporarily in anger.

Forced out of Winchester by overwhelming numbers early in March, Jackson had pulled back deep into the Valley and created a forty-mile cushion between his dwindling army and his opponent. As Jackson's superior officer, General Johnston had prodded Stonewall to close the gap to prevent the U.S. soldiers guarding Winchester from reinforcing the Army of the Potomac as it headed up the Yorktown Peninsula. Johnston had envisioned Jackson as an important decoy, but he believed that Stonewall's division was too understrength to perform offensive operations. On March 19 Johnston had ordered Jackson to head back toward Winchester to prevent the Union force from dividing there "by keeping as near as prudence will permit."[6]

Jackson proved to be more overzealous than obedient. Believing he outnumbered his opponent when he reached the outskirts of Winchester on March 23, Jackson had deployed half of his available artillery and hurled his nine regiments against a Union force that countered him with thirteen larger regiments. The result went down in the books as the Battle of Kernstown, a fiasco for Jackson that stripped away 22 percent more of his force and added two more of his cannons to the Union arsenal (four total artillery pieces since January). A strong rearguard performance and stifling darkness prevented Jackson from suffering more significant losses. Jackson had been licking his wounds since the battle—too weak in numbers to conduct any offensive operations.[7]

That Jackson had jeopardized Johnston's mission by risking his army in a poorly conducted battle—the exact outcome Johnston had advised against—would normally be met with a severe reprimand.[8] But no rebuke was forthcoming—far from it, in fact. Due to poor intelligence gathering by Union commanders after the battle and exaggerated concern by the U.S. War Department, Jackson's impetuous attack at Kernstown reaped an unplanned reward for Richmond. Believing that the Southerners had an eleven-thousand-man army in the Valley, Abraham Lincoln authorized a change in Union troop dispersal by increasing the protection of Washington and tripling the size of the Union force occupying the Shenandoah corridor. This was accomplished by stripping McClellan's army of twenty thousand soldiers who had originally been earmarked to join him on his Richmond campaign. Lincoln's overreaction awarded the Confederate War Department valuable time to protect the Southern capital. This strategic gain, achieved by happenstance, spared Jackson from virtually any criticism for his reckless action on the Confederate left flank in the Virginia theater.[9]

Although yet to realize his potential, Jackson impressed Jefferson Davis by his presence and its effects on the opposition. Let Jackson conduct an offensive, Davis proposed to his counsel, and the beneficial Kernstown aftermath could be repeated. This would give Johnston's army a better chance to defend Richmond. One of Davis's lieutenants reminded him that Jackson was vastly outnumbered and could be forced farther up the Valley. Although General Johnston that very night was lobbying for a rapid northern thrust, he did not wish Jackson to conduct it independently, instead preferring his Valley army to come to Richmond to take part in a grand offensive as part of his army. Johnston, therefore, would have objected to Davis's idea, although his conversation on the matter was never revealed.

Even those not supporting Johnston's plan appeared to agree that Jackson did not have the numbers necessary for Davis's alternative plan. Ironically, this included General Lee, who less than four weeks before the conference had suggested—without specifying Jackson as the mode—such a plan to Johnston: "Can you by a rapid forward movement threaten Washington and thus recall the enemy?" That March 20 query so mimicked Davis's philosophy as to suggest that the president, and not Lee, had brainstormed the idea, and Lee merely relayed it to Johnston. Although Jackson's rapid movement to Kernstown over the subsequent three days was a response to Johnston's order (sent to Jackson one day before Lee delivered the query to Johnston), the limited and temporary benefit of his March 23 attack at Kernstown dovetailed well with the hopeful intent of the suggestion

—"and thus recall the enemy." Noteworthy in Lee's transmitted question is the omission of the word "attack"; thus, Lee and Johnston (and perhaps Davis) were in agreement that the movement in itself would produce beneficial results for the hard-pressed Confederacy, the difference between their expectations being that Johnston expected only to hold troops in the Valley while Lee clearly expected much more.[10]

Although he supported the idea of a rapid northern movement in March, Lee appears to have changed his mind one month later. No one in attendance that night voiced support for Davis's plan for Jackson in the Valley; the prevailing opinion coming out of the meeting was that an offensive by Jackson was regarded as impossible.[11] Davis did not press the issue, and the meeting ended in the early hours of April 15 with Davis siding with General Lee to disallow General Johnston his request to undertake an offensive. On the contrary, Johnston's Yorktown defense would be strengthened to resist General McClellan's advance.

As for Stonewall Jackson in the Shenandoah Valley, neither he nor Maj. Gen. Richard S. Ewell—a peer who commanded a large division of eighty-five hundred soldiers that tarried on the eastern side of the Blue Ridge near Gordonsville—would be ordered to the defenses of Richmond.[12] Jefferson Davis was satisfied to maintain the status quo with the forces in and near the Shenandoah Valley, but he would never forget that in mid-April he suggested and wanted more for Jackson to do than to hold Union soldiers within the mountainous corridor.

Two days after the conclusion of the conference, the concern about troop disparity in the Shenandoah Valley proved legitimate. Overwhelmed by a growing Union offensive against him, General Jackson retreated from his two-week defensive line at Rude's Hill and established a new position for his army forty miles west at Conrad's Store, at the southern entrance to the Luray Valley, a mountain corridor bordered by saw-toothed Massanutten Mountain on the west and by the Blue Ridge looming on the east. Jackson chose the locale not only to protect his men from attack but also to draw them closer to General Ewell and his large division. Swift Run Gap opened the gate to link the two forces, a desire Jackson had harbored for two weeks.[13]

"If Banks is defeated it may greatly retard McClellan's movements." Jackson had authored this contribution to grand strategy back on April 5, ten days before Jefferson Davis appeared to introduce it at the overnight conference in Richmond. But Jackson had further separated himself from Banks, realizing that his division—perhaps six thousand soldiers in all—was no competition for an opponent who enjoyed nearly four times those numbers. Once he was granted approval in Richmond, Jackson planned to bring Ewell into the Valley. Jackson felt confident and comfortable that a united force approaching fifteen thousand could conduct an offensive operation against Union general Nathaniel P. Banks.[14]

Jackson was faced with a more immediate problem, one he decided to confront during the last week of April. Brig. Gen. Edward "Allegheny" Johnson visited Jackson's headquarters at Conrad's Store to apprise him of the threat to his and Jackson's district. Earning his nickname for his staunch defense in the Alleghenies the previous December, General Johnson grew concerned that his twenty-five hundred men present for duty in the Army of the Northwest were at risk for defeat by General John C. Frémont's advancing troops. Johnson's six regiments and two batteries were an army in name only; their only salvation from annihilation was a rapid infusion of troops at least equal in number to their own.[15]

Stonewall Jackson agreed, for he was also concerned about a potential linkage between Banks and Frémont that would produce a forty-thousand-man force. After conferring with General Ewell on April 29, Jackson headed his division southward on the Port Republic Road the following day, including seven hundred soldiers from the Tenth Virginia of Ewell's division, now infused into Jackson's third brigade. Ewell's division immediately filled the void left by Jackson's evacuation. Realizing that staying to the weather-gutted road would be too impractical for transferring his infantry and artillery, and left his supply train vulnerable to attacks from Banks's cavalry, Jackson quickly diverted his men through Brown's Gap and led them to Mechum's River Station on the railroad. Jackson's division at this time was as large as Ewell's, a force exceeding eight thousand men.[16]

He headed westward from there, stopping at Staunton for two days before continuing into the Alleghenies for a showdown with Union forces on a hill overlooking the mountain hamlet called McDowell. Before he departed Staunton to support Allegheny Johnson, Jackson wrote a letter to his favorite sounding board, Alexander R.

Boteler, a representative in the Confederate congress whose son—along with the son of Robert E. Lee—served in Jackson's artillery. In the letter, Jackson protested against the War Department's commissioning brigadier generals from colonels who had served in his brigades, in disregard of his admonitions against the political promotions. Considering these officers to hinder rather than help his operation, Jackson postured, "I wish that if such appointments are continued, that the President would come to the field and command them, and not throw the responsibility on me of defending the District when he throws such obstacles in my way."

Although his command was currently limited to a division, Jackson felt no qualms about airing his views about grand strategy. After informing Boteler about his confidence in General Lee and his satisfaction in Lee's efforts to strengthen him in the Valley, Jackson wrote, "I would like to see adopted the policy of abandoning for the moment one section of the country, in order to concentrate forces and sweep the enemy from another, and then return and crush him in the locality which had been abandoned, and thus keep our troops continually employed in successful work." He closed the issue by admitting, "But Genl. Lee sees things from a higher stand point than I do. I know but little comparatively outside my district."[17]

Those revealing insights spoke volumes about Jackson's military philosophy. He placed a premium on active campaigning, well attuned to how stagnancy can hurt an army in the field. Jackson also yearned for "successful work," a concept he had not experienced since the victory on the plains of Manassas nine months before. He also frankly admitted that the restrictions of his command responsibility prevented him from understanding the full theater of operations in Virginia; therefore, he knew he could not feasibly author grand strategy. Most importantly, Jackson believed in risk taking—abandoning one contested region to reinforce another with a hopeful return of a reinforced army to the original region. This is the wish he revealed to Boteler, a desire to have troops outside the Valley sent to him to sweep away the Union threat. With no promise of this from either Lee or Johnston, Jackson decided to materialize the idea within his own district. As April turned to May, he was abandoning the Shenandoah Valley, "to concentrate forces [with Allegheny Johnson] and sweep the enemy from another, and then return [to the Valley] and crush him in the locality which had been abandoned."

The Confederate maneuvers in the Valley did not go undetected by the Union. Within days of Jackson leading his division southward from Conrad's Store, General Banks learned that he was gone and that General Ewell's troops had slid into the Luray Valley. Banks's command had recently been reorganized as the Department of the Shenandoah, having transferred from their original designation as the Fifth Corps of the Army of the Potomac. In addition to a large cavalry force of thirty-five hundred horse soldiers and fifty-six cannons manned by more than one thousand artillerists, General Banks possessed two infantry divisions within his department. No two bodies of infantry could be more different. The First Division, Banks's original command dating back to the summer of 1861, was led by Brig. Gen. Alpheus S. Williams. In April 1862 its sixty-three hundred men were foot soldiers in name only—all marching and little fighting experience. The Second Division of the corps was the experienced one. Commanded by Brig. Gen. James Shields, the three brigades of this division consisted of veterans from the 1861 summer and autumn campaigns in western Virginia as well as the active campaign against Jackson's army during the winter months of 1861–62. General Shields's division had most recently defeated Jackson at Kernstown. By the early spring of 1862, they still carried the distinction of having marched and fought more than any other division of the Army of the Potomac.[18]

Much friction existed between General Williams's and General Shields's troops. Notwithstanding the differences between the two divisions, by their numbers alone they represented a formidable presence in the Valley. At the end of April, Banks's corps tallied twenty-two thousand officers and men present for duty, but Banks was frustrated at the lack of significant duty to be performed by this force, which was larger than all but three Confederate armies in America. Having pulled back to New Market after advancing as far south in the Valley as Harrisonburg, Banks was convinced from his intelligence sources that Jackson was either out of the Valley or about to evacuate it, ostensibly heading for Richmond to reinforce General Johnston's army on the Yorktown Peninsula. On April 30 Banks wired the U.S. War Department, concluding his succinct assessment of operations: "There is nothing more to be done by us in the valley."[19]

All the dispatches from the Department of the Shenandoah traveled northward from New Market to Harpers Ferry, where they were retransmitted eastward to Washington. On May 1 Salmon P. Chase, the secretary of the Treasury in President Abraham Lincoln's cabinet, stepped past the columned entrance way and entered the modest brick building housing the U.S. War Department. He entered the telegraph office and read the recently received telegrams. "Banks thinks his work done in Shenandoah Valley and wishes to advance," observed Chase after reading the dispatches, believing from one that Jackson was heading eastward with five thousand to ten thousand men. Naively accepting everything transmitted as factual, Chase still correctly surmised that no more than sixty thousand troops opposed McClellan at Yorktown, and a paltry rebel force stood between Maj. Gen. Irvin McDowell's Department of the Rappahannock, an army of twenty thousand soldiers and fifty cannons encamped north of its namesake river halfway between Washington and Richmond. "Strange that McClellan dallies & waits in eternal preparation," Chase scrawled in his journal; "Strange that the President does not give McDowell all the disposable force in the region & send him on to Richmond."[20]

That very day President Lincoln clarified what Secretary Chase considered "strange." Although his military experience had been limited to a brief stint as a captain of Illinois volunteers during the Black Hawk War thirty years before, Lincoln took it upon himself to be an active and involved commander in chief. His secretary of war, just three months into the job, was Edwin Stanton, formerly a renowned attorney. Together Lincoln and Stanton discussed strategy options, particularly concerning troop allocation. Lincoln had approximately 640,000 Union soldiers in all theaters in April 1862. By the end of the month, top military minds could see the Union advantages across all theaters. "The capture of N. Orleans & the impending victories at Corinth & Yorktown—preceded by the innumerable success [sic] on the sea-coast & the western waters . . . —point to the inevitable & early suppression of the great American rebellion," concluded Bvt. Lt. Gen. Winfield Scott in a letter handed to Lincoln on April 30. General Scott, an American military icon, went on to suggest a schedule for granting amnesty to the rebels who lay down their arms. Lincoln and his cabinet knew how premature General Scott's suggestions were. Secretary of State William Seward told Lincoln he answered Scott by claiming "the iron does not seem heated enough yet. We shall see a glow and hear some sparkles soon."[21]

Lincoln did not observe any indication of a glow emanating from

Maj. Gen. George B. McClellan's huge Army of the Potomac on the Yorktown Peninsula. McClellan had barely budged from his position near Yorktown. The army had advanced a mere twenty miles in six weeks with a yawning gap of nearly sixty miles between it and Richmond. Lincoln groaned at signs of further stagnancy on the Peninsula. Reading McClellan's late-April request for the large cannons—Parrotts capable of hurling thirty-pound rounds—that lined the trenches around Washington, Lincoln could hardly control his frustration. "Your call for Parrott guns from Washington alarms me—chiefly because it argues indefinite procrastination," telegraphed Lincoln to McClellan on May 1. "Is anything to be done?"[22]

The president decided to do whatever possible to prod McClellan to action. Like Secretary Chase, Lincoln read General Banks's dispatches to the War Department suggesting a new mission for his troops. In a separate telegram, General Banks advocated leaving five thousand troops in the Valley, advising the town of Strasburg as the preferred site over Winchester in the north or Harrisonburg in the south as the locale where those Union soldiers would be less subject to threats. Taking Banks's suggestions to heart, Lincoln decided to reallocate his forces in a manner that would appease McClellan. "The President has directed the transfer of General Shields, with his division, to your department," Secretary Stanton wired Maj. Gen. Irvin McDowell on May 1. Informing Banks of the same, Stanton ordered Banks to pull back from New Market to Strasburg.[23]

Once McDowell was reinforced by Shields's division and other scattered forces, he could boast an army exceeding thirty-five thousand soldiers and eighty-six cannons. McDowell's eventual destination would be Richmond. General McClellan's ranks would swell to one hundred fifty thousand men with the addition of McDowell's army. The three-to-one disparity in infantry and overwhelming firepower in artillery would place McClellan at a decided advantage, regardless of the defensive position chosen by the Confederates at Richmond.

Lincoln's decision should have eliminated McClellan's constant calls for troops and created the "sparkles" suggested by Seward to General Scott. The only one objecting to the May Day orders was the commander who originated the plan—General Banks. "I shall grieve not to be included in the active operations of this summer," he admitted to Stanton. Never expecting to be the one forced to remain in the

Valley, Banks learned shortly after receiving his instructions how vulnerable the holding force at Strasburg would become. Even before pulling his force back to Strasburg, Banks learned that Jackson had not headed to Richmond. This left Banks to fret that Jackson and Ewell together doubled what he had available after Shields departed.[24]

On May 15 Shields headed eastward out of the Valley, leaving Williams's forty-five-hundred-man division, two brigades of eight regiments, and nearly fifteen hundred cavalrymen under Banks's jurisdiction at Strasburg and along the Manassas Gap Railroad that struck the town from the east. Not one of the remaining Union soldiers appears to have taken note of a very sobering fact: they were the most inexperienced veterans in the war. Under arms for more than a year, they had marched and drilled; some of them had seen some brief skirmishes. But not one company of them had ever fired a gun in a Civil War battle.

The cascade of orders, troop movements, and events could be traced back to one sentence: "There is nothing more to be done by us in the valley." Three weeks after transmitting that assessment to the War Department, Nathaniel Banks well understood that he was a target; ironically, his force would have much to do in the Valley and would be the focus of a series of events that would send shockwaves emanating from the Shenandoah Valley to both U.S. and Confederate War Departments. With those twelve words, Maj. Gen. Nathaniel P. Banks authored his own ruin.

1

"CREATING A STIR"

S ince the beginning of the war, Jefferson Davis and Robert E. Lee
were never as concerned over the survival of the Confederacy as
they were on Thursday, May 22, 1862. Five weeks had passed since
President Davis had decided that the peninsula was defensible at
Yorktown, concurring with the adamancy of General Lee and countering the insistence of Gen. Joseph E. Johnston. The conference that
generated that decision had been based on a threat posed by McClellan's Army of the Potomac, sixty miles from the Confederate capital.
Now, one month and one week later, the enemy army was at the
doorstep of Richmond.

The closest major body of water protecting Richmond from Mc-
Clellan's advance was the Chickahominy River, the moat that flowed
southeastward, cutting across the Yorktown Peninsula at points ten
miles northeast of Richmond at Mechanicsville and gradually spread-
ing its distance as it worked its way toward the James River, outlining
the southern boundary of the Peninsula. Three days earlier, McClellan crossed thousands of troops at Bottom Bridge and was attempting
a crossing farther up the river near Mechanicsville. All of this had
been made possible by U.S. naval control of the James River. After the
Confederates withdrew from the Yorktown line and abandoned the
Norfolk naval yard early in the month (and destroyed its formidable

ironclad, the *CSS Virginia*), Union war ships advanced to Drewry's
Bluff, six miles south of Richmond. Johnston's fifty-three thousand
soldiers stretched across the peninsula twenty miles from Richmond.
With his left flank severely threatened, General Johnston decided to
retreat from his second defensive line across the Chickahominy to
the eastern suburbs of Richmond.[1]

With little opposition to the enemy at the Chickahominy, the
citizenry of Richmond had grown uneasy, Jefferson Davis included.
He sent his wife southward to safety, and prepared for the inevitable
battle that must be fought to save Richmond from Union capture.
The entire eastern arc of Richmond was threatened, from Drewry's
Bluff south of the capital to the hamlet of Mechanicsville, five miles
northeast.

President Davis and General Lee rode out to the latter on Thursday on the Mechanicsville Road. Reports of up to twenty thousand
Union soldiers across the river there had yet to be confirmed. Lee and
Davis arrived there in the afternoon, where they witnessed an artillery exchange. Davis was troubled not only at the light resistance
offered by Confederates on the eastern bank of the Chickahominy but
also by the ignorance of the defense as to who was in charge and what
plan was in effect. "My conclusion was," wrote Davis upon returning
to Richmond, "that if, as reported to be probable, [Union] General
[William B.] Franklin, with a division, was in that vicinity he might
easily have advanced over the turnpike toward if not to Richmond."[2]

Finally, Generals Johnston and Lee agreed that the Confederate
army needed to formulate an attack rather than be dictated to by an
attack from McClellan. They both understood that the attack must
occur soon, for even if McClellan continued to crawl as he had demonstrated over the past two months, the threat to Richmond extended beyond the Army of the Potomac and beyond Johnston's left
flank. Since May 8 Robert E. Lee had been concerned that General
McDowell was destined to be reinforced, posing a source of extra
pressure coming from the Rappahannock River fifty miles north of
Richmond. Over the next two weeks Lee learned that the source of
reinforcement would come from the Shenandoah Valley. By mid-
May, Lee had been informed that General Shields's division was heading down the Luray Valley to Front Royal, and that Banks had taken
the remainder of the Union's Valley army back to Strasburg. Since
both towns rested twelve miles apart on the Manassas Gap Railroad,

the obvious conclusion formulated by General Lee was that Banks would transport his army by rail to Alexandria. From there Lee believed Banks would reinforce McClellan either directly by water transport to the peninsula or indirectly by linking with McDowell's army, strengthening it on the right bank of the Rappahannock, and allowing it to cross the river and head southward to Richmond.[3]

Confederate War Department strategy had focused on one major goal: to prevent reinforcements from swelling McClellan's ranks, in order to allow General Johnston to have a fighting chance to beat the Army of the Potomac east of Richmond. One option to prevent McDowell from reinforcing McClellan was to strengthen the resistance on the opposite bank of the Rappahannock. Because Lee (and by extension, Davis) had hedged his bets that Banks would bypass McDowell at Falmouth and directly support McClellan by steamer transport down the Chesapeake Bay, Lee moved to negate the advantage of strengthening the defense at Fredericksburg and looked to wipe away McClellan's potential reinforcements from their source—the Shenandoah Valley.

Back in the mid-April overnight conference Jefferson Davis first suggested using Stonewall Jackson as an offensive weapon to thwart the Union strategy of reinforcement on the Yorktown Peninsula, and in doing so, to accomplish Confederate strategy. By the middle of May, Robert E. Lee had deemed Jackson strong enough to conduct an offensive. Jackson had reached Allegheny Johnson in time to achieve a rare feat for the Confederacy in the spring of 1862—a battle victory. Jackson won the Battle of McDowell on May 8 despite suffering nearly twice as many losses on the defensive than did Frémont's attacking brigades—commanded by Brig. Gen. Robert H. Milroy and Robert Schenck—attacking the Confederate defense on Sitlington's Hill.

Lee was pleased to learn that the immediate threat from Frémont was quelled as Jackson pushed him all the way down to Franklin, eliminating his ability to link with Banks. In the process Jackson absorbed the six regiments and batteries from the Army of the Northwest into his division (General Johnson was wounded in the battle and would not participate). He returned to the western edge of the Valley on May 17, prepared to attack Banks once he received orders from Richmond.[4]

General Lee had involved himself with Jackson's progress, frequently wiring dispatches from Richmond to Staunton, where they were carried by a courier to Jackson. Shortly before Jackson fought at McDowell, Lee received Jackson's strength report and must have been encouraged at the numbers on paper, for Jackson reported more than eight thousand infantry in his three brigades. Ewell had reported the same for his command three weeks earlier, so Lee determined that these divisions, plus the troops from the Army of the Northwest, bolstered Confederate strength in the Valley past eighteen thousand men, with battle losses factored into the calculation.[5]

Jackson's numbers convinced Lee that he could conduct an offensive operation in the Valley. Perhaps dictating the order from Jefferson Davis, Lee sent Jackson a dispatch on May 16, expressing the desire that he strike Banks in an attempt to keep him from leaving the Valley to support McClellan's occupation of the Peninsula. The Confederate War Department also approved of Jackson uniting with Dick Ewell to accomplish this goal. The notion was that Ewell and Jackson were necessary to operate together in the Valley, although Lee had warned Jackson, "But you will not . . . lose sight of the fact that it may become necessary for you to come to the support of General Johnston."[6]

General Johnston was not on the same page as General Lee on where the Confederate forces in and near the Valley should best serve. Since April, it can be assumed that Johnston wanted Jackson and Ewell to reinforce his army on the Peninsula. This assumption is based on the stated desire to bring up forces from South Carolina and Georgia to initiate an offensive. Within days of Lee telegraphing his mission to Jackson, Johnston wrote dispatches ordering Ewell and Gen. Lawrence O'Bryan Branch (heading a brigade of North Carolinians east of the Blue Ridge) to come to his aid at Richmond. For reasons never made clear, Johnston chose not to transmit his messages into the Valley by telegraphing them to Staunton; instead, he sent the dispatches by courier on horseback. This necessarily delayed delivery by two to three days a message that could have been received within hours of deciphering it at the telegraph office in Staunton. On May 18, perhaps after meeting with General Lee and President Davis, Johnston reversed his orders for General Ewell, allowing him to remain in the Valley, while General Branch would continue on to Richmond.[7]

Thus, while elements of McClellan's army approached within eight miles of Richmond from three directions on May 22, Jefferson

Davis, Robert E. Lee, and Joseph E. Johnston all planned to meet the direct threat from McClellan's army, while at the same time hoping that Jackson, with Ewell, could accomplish by planned strategy a similar outcome to that achieved two months earlier by his attack at Kernstown without planning—that is, to prevent Union forces in the Shenandoah Valley from leaving the Valley and to hold in place other Union troops earmarked for concentration at Richmond. All three Confederate giants shared the mind-set—that time was not on their side.

At Strasburg, General Banks felt the same way about his situation on May 22, 1862. Banks had come to the conclusion on that Thursday that his army would soon be assaulted. He had been well aware that Jackson had returned to the upper (southern) Valley after defeating Schenck and Milroy at the Battle of McDowell. He was warned by Frémont of Jackson's postbattle movements. Confederate prisoners, including infantry, brought in from both Jackson's and Ewell's commands further developed the strength and location of their divisions. Admitting his anxiety over Jackson's return, Banks expressed his views in a dispatch he wrote at the same time that General Lee and President Davis fretted over the vulnerability of Richmond. "From all the information I can gather," declared Banks, "I am compelled to believe that he meditates attack here."[8]

As the third-ranking officer of all the Union volunteer forces in the war, forty-six-year-old Nathaniel Prentiss Banks could attribute his appointment to one factor—his political influence. As a three-term Massachusetts governor and former speaker of the house, Banks held moderate political views that endeared him throughout New England, and that convinced him to seek the Republican presidential nomination in 1860. In 1861 he was passed over as secretary of the navy, a position Lincoln initially favored him for shortly after being elected. The president commissioned him a major general and provided him a large division, in order to place the former Democrat on a high tier and thus recruit his constituents and rally Democrats and moderates to support the war effort of the Republican administration. That Banks had no military experience did not dissuade Lincoln in his decision to place him in such a high military position, one that led to a corps, and subsequently a department, command in the Shenandoah Valley.[9]

Although his military experience was lacking, Banks did not ill fit his uniform. Physically, his presence was not commanding, for he was neither tall nor muscular; nevertheless; Banks's mien appealed to those who saw him for the first time. One observer declared, "He is by all odds the most impressive man, in countenance, language and demeanor, whom I have seen since the war commenced." Near Edinburg in the heart of the Valley, where Banks had participated in divine services in April, an observant staff officer studied the way the citizenry took in the general: "Immediately beside him stood a boy about twelve years old, ragged and snub-nosed, in the most independent and critical attitude, devouring the General with his eyes, measuring him from top to toe, probably guessing how long it would take him to grow into a major general. The scene was American."[10]

He was liked by the rank and file of his command, although no one considered him a top military commander. Brig. Gen. John P. Hatch readily contrasted Banks with a general he disliked. "Genl. Shields is a humbug of the first water," claimed Hatch, while "Genl. Banks although no great general is a good man and nice gentleman. It is unfortunate that he has not more educated military men on his staff." Alpheus Williams found Banks a hard nut to crack. "He is not very communicative, even to those near him in command," Williams wrote his daughter, "and although always pleasant and courteous, he cannot be said to be a companionable person."[11]

The greatest dissent against Banks came from the Second Massachusetts Infantry. Although recruited from Banks's home state, they felt no allegiance to their fellow Bay State commander. They blamed Banks for their stagnancy, and could not hold their frustration within their ranks. "To give Banks so small a force shows the estimation in which he is held," complained Capt. Edward G. Abbott, "Now while we are sitting here quietly at our ease other Mass. Men are fighting, doing what we should do. . . . We are no better than a home guard—When this war is over other regiments will laugh and sneer at us—Oh you were in Gen. Banks army."[12]

With the departure of Shields's division from the Valley six days earlier, Banks's "army" had been reduced to a division. It was his favorite division, for he had led these troops prior to his ascent to command the Fifth Corps of the Army of the Potomac, and subsequently to head the Department of the Shenandoah. The division, under Brig. Gen. Alpheus Williams, had been reduced to two infantry brigades after a third one had been transferred to Irvin McDowell's army at the end of March. The eight remaining infantry regiments hailed from Maryland, New York, Connecticut, Pennsylvania, Massachusetts, Wisconsin, and Indiana.

The spirit of Banks's army broke in the face of the May Day orders. "I have never been so low in faith and hopelessness as I am . . . in thinking over the conduct of the war and the management of public affairs," lamented David Hunter Strother, Banks's topographical engineer. New York native John S. Clark, another staffer, concurred. "It seems the wiseacres of Washington are standing trembling in their boots for fear Sesech will roll an overwhelming army on Washington and capture the President," he complained to his wife.[13]

Maj. Delevan D. Perkins also agonized tremendously over leaving New Market. The New York native served as Banks's chief of staff. He was one of several of Banks's aides who had assisted Col. Nathan Kimball during the battle of Kernstown in March, and his next major encounter occurred at New Market a little more than one month later. There Major Perkins had fallen in love. Her name was Annie. She was a captivating twenty-two-year-old cousin of Mrs. Mose, a farmer's wife forced to manage the three-hundred-acre homestead while her husband and sons served in the Confederate army. Annie happened to be visiting Mrs. Mose when Banks chose the house as headquarters. Within five days, she and Major Perkins began a speaking relationship that progressed to pleasant walks together. The orders to change base killed their relationship. The couple was reduced to tears when they parted company, never to meet again. "Major Perkins has had a desperate encounter," explained another staff officer to his wife, "and came off second best."[14]

The disappointment at the retrograde movement and frustration of inactivity was not isolated to the headquarters staff. Brig. Gen. Alpheus S. Williams, the division commander whose troops were to pull back to Strasburg, summarized the sentiment within the ranks: "[I]f the amount of swearing that has been done in this department is recorded against us in Heaven I fear that we have an account that can never be settled." Frustrated and depressed over the conduct of operations, General Williams described the miserable conditions to his daughter and vented, "I am getting terribly disgusted and feel greatly like resigning." A regimental officer was equally disappointed. "With that pitiful force to which Banks's 'army corps' is now reduced, and at that point fifty miles back of our recent advance, we have no other hope or purpose than protecting Maryland!" He sarcastically and rhetorically declared, "A proud sequel, is it not?"[15]

Adding to the misery of the Union soldiers was the reaction by many Virginian civilians to their occupation of the Shenandoah Valley. "Oh! how the people here do hate the Yankees!" admitted Col. John S. Clark to his family. Corporal John Anderson of the Second Massachusetts confessed in May that his outlook was affected by the citizens:[16]

> We are hearing glorious news from our army everywhere and I hope the war will be at an end soon—but I sometimes think that we are destined to disappointment in settling this trouble soon for I tell you what it is, the south hate us. They look upon us as invaders and will treat us accordingly, that is, will fight us as long as there is a particle of sight for them. Even the women of this lovely valley express their hatred of us in more ways than one, by words and actions. They tell us that we are destined to defeat and some of the lovely maidens in Winchester go so far as to spit in the faces of the soldiers.

General Banks realized his force was indeed anemic. Estimating Confederate strength opposing him at "not less than 16,000 men," Banks went on to delineate his force composition and location to the War Department in his May 22 dispatch. With five thousand infantrymen, sixteen hundred horse soldiers, and sixteen cannons, Banks complained, "We are compelled to defend at two points, both equally accessible to the enemy." Those two points were Strasburg and Front Royal, separated by twelve miles of Manassas Gap Railroad and also connected by a winding Virginia country road, both running east–west. The importance of the locations was twofold: each hamlet not only afforded railroad protection but also lined a north–south macadamized turnpike and provided access to the mouth of a valley within the Shenandoah Valley.

Commerce sustained Strasburg not only via the railroad but primarily by the Valley Turnpike (often called the Valley Pike), a ninety-mile-long road that ran between Winchester in the north to Staunton in the south. The pike was less than twenty years old in 1862 and was considered the most dependable road for wagon and passenger traffic. It was so efficient that it confused Northern generals in 1861 into believing that a railroad existed between Winchester and Strasburg.

Limestone walls closed in the pike on both east and west shoulders sporadically along its length, and mileposts helped travelers gauge their distances.

From Strasburg to Staunton, the Valley Pike ran in the middle of a valley, which still bore name Shenandoah Valley, though the Blue Ridge no longer formed its eastern boundary. Less than fifteen miles inward from the Blue Ridge loomed Massanutten Mountain, a fifty-five-mile sandstone chain that separated the north and south branches of the Shenandoah River. It was easily crossed at one gap near New Market. Three peaks formed the face of the ridge, the westernmost one being the dominant of the three. This was called Signal Knob, offering a telltale overlook to the activities at Strasburg below. The North Branch of the Shenandoah was the lesser of the two; it hugged the mountain on its northward course, bulging out northwestward to follow the ridge line, then turning sharply eastward less than one mile above Strasburg to curve around Signal Knob and the northern face of the Massanutten ridge. The Manassas Gap Railroad curved from westward to southward at Strasburg, running parallel to the Valley Pike on its western side until its terminus twenty miles south at Mt. Jackson. Another road, albeit a poor one, led travelers from Strasburg through the Alleghenies to Moorefield.

Because of the geography and road networks, Strasburg proved an important point of defense for Union troops. Banks recognized this in April and had set about to construct a fort to protect against an attack from the south. Forever known as Banks Fort, the earthworks rose between a creek and road due north of Strasburg, one thousand feet west of the Valley Pike. Directly across the east side of the pike from Banks Fort were General Banks's quarters at the George Hupp house, the former headquarters of Stonewall Jackson the previous March. At the Hupp house Banks superintended the continued construction of his namesake fort and spent a great deal of time reading and writing messages telegraphed to and from the U.S. War Department.

Most of Banks's available force was close by in Strasburg's environs. Infantry and cavalry were stationed five miles into the Valley all the way to Tom's Brook, where they protected the Union wagon train. Daily cavalry patrols trotted up to Woodstock, ten miles southwest of Strasburg on the Valley Pike. There they encountered Southern horse soldiers late on May 18 and on May 21, the night before Banks wrote his communiqué.[17]

Well aware of the presence of General Ewell's Confederate division deep in the Luray Valley, Banks felt he adequately covered this position at Front Royal, the town that formed the northern entrance to this fifty-mile-long corridor. The Luray or Page Valley was thinner than the Shenandoah directly west of it, measuring a mere six miles across at its most narrow segment. Cut by the South Branch of the Shenandoah, this bucolic valley boasted a good road for half its length. The River Road, as it was referred to by contemporaries, was macadamized like the Valley Pike, distinguished by a bed of crushed limestone called macadam from Luray to Front Royal, where it was then referred to as the Front Royal–Winchester Turnpike for the remaining nineteen miles to Winchester. South of Luray, the thinner, dirt road system was less dependable, particularly in wet weather.[18]

"I have on the Manassas Gap Railroad, between Strasburg and Manassas, 2,500 infantry, six companies cavalry, and six pieces of artillery," Banks informed the War Department as he continued his May 22 dispatch. The report, although accurate, was misleading, for it assumed that the majority of this military existed inside the Valley. It did not. Most of this command consisted of Brig. Gen. John W. Geary's brigade stationed at rail depots at Linden Station and Rectortown. Between Strasburg and Front Royal, Banks had spread out four companies of infantry. At Front Royal he placed nine hundred infantrymen and two rifled cannons, but no cavalry. So, although he admitted that Front Royal and Strasburg were "equally accessible to the enemy," Banks deliberately decided against an equitable distribution of troops to cover the entrances to each valley.[19]

The gist of Banks's May 22 dispatch was to create urgency at the War Department to reinforce him. "We are preparing defenses as rapidly as possible," he reported; "but . . . my force is insufficient to meet the enemy in such strength as he will certainly come, if he attacks us at all, and our situation certainly invites attack in the strongest manner." Banks pleaded for large rifled cannons to complete the fortification he was constructing—"a battery of 20-pounder Parrott guns will only place us on a level with the guns of the enemy" —and begged equally for infantry support.[20]

Knowing how dire his situation was, Banks had sent an adjutant, Maj. R. Morris Copeland, to Washington to make the case for reinforcement in person. Copeland conducted a twofold mission; the second was an attempt to organize and command a regiment of black troops. Copeland met with resistance on both accounts. Secretary Stanton nixed the black regiment and was irritated at Banks's request, telling Copeland that Frémont and McDowell had also pleaded for more troops; and according to Copeland, Stanton "did not believe Jackson was at all to be dreaded." Copeland refused to give up. He pressed Stanton to send Brig. Gen. James Cooper's Baltimore-based brigade to the Valley. Copeland wired Banks a telegram late on May 21 that Banks received the next morning: "I have seen the Secretary. . . . [Stanton] said there was not a man he could send, but, at last, said he would order to-morrow Cooper's brigade to join you. It is that or none." Banks would take it, but did not accept the "that-or-none" option. He sent Colonel Clark to press his case for more troops and to speak to President Lincoln and Secretary Stanton about the mission. Colonel Clark was on a B&O train heading to the nation's capital on May 22.[21]

As Banks continued his May 22 dispatch from the Hupp house, he knew that Cooper's thirty-eight-hundred-man brigade would be heading toward Harpers Ferry to join him in the Lower Valley, and his two aides may yet succeed in providing him even more troops. Under the best of circumstances, those troops could not reach Strasburg for at least four days; Banks felt it may be too late. "At present our danger is imminent," Banks stated to Stanton. His intelligence was accurate regarding Confederate strength, and Banks also invoked heady insight into the mind-set of the commander who opposed him:

> To these important considerations ought to be added the persistent adherence of Jackson to the defense of the valley and his well-known purpose to expel the Government troops from this country if in his power. This may be assumed as certain. There is probably no one more fixed and determined purpose in the whole circle of the enemy's plans. Upon anything like equal ground his purposes will be defeated.
>
> I have forborne until the last moment to make this representation, well knowing how injurious to the public service unfounded alarms become, but in this case the probabilities of danger are so great, that it should be assumed as positive and preparation made to meet it.[22]

As finely attuned as Banks's assessment was to his opponent's strength, focus, and determination, he completely underestimated

General Jackson's ability to move his large Valley army. That Thursday, the twenty-second, Banks informed Secretary Stanton he believed Jackson would close in within twenty-five miles of him at New Market, up the Valley Pike from Strasburg. He also maintained that Ewell remained at Swift Run Gap, nearly sixty miles from the Front Royal garrison he had established. Little did he realize, that very day both Jackson and Ewell would be united in the Luray Valley, much closer to striking distance of Union positions than he ever fathomed was possible.[23]

General Jackson awoke early on the morning of May 22 at the Mauck Meeting House, a colonial-era church in the hamlet of Hamburg, two miles east of the South Branch of the Shenandoah River. Hamburg, according to a Cincinnati newspaper reporter who passed through it one week earlier, consisted of "four houses and a blacksmith shop, population about ten white people and forty negroes." Jackson stood two miles from the South Branch of the Shenandoah and two miles from Luray. Twenty-five miles down the Valley stood Jackson's military objective: Front Royal.[24]

He met with General Ewell early that morning; both agreed to place Ewell subordinate to Jackson's instructions. For the first time since taking independent command in the Shenandoah Valley, Jackson could now claim the leadership of the fourth-largest Confederate army in the field. By prior arrangement—and date of commission— Jackson absorbed Ewell's command with his original division. The six regiments collected from Allegheny Johnson's Army of the Northwest, along with the batteries, joined Ewell's division as they entered the Luray Valley. This particular day would be the first in which all commands would be united: eight infantry brigades containing twenty-seven regiments and two battalions, eleven batteries of artillery with forty-eight cannons, and two cavalry regiments with four companies of a third.[25]

The movement into the Luray Valley had begun the previous day, but several thousand infantry and cavalry remained at New Market or in the gap on the morning of May 22. This included the tail formed by the Stonewall Brigade, under the command of Brig. Gen. Charles Winder. His Virginians had bivouacked on the town side of New Market Gap. General Winder marched his men up and through the gap beginning at 6:00 A.M. Cavalry and horse artillery came in behind them. Only detached companies of the Seventh Virginia Cavalry

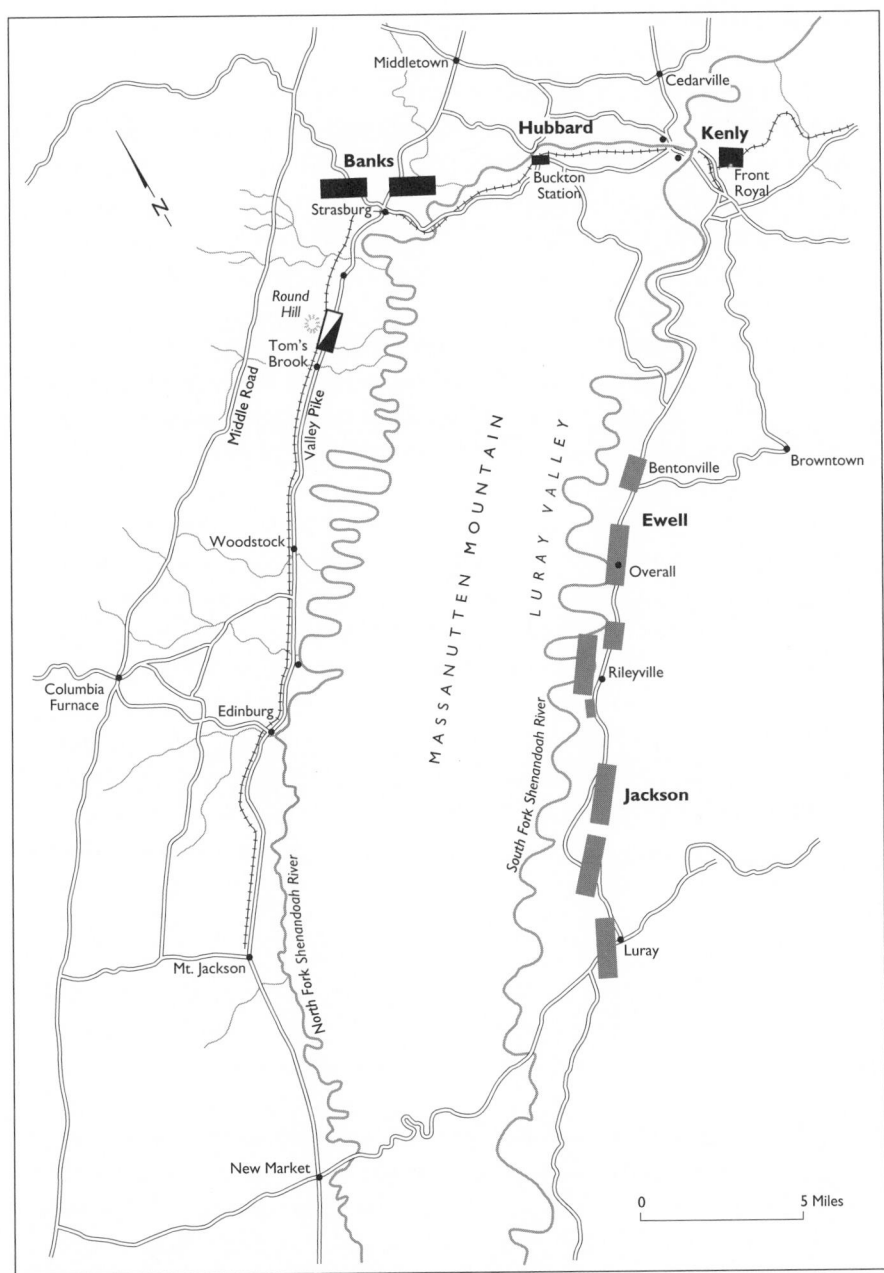

Position of forces in the Valley, 2:00 P.M., May 22, 1862

would patrol the Valley Pike by day's end; the remainder moved northward on the River Road through Luray and beyond.[26]

By all indications, the decision to march the entire army into the Luray Valley materialized late on May 20. Jackson's mission in the Valley was spelled out in a May 16 dispatch written by Gen. Robert E. Lee—perhaps dictated by President Jefferson Davis. "Whatever movement you make against Banks do it speedily," Lee had ordered, "and if successful drive him back toward the Potomac, and create the impression, as far as practicable, that you design threatening that line."[27]

Upon receiving those instructions, Jackson had ordered General Ewell to march his remaining brigades from the Luray Valley to the Valley Pike and join Jackson's division between New Market and Mt. Jackson—twenty miles from Banks and his Strasburg force. (Two brigades of Ewell's command had already joined Jackson's men near New Market.) Jackson also sent his engineering staff and some of his cavalry northward to determine Banks's strength and exact positions at Strasburg. He also expected reinforcements from General Branch's brigade. But General Johnston had recalled Branch during his attempt to enter the Valley; and after Ewell had sent most of his division to Jackson he had also learned he had been recalled. The mixed messages to Jackson from the War Department and General Johnston was made unnecessarily confusing by General Johnston's two- to three-day delay in delivering horse-carried instructions from Richmond (having chosen not to send his orders by telegram). Jackson felt he could override this by getting approval from General Lee by telegraph, but even wired transmissions required a forty-mile trip to carry from Staunton to New Market, making it exceedingly difficult to conduct a two-way "conversation" during the same calendar day. So that Tuesday morning (May 20), when Jackson requested Lee "to please answer by telegraph at once," Lee's response was not dated until the twenty-first, and may not have reached Jackson until Thursday morning, May 22, in the Luray Valley. By then Jackson had received Johnston's May 18 dispatch, which told Jackson and Ewell that if conditions were favorable to dispose of Banks, "then attack."[28]

Jackson never revealed the exact reason for his very late decision to head into the Luray Valley. He may have been concerned that Banks was too well dug in at Strasburg, perhaps with reinforcements from Harpers Ferry. The sudden removal of General Branch's soldiers factored in as well, for Jackson had been counting on those North

Carolinians to bolster his own strength. Even before his engineers had returned with news of enemy strength and disposition at Strasburg, Jackson already was looking eastward to the thinner Luray Valley. He did not know the exact composition of the Union force at Front Royal, but expected it to be weaker resistance than Strasburg. He convinced himself that he could strike the garrison there by surprise, an option unlikely if he headed down the Valley Pike to Strasburg. An additional advantage for Jackson was the opportunity to gain the flank and rear of Banks's Strasburg defense using the Massanutten ridge to shield this movement with a quick strike at Front Royal, offering him a better chance to subdue Banks than to assault him straight on.[29]

Ironically, the only reason Jackson could entertain the option of transferring into the Luray Valley was the failure of his cavalry one month earlier. Ordered to burn Columbia Bridge, White House Bridge, and Red Bridge on April 19, they had only been successful in the latter endeavor. Columbia Bridge and White House Bridge, eight miles apart, remained unscathed. Shields's division of blue-clad soldiers crossed over White House Bridge on May 13, and Jackson followed the Union march eight days later. Had all the bridges been burned as ordered four weeks earlier, Jackson may have forgone this option if he were forced to consider the sluggish crossing necessitated by a pontoon bridge.[30]

Jackson's force had nearly tripled in two weeks with the infusion of Ewell's and Johnson's brigades. This command structure would have inherent impediments. Jackson retained the brigade structure of the former Army of the Northwest, but placed the two brigades of that former army directly under Ewell's jurisdiction. Thus, Ewell's command burgeoned past eight thousand soldiers with the addition of the six regiments that fought at the Battle of McDowell. His five brigades included an organization called the Maryland Line, which was headed by Brig. Gen. George H. Steuart and consisted of one infantry regiment (the First Maryland) and a four-gun battery (the Baltimore Light Artillery). The remaining four batteries, eighteen cannons, existed as a separate entity from the infantry brigades.

Conversely, Jackson chose not to relinquish command or reorganize the structure of his original division, placing him as both an army and division commander whose three brigade commanders answered directly to him. Complicating the picture was Jackson's deci-

sion not to partition off his artillery in a separate command, leaving
the five batteries attached to the brigade commanders. But Jackson
did employ a new staff position: chief of artillery. Lt. Col. Stapleton
Crutchfield, a twenty-six-year-old former Lexington neighbor and
Virginia Military Institute (VMI) faculty mate of Jackson's, was given
the nod to handle the deployment of Jackson's forty-eight cannons.
Crutchfield's jurisdiction included the three cannons belonging to
the horse artillery, commanded by Capt. Roger Preston Chew, still a
teenager in 1862. Jackson's cavalry lacked a chief. Col. Turner Ashby
commanded twenty-one companies of the Seventh Virginia Cavalry.
Ashby's behemoth regiment, beginning on May 22, was joined by the
fourteen companies of the Second and Sixth Virginia Cavalry from
Ewell's division.[31]

The morning progressed smoothly, so well that the vanguard of
Jackson's column stopped marching near Bentonville at noon, near
the turnpike post informing them they were nine miles from Front
Royal. These men—Trimble's brigade—were spared the hardship of
eating dust in the rearward portions of the column as those soldiers
endured the second straight eighty-degree day of hard marching. Lifting the spirits of the Confederates was the reaction of the Luray Valley citizenry. The civilians were entertained by the second spectacle
in ten days watching thousands upon thousands of soldiers tramping
past their homes. Mostly sympathetic to the Confederates, these Valley residents generally had stood quietly by when Shields's blue-
coated division trekked down the Valley on May 12. The reaction to
the Southern soldiers was quite the opposite. A Confederate horse
soldier raved that "all along our route the loyal women of that beautiful valley, from the gray-haired matron to the fair, blooming maiden,
flocked to the roadside to cheer us on our way." A member of Jackson's staff was equally touched. "As we moved down that beautiful
Luray Valley, one of the loveliest spots the sun shines upon," crowed
J. William Jones, "the people received us everywhere with the live-
liest demonstrations of joy, and supplied us with food of every description." The demonstrations along the roadside put more bounce
into the steps of the Confederate infantry.[32]

Not all the citizens in the Luray Valley sympathized with the
Confederacy. As he had done in Winchester, Jackson arrested Unionists he felt detrimental to the Southern cause. These included two
men surnamed Haynes and Beehler, the former a father of five who

lived about halfway between Front Royal and Luray. Unfortunately for the two, they would suffer at the hands of their Valley neighbors after Jackson's army had passed and gone. The two would be executed in Luray, their bodies never returned to their families. Civil war existed in its most literal sense here in the spring of 1862.[33]

The marching for everyone ended in the afternoon. Ewell's division sprawled for nearly ten miles from Bentonville back to Compton's Creek; Jackson's old division encamped for five miles up the road from there, extending past Luray. Although he had several hours of daylight remaining with foot soldiers only three hours' march from Front Royal, Jackson chose not to approach any closer for May 22, ostensibly in an effort to allow one of his "eyes" to return to him.

Those "eyes" belonged to his two cartographers. Although his army was united in the Luray Valley, his staff was not. Neither Jedediah Hotchkiss nor Lt. James K. Boswell, the chief engineer of Jackson's army, had reported to Stonewall since he had detached them on their reconnaissance from Mt. Solon four days earlier. Jackson had sent for Hotchkiss and Boswell to join him in the Luray Valley on May 22, but the directive reached the topographical officers too late for them to join the army; they finished their day on separate missions across Massanutten Mountain. Jackson's decision to advance down the Luray Valley was so quick to produce a negative consequence, for he now trod into unfamiliar territory. "As a rule he did not refer to maps in the field, making his study of them in advance," recalled Jed Hotchkiss about Stonewall Jackson. "He undoubtedly had the power of retaining the topography of the country in his imagination." Unfortunately for General Jackson, his imagination could not accentuate the topography around the mouth of the Luray Valley. He had made several trips up and down the Valley Pike (three times in the past two months) and had committed the route and its crossings to memory, but Jackson had little knowledge and understanding of the roads and distances between Front Royal and Winchester. He needed details about the crossroads that connected the Front Royal–Winchester Pike with the Valley Pike west of it to continue his campaign against Banks.[34]

Jackson's headquarters staff had never been larger than it was in May 1862. He had no fewer than a dozen staff personnel working for him as he transferred into the Luray Valley. But only six of them had more than one month of experience to perform the functions assigned to them, and half of these veterans were conflicted on the eve of an important thrust into the Lower Valley. Maj. William Allan, Jackson's chief ordnance officer, learned that very day during the march toward Front Royal that his mother had died at his Winchester home in April; he obviously would be distracted. Maj. John Harman, the division's irascible quartermaster, had also suffered personal loss with two children succumbing to scarlet fever and a brother at death's door from a wound at the Battle of McDowell. Jackson refused him a leave of absence during the active campaign, and refused to explain objectives to Harman that would have eased his supply missions. Fed up with the grief, the demands of his duties, and the coldness of his boss, Harman submitted his resignation to Jackson in mid-May. He withdrew it when Jackson got the message and treated Harman with more kindness and tact.[35]

At the same time that Harman resigned, Jackson's chief engineering officer also tried to leave Jackson's army, but for a different reason. Lt. James K. Boswell had served Jackson since February, but sought a transfer in May—not because of a gripe with his superior but due to the lack of work he could conduct as an engineer skilled at the craft of fortifications. "There is nothing but Topg. Duty to be executed in this command," complained Boswell to a confidant on May 14, "and as you know *I am a very poor draftsman*" (emphasis added). Based on his frank self-assessment, Boswell's maps may have been incomplete, inaccurate, or poorly drawn. Regardless, he wished to be transferred to another department. It is unknown if Jackson was aware of Boswell's discontent. Before he entered the Luray Valley to flank Banks at Front Royal, Jackson had sent Boswell to determine Banks's strength at Strasburg. Boswell complied by counting Banks's men from atop Signal Knob for several hours on May 21. Although the mission seemed to placate Boswell, this would prove to be another duty ill-suited to the fortifications engineer.[36]

The other staff officer who felt inadequate for his position was Reverend Robert Lewis Dabney. The theologian was a longtime friend of Jackson's who had housed the general's pregnant wife at Hampden-Sydney College in the latter weeks of the winter of 1861–62. When Dabney sought a position at headquarters, Jackson rewarded him with a commission of major and the position of assistant adjutant general—his chief of staff. Dabney had only a smidgeon of military experience, which failed to carry over to this all-important duty. One month later, in the Luray Valley, Dabney still failed to impress anyone. A colonel in the Stonewall Brigade laughed off Dabney's appointment as an example that headquarters "are no longer omniscient." Lt. Henry K. Douglas was equally dismissive, long afterward claiming that no one knew what Dabney ever did, and believing that Maj. Alexander Swift "Sandie" Pendleton actually performed many of Dabney's duties. It did not help solidify Dabney's military bona fides to see him shading himself with an umbrella while on horseback. The spectacle earned audible jeers from the troops.[37]

Jackson was more dissatisfied with other elements of his army than his questionable appointments at headquarters. His chief complaint was the lack of discipline in the score of companies serving in the Seventh Virginia Cavalry, commanded by Col. Turner Ashby. Ashby was about to be promoted to brigadier general, another annoyance to Jackson, who lamented over the lack of control he exerted over the troops. Jackson also was hamstrung by the authorization Ashby obtained from the former secretary of war, Judah P. Benjamin, to recruit infantry and heavy artillery, in essence allowing Ashby to command an army within Jackson's army. Like Harman, Ashby had resigned in April after learning that Jackson tried to divide his command and prevent Ashby from reenlisting former infantrymen into his unit. Maj. Oliver R. Funsten, the only other field officer of Ashby's unwieldy regiment, also resigned as a symbol of solidarity. This served notice to Jackson that the entire body of horse soldiers could mutiny if he pressed the issue. Jackson backed down from his plan and Ashby withdrew his resignation, leaving the cavalry problem unresolved. But Jackson still had not given up on converting the Seventh Virginia Cavalry into a more disciplined and organized force. Even after assuaging Ashby, Jackson bypassed him by requesting that the Confederate War Department organize Ashby's twenty-one companies into regiments.[38]

Notwithstanding the friction and headaches produced by Jackson's confrontation with his staff and subordinates, these issues were not Jackson's greatest problems. The largest impediment to the Confederate Valley army—a problem Jackson likely had yet to appreciate—was the condition of his infantry, particularly the all-Virginia division under his command since March. Two weeks earlier, in the midst of a heavy march, Jackson had revealed that he liked to "keep our troops continually employed in successful work." The work had been continuous and had been successful, but three nonstop weeks of marching and fighting in some of the most arduous country in Virginia had exacted a toll on Jackson's "foot cavalry." After taking the month of April to rest and repose, Jackson's infantry logged two hundred miles in the twenty days between May 3 and 22. The effect on regimental ranks was shocking. Jackson claimed peak strength on May 3 in the three brigades that had served with him since the first day of the campaign: 8,597 aggregate infantry, an average of 740 officers and men per regiment with only one regiment (the eight-company Twenty-seventh Virginia) having fewer than 500 troops. Considering that only 2,400 men and boys from the same force walked off the Kernstown battlefield on March 23, Jackson's ballooned strength six weeks later included new recruits not expected to tough it out if confronted with hardships, no matter how strictly Jackson enforced discipline within his command.[39]

But no one could have predicted the mass desertion and breakdown that would hobble Jackson's force during the first three weeks of May. On May 3 Jackson claimed the Stonewall Brigade had 3,681 troops in the five Virginia regiments. By the time the brigade's members plopped down in the Luray Valley twenty days later, fewer than 1,600 foot soldiers, rank and file, had completed the two hundred miles of marching into the Alleghenies and back to that valley. No attempt had been made to account for the 2,000 soldiers that deserted and straggled over the previous twenty days. The loss of 55 percent of the force is more astounding considering that the brigade did not suffer casualties at the Battle of McDowell on May 8.[40]

Brig. Gen. Charles Winder claimed he "had a pleasant day" on May 22. He had halted his command near noon after completing an eighteen-mile march at the helm of the Stonewall Brigade. He was treated to lunch by a hospitable citizen in Luray. Relieved that his men sat out a heavy afternoon march in hot weather, Winder described the rest of his Thursday as "quite gratifying—really enjoyed myself."[41]

His subordinate commanders did not share the same sentiments. Those who did not desert or straggle from Jackson's division were in poor physical condition in the Luray Valley. It was serendipitous for Jackson that the fresher legs of Ewell's original division spearheaded the march toward Front Royal. Although equally relieved about not marching the rest of the day, Lt. Col. Lawson Botts, temporarily in command of the Second Virginia Infantry, still feared for the health of his command, particularly after receiving Winder's order to prepare for a big day of marching in the predawn hours of Friday, May 23:

> I have received your circular ordering Reveille at 2½ AM, Brigade to move at 4, with cooked rations for three days. . . . I immediately called upon the commissary of the Reg. To know if he could issue at once rations for three days. He replied that he had no rations except for one day. . . . As the commandant of the Reg., I deem it my duty to state that the men are much fatigued by the constant marches they have made & need rest, that, were it possible to issue the rations, at once, it would be impossible for the men, with limited supply of cooking utensils, to cook them and obtain any rest tonight. This loss of rest, followed by a forced march tomorrow, would so exhaust them as to hazard the hard-earned Reputation of the Regiment.[42]

The other brigades of Jackson's division were equally broken down. "We have been constantly marching, fighting, and watching for more than a month," complained Samuel V. Fulkerson, in charge of Jackson's third brigade, "and the consequence is that we are all broken down, with fatigue, loss of sleep and irregularity in eating." He wrote that plaint to his sister on May 16, and even though the whole army rested for the day—to commemorate a day set aside by President Davis for humiliation and prayer—Fulkerson's men could not have considered themselves rested after logging sixty miles over the final four days. Like the regiments in the Stonewall Brigade, hundreds of infantrymen disappeared from the third brigade during the first three weeks of May. Near Luray on May 22, Fulkerson's former regiment, the Thirty-seventh Virginia, was perhaps down by half the number compared to what was tallied on May 3. So was the Tenth Virginia in Fulkerson's brigade; the colonel informed his wife that his regiment's strength was down by 50 percent. "Jackson is killing up all my men," he railed. In all, fewer than five thousand men of the eighty-six hundred tallied in Jackson's division on May 3 entered the Luray Valley on May 22.[43]

The regiments formerly belonging to the Army of the Northwest felt a similar strain. A Virginian belonging to that force informed his diary that Thursday he was on the pike leading to Front Royal. He finished his May 22 entry with a self-assessment likely shared by most of his old army mates: "Almost tired to death." Given the noted troop reductions exceeding 50 percent, and considering the condition of those who remained with their regiments, the weather, terrain, and marching demands during the first three weeks of May had weakened Jackson's army more than could be expected from the most heated and vicious battle.[44]

The condition of the soldiers, as alluded to in their diaries and letters, was worsened by breakdowns in the commissary and quartermaster departments, despite yeoman service performed by the officers tending to those specialties. Supply also affected the cavalry. Major Harman pleaded for days to alleviate the corn and oat shortages in the region by sending enough forage to feed more than one thousand horses and mules serving the army in transport wagons and cavalry. Many of the supply wagons were inoperable or barely operable and in desperate need of replacement. By the afternoon of May 22, the army wagons stood eight miles north of Luray. Major Harman wrote his brother (also attached to the quartermaster department) to send shoes and nails for the horses, in addition to the pleas for forage. Informing his brother that a big battle was expected the next day, Harman wrote, "God grant that we may be enabled to make a good lick." No doubt he hoped the lick would be big enough to scoop up U.S. government supplies to alleviate his woes.[45]

Ewell's command—specifically those comprising the division before the infusion of the regiments from Allegheny Johnson's command—had the freshest legs and were generally better supplied than the rest of Jackson's command. But Ewell also suffered from desertions, although not to the extent infecting Jackson's division. Perhaps 1,000 to 1,500 new recruits that had swelled Ewell's command in mid-April found a way to disappear during May. All together, Jackson's numerical strength in the Luray Valley was at least 4,000 fewer men than expected by the Confederate War Department—his actual numerical strength present for duty could not have exceeded 14,000 officers and men, and was likely closer to 12,000 effectives.[46]

Not surprisingly, Trimble's brigade, Taylor's brigade, Elzey's brigade, and the Maryland Line marched in advance down the Front Royal Road, despite the fact that no one in these commands was native to the area as was the case with the force inherited by Ewell on May 22. Notwithstanding the better conditioning and supply, the most hampered regiment in Jackson's entire army marched within Ewell's division—the First Maryland Infantry. The regiment had no shortages or physical problems that stood out more than any other in Ewell's original command. As this regiment settled in around the banks of Compton's Creek, they were in crisis. The regiment was in mutiny!

What was known by all was that a problem festered for nearly one week within the First (CSA) Maryland Infantry. The previous Saturday, one company had been disbanded over the protests of Col. Bradley T. Johnson, the newest commander of the First Maryland. Johnson discharged twenty soldiers from two other companies the following Wednesday, but the soldiers in four other companies were also insisting on their discharge at the same time, claiming they had signed up for only one year. When Johnson showed them that their muster rolls stated "for the war," the infantrymen complained that they were misled into signing up for a longer term of service than they had intended.[47]

All of this stemmed from the recent passing of the one-year anniversary of the enlistment of the First (CSA) Maryland Infantry. Although the newly passed Confederate Conscription Act forced all eligible male residents of the Confederate States of America to serve in their armies for three years and extended previous one-year enlistments to three years, the act did not apply to Maryland regiments. As a border state, Maryland was considered a nonresident of the Confederacy; therefore, its soldiers were exempt from this forced continued service.[48]

No Maryland native was more devoted to the Southern cause than thirty-two-year-old Bradley T. Johnson. A Princeton graduate and prewar lawyer from Frederick, Johnson had helped recruit the regiment one year before. He had always dished tremendous accolades on his regiment by boasting that it embodied the faith and pride of the state while at the same time deriding those Maryland soldiers forming Union regiments as devoid of courage and chivalry. Johnson had begun his service with the First (CSA) Maryland as a major, but had risen so quickly with the promotions of its original colonel and lieutenant colonel (George Steuart and Arnold Elzey) that Colonel Johnson found himself without a major to take up his original duties in his regiment.

On May 22 Colonel Johnson also found himself without an organized and unified command. Johnson bristled when half of his regiment threw down their arms and refused to serve beyond their expired term of enlistment. It was "the worst possible condition," recalled a Marylander, "one-half under arrest for mutiny, the rest disgusted with the service, and the colonel disgusted with them." Although Generals Ewell and Jackson were aware of Maryland's enlistment predicament, a company officer maintained that the mutiny "was kept concealed from General Jackson, as it was still hoped the men would return to reason."[49]

Jackson took his headquarters one mile north of the disgruntled Marylanders, near the town of Rileyville. General Ewell stayed with the vanguard, a few miles north of Jackson at Bentonville. Jackson did not meet with Ewell that night, but issued orders to march at dawn—Trimble's brigade was to hold its place in front until the column closed ranks behind. Everyone was expected to carry two days' cooked rations in their haversacks while a third ration would travel behind the entire column in a designated wagon. Only ambulances and ammunition wagons were allowed to move with each regiment. Jackson clearly expected action on the morrow.[50]

It is apparent, however, that he had not formulated a battle plan. A crossroad ran eastward from Bentonville, connecting to a road parallel to the turnpike; this road offered a central approach to town. Jackson shunned this approach; either he was unaware of the alternate roads into town or he planned to move by the river road directly into the town. Neither Hotchkiss nor Boswell had entered the Luray Valley that night, forcing Jackson to plan a blind approach to Front Royal. Sometime during the night, a lone Seventh Virginia cavalryman galloped down the road and silently slipped into Front Royal. His mission was to determine exactly where the U.S. troops were stationed and also to ascertain their composition.[51]

Reveille sounded at 2:30 A.M. on May 23. The army was up and ready to move at first nautical light—the light before dawn—which crept into the Luray Valley at 4:30 A.M. Taylor's Louisianans, for reasons unknown, were already moving to the front, ordered to spearhead the assault in front of Trimble's brigade. Shortly before 5:00 A.M., the column closed ranks. From one mile north of Bentonville to three miles north of Luray, Southern soldiers, cannons, and wagons crowded onto thirteen miles of the turnpike. Stonewall Jackson initiated the march by riding to the front of his army bareheaded. As he trotted down the line, his troops acknowledged him with a "rebel yell." The spirited response proved contagious as even headquarters personnel cheered their commander as he worked his way to the front. "We, too, at once took up the shout," fondly recalled J. William Jones, "and gave a hearty greeting to the great captain, who had come to lead us to victory, and the mountains echoed and reechoed with the glad acclaim."[52]

At the Hupp house in Strasburg, General Banks slept during the early morning hours of May 23. He retired the previous evening without a response from the War Department to his immediate plea for troops. He awoke that morning assured and concerned that Jackson had closed within twenty-five miles south of him at Strasburg. He had no idea that Jackson personally led a 13,000–14,000-man army, concealed by Massanutten Mountain and determined to destroy his flank before the morning was over.

The *Lexington Gazette*, Jackson's hometown paper deep in the Valley, had been trying to follow the progress of its most noteworthy citizen. "We know little of Gen. Jackson's movements," admitted the most recent issue of the paper, "but we are expecting to hear of him creating a stir, somewhere between Harrisonburg and the Potomac before many days."[53]

Stonewall Jackson was determined to meet those expectations.

2

THE BATTLE OF
FRONT ROYAL

A s the morning sun glared across the broad Potomac waters during the seven o'clock hour of May 23, 1862, Abraham Lincoln
stepped out of his steamer at Aquia Landing. The president, accompanied by Secretary of War Edwin Stanton, shook hands with Maj.
Gen. Irvin McDowell and Col. Herman Haupt, then all boarded a
baggage car. As the spring season entered its third month, the capital
and Tidewater region received a summer weather preview with temperatures climbing well into the eighties for two consecutive days.
This Friday promised more of the same with a comfortable morning
and a cornflower blue sky.[1]

The sanguine weather matched the Union's prospects for the
war's end as United States forces achieved significant gains in nearly
all theaters of operation. The western armies followed up their victory in the horrific Battle of Shiloh by closing in on the vital railroad
junction of Corinth, Mississippi. After wresting New Orleans from
Confederate control, the Union navy threatened to take the Mississippi River completely away from the South as Admiral David Far-
ragut closed in on Vicksburg with a fleet of warships.[2]

Union successes mounted that very morning. In the Alleghenies,
Col. George Crook defeated a small Confederate garrison guard at the
town of Lewisburg in western Virginia, thus opening the door for a

Union advance to threaten the Confederate rail lines at Salem. Even General Frémont, who had been driven back to Franklin by Stonewall Jackson, showed signs of stirring again in the western Virginia mountains. Despite General Schenck's and General Milroy's setback at the Battle of McDowell, Frémont appeared ready to redouble his efforts to march into Tennessee and seize Knoxville and the Virginia and Tennessee Railroad.[3]

Buoyed by the numerous gains achieved by his armies, Lincoln and his escorts rode the rails from Aquia Landing to Falmouth, opposite the Rappahannock River from Fredericksburg. The object of the president's mission was to hold a grand review of General McDowell's reinforced Army of the Rappahannock. McDowell boasted a force of thirty-eight thousand and eighty-six cannons, including Shields's division of westerners (comprising Indiana and Ohio units) who joined his army the day before. After reviewing McDowell's men, Lincoln intended to send them southward to cooperate with General McClellan's advance on Richmond. With one hundred fifty thousand Union soldiers descending on the beleaguered city from two directions, no one could fault President Lincoln if his spirits had lifted this day.[4]

Sixty-five miles due west of Aquia Landing on the morning of May 23, Stonewall Jackson's army approached Front Royal at the mouth of the Luray Valley. Marching four abreast as they snaked northward along the River Road, Jackson's column stretched a dozen miles from head to tail. The head of the column left Bentonville at 5:00 A.M. Ewell's division marched in the van. Brig. Gen. Richard Taylor's Louisianans led Ewell's column followed by Brig. Gen. Isaac Trimble's mixed brigade from four states. Col. Arnold Elzey's Virginians and Georgians came next with Col. William C. Scott's Virginia brigade behind them. By 6:30 A.M. Taylor's brigade marched through Spangler's Crossroads and splashed across Gooney Run. Front Royal was a mere five miles ahead of them.[5]

The "Wise Troop," Company H of the Sixth Virginia Cavalry, led the entire army as they trotted over the pike. Jackson and Ewell's headquarters staff rode horses directly behind them. The single most advanced Confederate horse soldier this day was Lt. William "Walter" Buck of Company E, Seventh Virginia Cavalry. Raised in a house three miles south of Front Royal with a prominent uncle living in the town, Buck had intimate knowledge of Front Royal and the thoroughfares leading to and from it. Ashby had sent him on a special reconnaissance the previous night or at dawn to determine the size and composition of the Union garrison stationed there. Buck had slipped into town, studied the force, and wrote a brief report. After receiving and reading his lieutenant's dispatch, Ashby immediately forwarded the note to Jackson.[6]

Stonewall ordered his army to halt. Learning from the intelligence that a paltry force consisting predominantly of "one regiment of Marylanders" was encamped north of town, Jackson adjusted his force for his offensive. "Colonel Johnson will move the First Maryland to the front and attack the enemy at Front Royal," dictated Jackson to his adjutant. "The army will halt until you pass."[7]

Jackson's intentions were inscrutable. He wished to spearhead Ewell's assault with his lone Maryland infantry regiment pitted against their hated brethren fighting for the North. Likely aware of the dissension in the ranks of the First (CSA) Maryland, Jackson sent the directive for no other viable reason than to instill élan into the disgruntled troops. But even had Jackson known that the regiment was in mutiny, he was unaware that they no longer marched within Ewell's division; instead, they took up the rear, having allowed the rest of the army to pass them. His order, therefore, would force an hours-long halt to allow a courier to deliver the message to the rear, then for the Marylanders to reach the front, thus delaying his attack against Banks's flank from morning to afternoon.[8]

Jackson's courier delivered the assault order shortly after 8:00 A.M. Johnson read the note, then turned to his regiment. A gifted orator, Johnson's skills would be tested in an all-out effort to unite his command. He read Stonewall's dispatch aloud, then faced his men, his piercing eyes and trimmed goatee presenting a formidable appearance. "You have heard this personal order from General Jackson and you are in a pretty condition to obey it," he began. Johnson exhorted his disrupted command, calling them the sole hope for Maryland. Then Johnson shifted his verbal tactics by shaming his men for their dereliction. "I shall return this note to General Jackson with the endorsement, 'The First Maryland refuses to face the enemy,'" threatened the colonel, "for I will not trust the honor of the glorious old State to discontented, dissatisfied men. I won't lead men who have no heart." Johnson told his regiment that he would lead just ten men into this battle, if that were all that would follow him into the fight. He claimed that there was too heavy a debt to pay for the Southern soldiers held in Northern prisons. He closed his impassioned speech by challenging those men under guard. "Never again call yourselves Marylanders!" he declared. "No Marylander ever threw down his arms and deserted his colors in the presence of the enemy—and those arms and those colors given you by a woman! Go!"[9]

It worked! The men under guard pleaded to be allowed to get their guns while the men in the ranks promised to meet his challenge. The First (CSA) Maryland shouted with passion, a command united with a single purpose. Johnson had pulled the right strings to motivate his men. His mixed denunciation and appeal was delivered in such a way as to never leave the memories of those who listened to him that morning. Thirty-five years after the fact, one of his men rated Johnson's memorable speech "as the most effective eloquence to which it has been my fortune to listen."[10]

After the men grabbed their guns and filed into line, Johnson led them forward. They marched past Jackson's Virginians, who boisterously cheered them on as the 250 Marylanders quickened their pace to three and one-half miles per hour. "The men seemed to tread on air," noted Colonel Johnson with renewed pride in his men.[11] Despite the blistering marching rate, the First (CSA) Maryland required more than three hours to take their position in the van of the army.

Clearly, Jackson did not order a protracted halt within picket distance of an attack point simply to finesse his attacking column. Nor did it make sense to purposely delay his plans to spearhead an assault with a depleted and demoralized regiment of unknown fighting ability. It is more apparent that the shifting of the First (CSA) Maryland to the front was ordered to bide his time. He had marched at the break of dawn, but now was forced to delay all of his plans for May 23.

Jackson's decision to advance down the Luray Valley had met with its first negative consequence, for he was now treading into unfamiliar territory. He needed details about the crossroads that connected the Front Royal–Winchester Pike with the Valley Pike west of it to continue his campaign against Banks. But neither Jed Hotchkiss nor Lt. James Boswell—the best sources of that vital information—had reported to Stonewall since he had detached them on their reconnaissance from Mt. Solon four days earlier. Jackson had sent for Hotchkiss and Boswell to join him in the Luray Valley on May 22;

however, the directive reached the topographical officers too late for them to join the army that morning. Now Jackson suspended all movements, ostensibly in an effort to allow one of his "eyes" to return to him. The decision indicated how lightly he regarded the upcoming engagement at Front Royal, and also accentuated the importance he placed on what was to happen after the town was seized.[12]

While Colonel Johnson's regiment hastened to the front, the remainder of the Valley army stepped away from the River Road. Artillerists took their guns and caissons into the lush fields where their horses ate the clover. The infantrymen piled their knapsacks into available wagons to place the troops in fighting trim. (Much grumbling was heard from the men as they were forced to part with their surplus accoutrements.) Jackson stripped his army down to one ration wagon per regiment plus ambulances and ammunition wagons. The night previous he had issued General Orders No. Fifty-one, demanding that two men from each company be detailed for hospital duty and specifying that no man is to leave ranks "for that or any other purpose during battle." As an added measure, he ordered company rolls to be called after the engagement.[13] Perhaps aware of his desertions, Jackson was clamping down on his men as they were about to enter the heart of the campaign.

As the respite dragged through the morning, Jackson took the time to learn about the approaches to town. Two roads took them into Front Royal. Continuing on the River Road was the most direct avenue into the town, but this thoroughfare restricted troop deployment. The South Branch of the Shenandoah hugged the western side of the macadamized road and towering rugged terrain closed off the eastern side. One mile from Front Royal, the road left the river and ran across a low divide before it gently descended into the open Happy Creek valley. Jackson had previously learned of a direct northward approach to town called the Gooney Manor (or Browntown) Road. This well-graded turnpike, complete with tollhouses, meandered through an elevated shoulder in the foothills of the Blue Ridge. It offered a centered approach to the town with ample room to deploy troops on both sides. Because very few byroads interconnected the River Road with Gooney Manor Road, the latter track offered Jackson the best chance to surprise his adversaries and prevent them from fleeing eastward through Manassas Gap. What Stonewall did not know at the time was how to get his army into Front Royal from where he stood.

With no decent maps for Jackson to brand into his memory and imagination, his next choice was to rely on citizens to guide them into town. Asbury Chapel, off to the right of River Road and in front of the army, stood near to General Jackson. Isaac King, a militia colonel living across the river from the church, had gone there to watch the impressive Valley army march by. Jackson noticed the colonel sitting on the fence in front of the church, rode up to him, and inquired for a guide to direct the army to the Gooney Manor Road and subsequently to Front Royal. King told Jackson that the best guide he knew was a lieutenant in his army, Samuel J. Simpson, Seventh Virginia Cavalry, Company E.

Company E, recruited as "Bowen's Mounted Rangers" consisted predominantly of Warren County natives. Colonel Ashby reaped a benefit for Jackson by using Walter Buck; now another company officer would provide a similar favor. Jackson called up Lieutenant Simpson, who grew up near the Gooney Manor Road. Simpson galloped to the front and informed Jackson that a nearby mountain road, running due east from the River Road, bisected the Gooney Manor Road. This perpendicular road was immediately south of Asbury Chapel and in front of Taylor's halted brigade.[14]

Jackson took in this information and changed his battle plan. He had awoken that morning intending a two-pronged advance into Front Royal, with Ewell's division marching on the Gooney Manor Road and the rest of the army heading straight into town on the River Road. That all changed as Jackson revealed his new plan to General Ewell. According to Campbell Brown (who apparently was privy to the discussion), Jackson decided to divert the entire army from the River Road to continuously feed troops onto the Gooney Manor Road.[15] The revised plan reduced the number of troops Jackson could amass upon the battlefield at one time, which served one of his ostensible purposes. Jackson could dispose of the Union garrison without exposing more than a brigade or two of his army. Therefore, any Federal soldier who escaped could not reveal to General Banks that Jackson's entire force was in the Luray Valley. By filtering his army onto one centered road, Jackson also guaranteed a simple one-column march through Front Royal, which was more likely to plant his men firmly on Banks's flank before nightfall.

The eleven o'clock hour passed with the First (CSA) Maryland still marching to the front, and no sign of either Jed Hotchkiss or

Lieutenant Boswell. In the meantime Jackson had sent a directive for his cavalry. The Sixth Virginia and remaining four companies of the Second Virginia (the other companies were detached with Colonel Thomas Munford) directed their mounts toward Spangler's Crossroads. Lt. Col. Thomas Flournoy of the Sixth Virginia Cavalry took charge of this force. Colonel Ashby soon arrived at the crossroads with five available companies of the Seventh Virginia Cavalry. Jackson had directed the entire force of approximately six hundred horse soldiers to cross the South Branch at McCoy's Ford and head toward the Manassas Gap Railroad between Strasburg and Front Royal. Jackson ordered Ashby to strike Buckton Station, ten miles from Spangler's Crossroads, and destroy the telegraph lines and damage the railroad there. Flournoy would strike the tracks closer to Front Royal. Jackson also ordered them to check any advance of Banks's army from Strasburg and to block the pending retreat of Union forces from Front Royal.

As the morning waned toward noon, Jackson's cavalry galloped westward from Spangler's Crossroads toward the river, thousands of hoofbeats thundering toward McCoy's Ford. Remaining at the front with the headquarters staff was Company H of the Sixth Virginia Cavalry and two officers of the Seventh Virginia Cavalry, Lieutenants Simpson and Buck of Company E.[16]

Soon after Ashby and Flournoy embarked on their missions, a crescendo of cheers emanated from behind General Jackson to announce the arrival of the First (CSA) Maryland Infantry. "We passed two divisions without making a halt, marching twelve miles on a stretch, seven of which we made in two hours," boasted one of the Marylanders, who raved at the "great enthusiasm as we passed through the army at our rapid, swinging Zouave step, singing 'Baltimore, ain't you happy?' " The sun peaked in the clear noon sky as the mercury rose toward the eighty-degree mark. The Marylanders took their position at the front of the line while the infantry behind them stepped back onto the River Road, four abreast. After a brief rest for the Free State soldiers, the column began to march. They immediately peeled off the River Road onto the mountain road. There they began their ascent up Dickey's Hill in the western foothills of the Blue Ridge.[17]

The 380-foot climb took them only one-fifth of the way to the summit; nevertheless, it tortured the soldiers, particularly the Marylanders who had virtually no rest after hustling for more than three hours to get to the front. Briny sweat soaked their uniforms, and their hearts pounded within heaving chests as their lungs strived to capture oxygen from the warm, stagnant air. The men trudged through thick woods for one and one-half miles of thigh-burning incline between the River and Gooney Manor Roads, not enough room to hold simultaneously the headquarters staff, advanced cavalry guard, Maryland troops, and approximately six hundred four-man lines created by Taylor's brigade. The remaining infantry and artillerymen repeatedly lurched to a halt as successive quartets managed their way onto the unforgiving byroad.

By 1:00 P.M. the First Maryland reached the Gooney Manor Road, the intersection marked by the simple home of Mrs. King (Colonel King's mother) on the northwest corner and James Garrett's residence across from the T intersection. There, three and one-half miles south of Front Royal, the troops wheeled to the left and soon exited thick woods into open rolling fields on each side of the road. The view here was spectacular: jagged Massanutten Mountain looming to the west and fresh spring growth sprouting from the trees and shrubbery. What the Southerners had yet to see was an enemy soldier. Colonel Johnson sent out Company D on the right and Company G on the left to skirmish on each side of the road. The thirty members of the Wise Troop also advanced in front of the column on the road. Colonel Johnson and Generals Ewell, Taylor, and Steuart also rode forward to reconnoiter.[18]

Stonewall solidified his plans for May 23 when Lieutenant Boswell trotted to Jackson's side one-half mile down the Gooney Manor Road. Boswell found his superior after completing a circuitous daylong journey from Massanutten's northern tip to Woodstock, across New Market Gap and down the Luray Valley. Boswell reported to the general what he discovered at Signal Knob, but he woefully overestimated enemy strength across the Massanutten ridge at twelve thousand men in three divisions encamped between Strasburg and Tom's Brook (Banks had only one division of half as many men). Boswell also confirmed that Union soldiers "were busily engaged in fortifying the Round Hill just in rear of Strasburg."[19]

Jackson immediately put Boswell to work on a new and vitally important function: sketching the region between Front Royal and Winchester. He ordered Boswell to make a similar map for General

Ewell, ostensibly planning to divide his force once he reached the junction of the river branches. Jackson needed the maps for his subsequent operation against Banks once he swept away the Front Royal garrison. He desired that operation to come off this day. Six precious hours of daylight remained on Friday for him to accomplish the objective.[20]

Jackson's best-laid plans did not prevent Union high command at Front Royal from being apprised of the attack. Lt. Col. Charles Parham, Twenty-ninth Pennsylvania Infantry, decided to ride out to see the officer in charge of the force guarding Buckton Station. But Parham's horse changed his plans when the mount fell, its entire weight landing on Parham's pinned leg. In intense pain and unable to ride any farther, Parham returned to his headquarters at "Riverside," the elegant Richards house between the two river branches.

As soon as he returned to "Riverside," Parham received one of his bridge guards. The sentry brought a boy who had requested a pass for himself and his mother to see the boy's father, who worked north of the river branches. Parham questioned the boy and quickly realized the lad had valuable information, so he called for the boy's mother to elaborate. She soon arrived and completed the boy's story. They lived near Bentonville, ten miles south of Front Royal, and had come north to warn their father, a known Unionist, that fifteen thousand rebels were marching toward Front Royal to burn the bridges, drive the Yankees out of the Valley, and capture General Banks. Stragglers and a deserter had confirmed the information to her on her journey northward.

Stunned at his valuable intelligence coup, Parham accepted her story, for it confirmed warnings he had received from other pro-Union residents of the town. As Jackson's men advanced on the Gooney Manor Road, Parham relayed his information to Colonel John R. Kenly and advised him to send his First (USA) Maryland pickets farther out on the roads south of town and hold his men in readiness in town. Parham then wrote his warning to General Banks in a three-page dispatch that detailed what the woman and her son told him.[21]

At the same time that Parham was forewarned of an attack, Ewell's men struck an unwary Union picket as they closed in on Front Royal, one and one-half miles south of the village. The Northern sentinel, wearing a red shirt, had constructed a shelter by stretching his blanket between two fence posts. This was standard practice for the Union pickets there. (A few days earlier, a passerby noted that "half of them [were] asleep in the grass, and the rest fishing and bathing in the brook.") The picket appeared puzzled at the horsemen who approached him. Finally deducing who they were, he reached for his musket, but the Virginia cavalrymen were on him and two of his company mates before he could raise his weapon.

Hustled to the rear, the prisoners marched past Colonel Johnson, who gruffly asked the red-shirted captive what regiment he belonged to. Hearing the words "First Maryland" within the sentinel's thick German-accented response, Johnson pointed to his men and defiantly corrected the prisoner, "*There*'s the First Maryland!" General Steuart picked up on Johnson's response. He wheeled around, faced his former regiment, and shouted, "My boys, it's the First Maryland!" General, colonel, and private had learned for the first time that they were about to face off against Yankee Marylanders; each side considered the other as traitors to their cause.[22]

As pickets from Company H and I of the First (USA) Maryland Infantry scampered back toward Front Royal, the Confederate pursuit came to a brief halt on the last ridge before the descent into town. As the First (CSA) Maryland deployed into line of battle, General Taylor aligned his infantry brigade behind them. Maj. Chatham Roberdeau Wheat's Louisiana battalion remained on the road directly behind Johnson's men. Behind them marched the Sixth Louisiana. Apparently through orders from General Ewell, Taylor split his force by directing the Seventh, Eighth, and Ninth Louisiana regiments off the Gooney Manor Road and deploying them in lines in the open fields to the west. This allowed room for the next brigade in line to begin its advance from the mountain road onto the Gooney Manor Road. General Trimble's men closed ranks and proceeded to fill the space.[23]

Generals Jackson and Ewell quickly took in what lay in front of them while their staffs chatted and gossiped as they sat on their mounts behind them on the road. Lt. Henry Kyd Douglas, one of Jackson's aides, caught sight of a woman running toward them from the northeast. The woman ran up, gesticulating madly, and when Douglas called Jackson's attention to her, Stonewall granted his young aide permission to intercept her. Douglas did so and immediately identified the woman as Belle Boyd, a citizen of the town who prided herself as a Confederate spy.

Boyd caught her breath for a minute, then urged Douglas to tell Jackson that only one regiment of Maryland troops was in the vicinity with "several pieces of artillery and several companies of cavalry." She continued, "Tell him to charge right down and he will catch them all." Satisfied that she had accomplished her duty, Boyd turned around and ran back circuitously toward the town. Douglas considered Boyd's information vital, obviously unaware that Jackson held a dispatch that contained the same infantry information with much reduced (and more reasonable) artillery and cavalry estimates. Miss Boyd, therefore, provided no new information to alter the plans of General Jackson and his army.[24]

At the same time that Belle Boyd rushed out to provide information to General Jackson, Charles Parham finished off his dispatch to send to General Banks. "I do honestly believe they are near here in large force and will try to take us . . . and then push on to Winchester over the pike and get in your rear," wrote Parham while lying in pain in his bed. "Although I cannot stand," Parham closed, "still I am preparing to give them a warm reception. I wish it to be distinctly understood that I am not frightened at trifles, but do believe the above, and deem it proper for you to be informed of the report."[25]

Tremendous excitement rippled through Front Royal in the moments preceding the Confederate attack. The sight of Union pickets scurrying toward the confluence of the Shenandoah River branches alerted the townspeople to look toward the hills south of the courthouse. There they saw the head of Jackson's column halted briefly on the brow. "Oh my God!" cried one of the Front Royal women, "The Southern army is upon them—the hill above town is black with our boys!" In the northern corner of the town, near where the railroad crossed Happy Creek, young Tom Ashby and five of his playmates had been building a dam to cool themselves in the heat. Suddenly a Union sympathizer rushed back toward the Union infantry camp by following the course of the creek. Hearing the report of a musket in the distance, the boys jumped out of the water, briskly put on their clothes, and returned to the village. All were aware that something huge was about to happen.[26]

It took a few more minutes for the Union high command one mile north of Front Royal at the South Branch camp to come to the same conclusion. Colonel Kenly's force had been lounging in their camp near the Van Nort home when a frantic Union sympathizer—a black man on horseback—galloped into the camp and insisted that the rebels were taking the town. Lt. George Thompson, Company D of the First (USA) Maryland, interrogated the frightened citizen and ridiculed him, convinced that the man was overreacting to the presence of a known guerrilla party that was likely engaging the pickets in a skirmish. Lt. Col. Nathan Dushane and another soldier mounted their horses and rode into town to check out the story. On the peninsula between the river branches, Capt. William Davis of the Twenty-seventh Indiana and Lt. Ephraim Giddings of the Third Wisconsin had ridden to Riverside from their Buckton Station outpost to see Lieutenant Colonel Parham. They had received instructions and were about to head back to the railroad post. This temporarily prevented Parham from handing his dispatch to a courier or telegraphing it directly to General Banks—a delay with far-reaching consequences.[27]

Hearts pumping from a combination of adrenaline surge and exertion, the First (CSA) Maryland impatiently awaited the order to take the town. They watched the Wise Troop chase after fleeing pickets from Companies H and I of the First (USA) Maryland. Company F of the Union regiment (the provost guard) did its best to prevent the Confederate Marylanders from seizing Front Royal. Capt. Robert W. Reynolds posted his men in the southernmost of three large hospital buildings across the street from the courthouse. From the upper-floor windows, Reynolds's men held the first wave of Confederate attackers in check with a shower of balls from their smooth-bores. Watching the scene unfold from the brow of the hill seven hundred yards south of the hospital, General Steuart turned to Colonel Johnson and asked, "Can't you take that building?" "I think so," came Johnson's reply. Colonel Johnson wheeled toward his Confederate Marylanders and proclaimed, "Men, you see that house? You are to take it. Forward, double quick charge!"[28]

"You never in your life heard such a fiendish yell of joy as it was given when we received the order to charge," claimed Capt. William Murray of Company H. "At the command my feet became as light as my heart," he continued, "and for 300 yards I beat most everything except the Yanks." Sergeant James Thomas of Company B did not enjoy "light feet." So worn out from the grueling fifteen-mile march leading up to the moment, Thomas and some of his company mates realized that they could do no more. "To my regret," he admitted in his journal, "I was forced to stop before I got through the town."[29]

The Confederate Marylanders received a lively surge of support from the most colorful unit in Jackson's army. They were officially known as the First "Special" Battalion of Louisiana Infantry, but everyone called them either the "Louisiana Tigers" or "Wheat's Tigers." Most of the battalion was recruited from New Orleans and was made up predominantly of Irish immigrant dockworkers and other inhabitants of the southern edge of the city. The "Tiger" appellation came from the designated name of Company B—"The Tiger Rifles"—the only Zouave company in Jackson's army. Sporting a blue jacket over a red shirt and vertically blue-striped trousers tucked into horizontally striped socks, the "Tiger Rifles" not only lent their name to the battalion, but also infused their raucous behavior into the other battalion companies. "They neither fear God[,] man or the Devil," wrote a Virginia soldier about the Tigers in his diary, while another observer assessed them as the "lowest scum of the lower Mississippi." An Alabama soldier believed their nickname was perfect. "Tigers they were, too, in human form," he wrote, "I was actually afraid of them, afraid that I would meet them somewhere and they would . . . knock me down and stamp me half to death."

Fellow soldiers had good reason to fear the Louisiana Tigers, for they learned that these "wharf rats" were men to stay away from between battles. Notorious as mischievous brawlers, the Tigers wreaked havoc within their own army frequently during the war's first year. Confederate captain George McCausland became a fatal example of this after he had foolishly cast dispersions upon the Louisiana battalion. A Tiger officer, Capt. Alexander White of Company B (who spent time in a penitentiary for pistol-whipping a steamboat passenger prior to the war), took offense, challenged the officer to a duel, and shot him to death. "They were always ready to fight," opined a South Carolinian, "and it made little difference to them who they fought."

The renegade unit carried the most misleading battle flag in the Confederate army: a standard depicting a lamb with the legend "as gentle as" festooned above it. The Tigers were armed with 1841-pattern Mississippi rifle muskets but were known to brandish an even more distinctive weapon in battle—Bowie knives. They were one of only a few battle-tested units in Ewell's division, gaining a great deal of fame for their stellar performance in Evans's brigade at the Battle of Manassas. An English reporter had taken careful note of

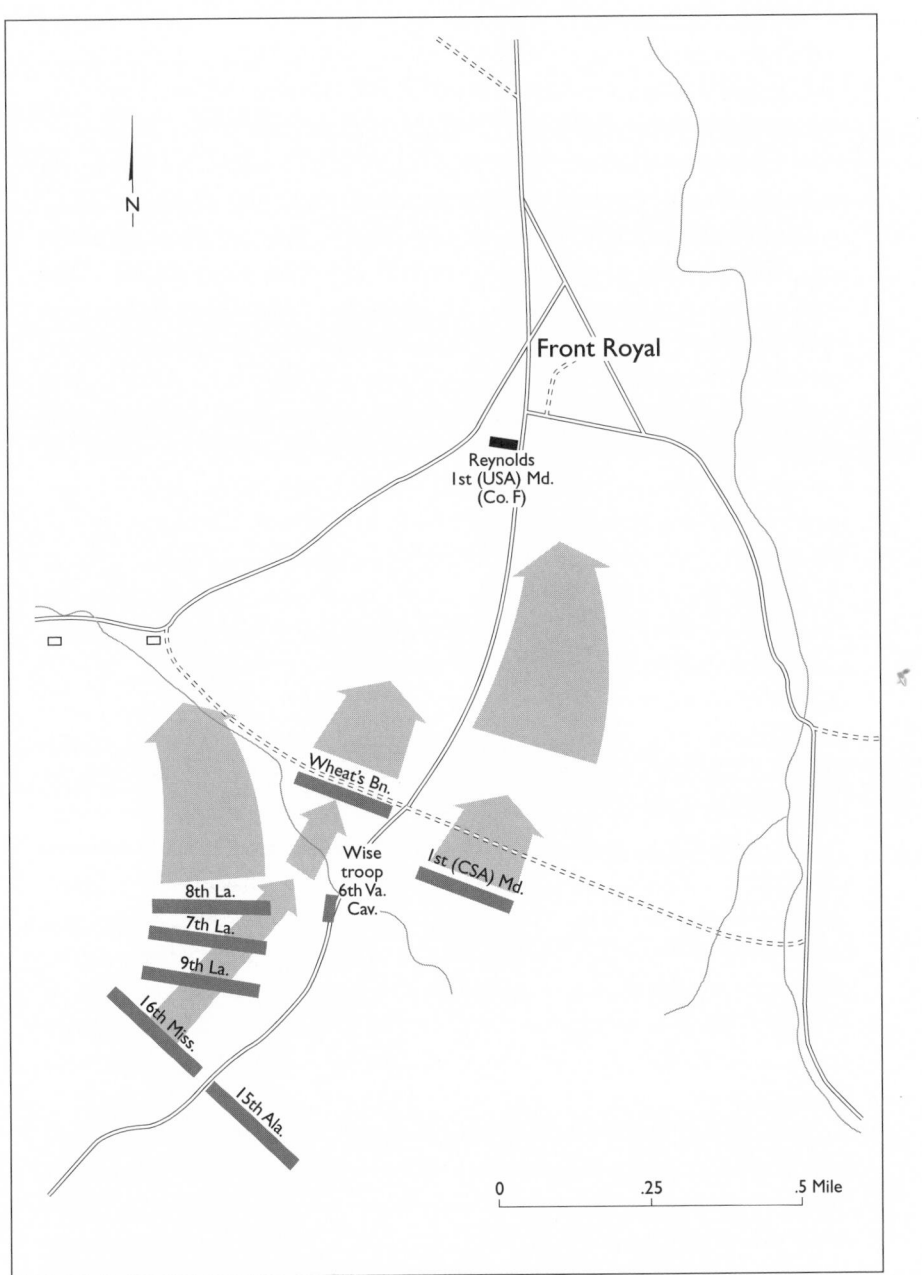

N

Front Royal

Reynolds
1st (USA) Md.
(Co. F)

Wheat's Bn.

Wise
troop
6th Va.
Cav.

1st (CSA) Md.

8th La.

7th La.

9th La.

16th Miss.

15th Ala.

| 0 | .25 | .5 Mile |

Front Royal: Opening Action, 2:00 P.M., May 23, 1862

the Tigers' unique battle style. He observed that they "would keep up
a lively fire from the woods, creep through brush, make a sudden
charge, upset a cannon or two and retire. Again, they would maintain
a death-like silence until the foe was not more than 50 paces off; then
delivering a withering volley, they would dash forward with un-
earthly yells and [when] they drew their knives and rushed to close
quarters, the Yankees screamed with horror." Perhaps the most fit-
ting battle cry for the battalion could be adopted from the lingering
words of a wounded lieutenant at Manassas: "Tigers, go in once more,
go in my sons, I'll be great gloriously God d—d if the s-s of b—s can
ever whip the Tigers!"[30]

The commander of the Louisiana Tigers was one who was well
suited for the arduous duty of keeping these seemingly unmanage-
able men in line. Maj. Chatham Roberdeau Wheat was arguably the
most experienced soldier to enter the Civil War, having served in
Mexico and four revolutions during the fifteen years prior to America's ultimate conflict. His euphonious first and middle names were
the maiden names of each of his grandmothers. A Virginia native and
the son of an Episcopal minister, "Rob" Wheat looked every inch the
leader of men. The thirty-six-year-old was a dark-complexioned
giant—six feet four inches tall and weighing as much as 275 pounds—
but he bore his tremendous frame so gracefully that one of his comrades christened him "a mounted Falstaff." Wheat balanced his commanding physical presence with a gentler personality. Gifted with
intelligence and charm, the worldly Wheat was a favorite among his
fellow officers and men. "It required the iron hand of discipline tem-
pered with fatherly kindness, to make soldiers of them," remarked a
Confederate officer after the war. "Wheat had these two good qualities of a commander in a remarkable degree. His men loved him—and
they feared him—the power or spell he had over his men was truly
wonderful."[31]

Wheat had been severely wounded in the first great land battle of
the war at Manassas ten months earlier when a bullet tore through
his lung. He beat the grim odds given him by his attending physician
and recuperated at Culpeper, Virginia, then returned to his command
in March. Wheat was back in the saddle, leading his Tigers in a skirmish against the Thirteenth Indiana on May 7. Two weeks and two
days later, on the Gooney Manor Road, Wheat received his attack
instructions with pleasure and vigor. He had served under Gen. Win-

field Scott in Mexico and Giuseppe Garibaldi in Italy; now for the first time it was for Stonewall Jackson in the Shenandoah Valley.

Brandishing his sword, Wheat trotted forward, his men following closely behind him. As General Jackson and General Ewell stood on the road, the Louisiana Tigers approached on their left. "I shall never forget the style in which Wheat's battalion passed us," recalled Campbell Brown six years later. "[Wheat] was riding full gallop, yelling at the top of his voice, his big sergeant-major running at speed just after him, calling to the men to come on, and they strung out . . . all running, all yelling, all *looking* like fight." Coming in on the left of the First (CSA) Maryland, the Tigers added color, excitement, and terror to the charge with their unique fighting style. " 'Twas beautiful to see them—firing, dropping on the ground, and firing—all the time creeping up while the enemy blazed away from under cover of the town," admired a Confederate in the town at the time.[32]

The Union Marylanders proved no match for this onslaught. Many scampered northward toward the river, which induced one of the citizens to deride them as "a flock of sheep." Within minutes the Confederates seized the hospital, punishing their opponents in the process. Two Federals lay dead while several others were wounded and captured, including the provost marshal—Captain Reynolds. Incapacitated by merciless blows to his testicles and the small of his back (likely delivered by the Tigers), Reynolds was escorted away as a prisoner of war. Company H of the Sixth Virginia Cavalry rode up, and both Confederate infantry and horse soldiers spilled onto the streets and flowed northward through Front Royal. "We drove them through the town," proudly wrote a Confederate Marylander to his mother, "all the time howling like demons."[33]

The powerful reaction by the citizens of Front Royal caught the soldiers by surprise. Oblivious to the danger of errant shots buzzing around them, the secessionist women ran out into the street to greet their liberators, waving their bonnets, cheering and screaming. Some took in those soldiers who were too spent to continue, while others aided the Confederates by pointing to areas where Union soldiers were hiding. "I love to think of all the nice things the nice ladies offered us going [through]," recounted one of Johnson's men, "and hate to think how foolish I was not stopping and getting some." For the boys who lived in Front Royal, the action would leave a lasting imprint in their memories. Witnessing the disorder on both sides and irregular small arms fire, Tom Ashby assessed the Front Royal skirmish as "more like a police riot than a fight between soldiers."[34]

Lt. Walter Buck had performed the necessary reconnaissance earlier that morning; now he bore witness to a battle waged in his hometown. He clattered through the streets of Front Royal and made his way to "Bel Aire," the home of his cousins in the northeast corner of town. The Bucks were beside themselves with joy at seeing their relative. The youngest children rushed up and kissed his hand while one of the older cousins, a teenager named Nellie, just stood there and sobbed. "Why Nellie, child!" exclaimed Lieutenant Buck at the reaction. "Crying? Cheer up! Now is the time to be laughing. Jackson's army is coming and we're going to drive the Yankees away from you."[35]

Given how easy it was for the Confederates to sweep their opponents from the town, no Southerner expected the resistance that Kenly was about to offer them north of Front Royal. Lieutenant Colonel Dushane of the First (USA) Maryland had ridden to the town at Kenly's request to confirm the frantic citizen's story. He immediately galloped back to camp and told his colonel the report was true. The time inched to quarter past two when Kenly ordered the long roll to beat. Startled due to the lack of prewarning from his pickets, Kenly suffered from General Banks's oversight of not providing him any cavalry. With cavalry, Kenly would likely have learned of Jackson's approach as early as 7:00 A.M. Receiving his first warning from Lieutenant Colonel Parham six hours later, Kenly realized he had no time to do anything else except to stay and fight. His vital position on the flank of Banks's army also influenced his decision. "I prepared to hold the position as long as possible," explained Kenly, "for I was certain that if I did not check Jackson's advance . . . Banks was lost." He dispatched a courier to ride to Strasburg and inform Banks of the attack.[36]

Behind Kenly, on the peninsula between the two river branches, ailing Lieutenant Colonel Parham of the Twenty-ninth Pennsylvania took charge of his two companies and Captain William Mapes's pioneer company from the Twenty-eighth New York. Keeping the two company officers from the Buckton Station garrison with him, Parham ordered his horse to be saddled, then he painfully mounted and positioned his force. Mapes's pioneers crossed the North Branch bridge and climbed Guard Hill, the dominant height that loomed over the river's north bank. Companies B and G of the Twenty-ninth Pennsylvania remained north of the rivers, covering the wagon and railroad bridges over the confluence. Two locomotives sat in the River Station depot at the time Jackson's men struck the town. Parham ordered the trains to head out to Strasburg.[37]

Kenly took his six companies of infantry and ordered them onto Richardson's Hill. A section of Battery E, Pennsylvania Light Artillery, under the command of Lt. Charles A. Atwell, occupied the military crest on the east side of the Front Royal–Winchester Turnpike with two ten-pounder Parrotts. Remnants from the three outpost companies rushed back toward the height from the captured town. In all, Kenly's defense south of the river confluence amounted to seven hundred infantrymen, rank and file, with thirty-eight artillerists. Not realizing that he was outnumbered by twenty to one, Kenly determined to hold his position to buy as much time as possible. At approximately 2:15 P.M., Atwell's guns opened fire as Confederate infantry and cavalry reached the northern outskirts of the village.[38]

The effect was nothing less than devastating. Rounds careened off buildings. One shot smashed into the Happy Creek mill, between a line of railroad tracks and the Bel Aire estate, and spooked the horses of the Wise Troop standing directly east of it. Lieutenant Buck ordered his cousins to get into the basement of their house. But curiosity seized Lucy and Nellie Buck, and they returned to the porch of Bel Aire in time to watch a shell explode as it struck their barn. "The sound was rather pleasantly exhilarating and I watched the discharges with positive enjoyment," Lucy explained in her diary.[39]

Colonel Johnson detached three companies of the First (CSA) Maryland to advance against Kenly's commanding position. Lt. Col. Edward R. Dorsey took charge of the front-line skirmishers. Companies A and D flanked on each side of the color guard (Company H) and marched toward Richardson's Hill. Wheat's battalion formed up on the left of the Marylanders and also moved out. The remaining one hundred Marylanders formed on the edge of town as three hundred Confederates advanced toward Kenly's position in a broken line extending from the Front Royal–Winchester Turnpike on the west to Happy Creek on the east.

As the Southerners entered a meadow in the flat land north of Front Royal, Atwell trained his guns on them. "His shells began to tell in our ranks," admitted Pvt. Washington Hands in Company D. One projectile burrowed into the ground practically underneath the

Maryland color guard. When it exploded, clods of earth flew all around and the line wavered as the flags fell to the ground. A wary lieutenant scooped them up and continued forward despite the shelling. As Captain Murray of Company H explained to a friend, the "shells did fly most uncomfortably near."[40]

The Confederate skirmishers found an east–west stone wall near the foot of Richardson's Hill. They took cover behind it and flattened themselves as best they could as Federal shells raked across the open valley between the town and the hill. The Louisianans hugged the ground so closely that their heads lay against it. The Wise Troop galloped forward from Front Royal; but after reaching that fence, they, too, could go no farther. Watching a round take out the horse from underneath the lieutenant commanding the horse soldiers, a cavalryman admitted that "the shells [came] quicker than I thought two guns could shoot." The thirty horse soldiers soon returned to town to resume their original duty as General Ewell's escort.[41]

Colonel Kenly countered the offensive of his opponent. He ordered Lieutenant Colonel Dushane to cover his right flank with two companies of First (USA) Maryland. Dushane's companies crested the hill to harass Wheat's Louisianans east of the turnpike. Maj. John Wilson took one company and deployed it on the pike. Two more companies took up a position in front of the railroad bridge. The remaining four companies (including remnants from the picket companies) supported the Parrotts on the crest of the hill east of the turnpike. As the time passed 3:00 P.M., Kenly stood firm in his defense, surprisingly receiving no counterfire from any opposing batteries.[42]

Stonewall Jackson's chief of artillery committed an unconscionable error that prevented a swift Confederate victory at Front Royal on May 23. A former student of Jackson at VMI, Stapleton Crutchfield had graduated first in his class in 1855, then joined Jackson on the teaching staff at the institute for the remainder of the decade. Tall and thin, he had officered three different regiments prior to being awarded the Valley army's chief of artillery position two weeks prior to the Front Royal battle. But Crutchfield's casual tendencies conflicted with the personal traits essential to perform his duties. Alluding to his habit of being a late riser, one of Jackson's aides called Crutchfield a "descendant of the man who invented sleep." Crutchfield's less-than-enthusiastic approach to his duties induced Campbell Brown to assess him as "a competent but lazy officer."[43]

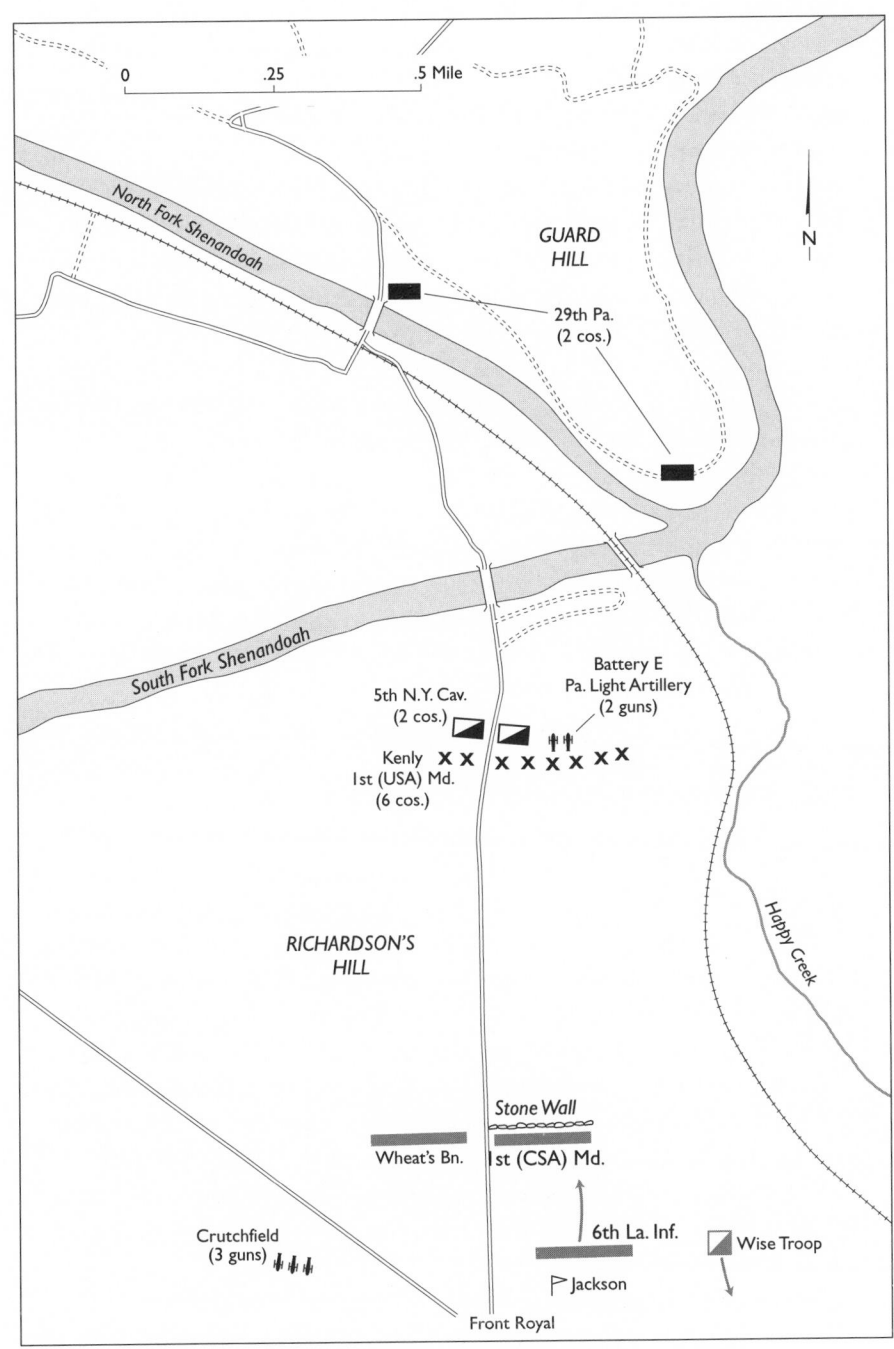

0   .25   .5 Mile

North Fork Shenandoah

GUARD
HILL

N

29th Pa.
(2 cos.)

South Fork Shenandoah

Battery E
Pa. Light Artillery
(2 guns)

5th N.Y. Cav.
(2 cos.)

Kenly   X X   X X X X X   X X
1st (USA) Md.
(6 cos.)

RICHARDSON'S
HILL

Happy Creek

Stone Wall

Wheat's Bn.   1st (CSA) Md.

Crutchfield
(3 guns)

6th La. Inf.

Wise Troop

Jackson

Front Royal

Front Royal: Kenly holds his position, 2:00–4:00 P.M., May 23, 1862

Perhaps the "lazy" tag was undeserved, but Crutchfield left no legacy as a model of preparedness at Front Royal. Lieutenant Simpson escorted Crutchfield from Gooney Manor Road to a commanding ridge that skirted the western side of the village. Placement of guns on this height was guaranteed to suppress his opponent one mile away on Richardson's Hill, which was a lower height northeast of the newly designated site. Pleased at his position, Crutchfield decided to stick with only rifled pieces and called up the first battery available, but when the cannons arrived after their tortuous journey up the side road, Crutchfield was dismayed to find only six- and twelve-pounder smoothbores in the battery. Leaving this battery on a knoll three thousand yards away from Richardson's Hill, he sent orders for the next battery to make the journey to the hill. Captain Alfred R. Courtney responded with his four guns. When the battery arrived, only one piece was found to be rifled. Crutchfield extracted this gun, set aside the others, and ordered its commander, Lt. Joseph Latimer, to fire. Although this cannon was able to exchange shots with Atwell's Parrotts, Crutchfield lamented that it was "unequal to the task of silencing their guns."

As the time approached 3:30 P.M., Crutchfield impatiently awaited the arrival of the next battery. "The division of Major General Ewell had only joined us a day or so previous, and I was, therefore, unfamiliar with the composition of his batteries, which I afterward found to contain but three rifled guns in all," a dismayed and apologetic Crutchfield explained in his after-battle report.[44] Crutchfield failed to explain why he had failed to learn the composition of Ewell's batteries, twenty-two guns in all. Despite knowing that Ewell's division was to lead the assault since dawn, Crutchfield never made the effort to familiarize himself with the type of guns Ewell had—the most important duty for the artillery chief! The oversight was more damning when the five-hour halt was taken into account. Crutchfield's whereabouts and activities during the respite obviously did not include a study of the guns he was destined to command in battle.

Stonewall Jackson agonized at the lack of artillery power displayed by his army at Front Royal. On March 23 at Kernstown, he had faced similar circumstances and had personally deployed his division artillery on the military crest of Sandy Ridge. It had taken him merely one hour that day to deploy a mix of rifled pieces and smoothbores—at least thirteen guns in all—which effectively suppressed ten

ten-pounder Parrotts on Pritchard's Hill a mile away. Exactly two months later, the two heights near Front Royal stood one mile apart as they did at Kernstown, yet no suppression of two enemy Parrotts had occurred more than one hour into the battle. Impatient for more infantry and artillery to counter the unexpected resistance, Jackson turned to an aide and barked out the instructions to "order up every rifled gun and every brigade of the army."[45]

The protracted action excited and horrified Front Royal's populace. The ubiquitous Walter Buck took advantage of his familiar surroundings, shouting to the town folk to get out of danger. Riding by young Tom Ashby, Buck chided the curious boy for remaining in the open and instructed him to run home as fast as possible and tell his family to take cover in the basement. Without waiting, Buck wheeled his horse around and galloped to Ashby's home to deliver the instructions himself. But Ashby could not follow Buck's order. Distraught by the menacing artillery fire, the boy decided against running the gauntlet of five hundred yards of open space between him and his family's home. Instead, the boy shared the cover of a locust tree with a Confederate soldier, in front of a house occupied by a widow and several small children. For more than an hour, Ashby remained behind the tree, as the cries of children and explosion of shells rent the air around him. "I sat behind that tree believing in my childish fear that every shell was directed at that old house and tree," Ashby distinctly recalled fifty-two years later.[46]

Until more Confederate artillery could unlimber on the dominating height west of the village, the unequal contest allowed Kenly to maintain his position with a meager assaulting force opposing him. A breakdown in Confederate infantry deployment was growing more apparent with each passing minute. For the first hour and a half, one depleted Confederate regiment and one battalion bore the brunt of the action in and around Front Royal. The Seventh, Eighth, and Ninth Louisiana also had been deployed to the west and south of town but had not been seriously engaged. Another regiment from the Pelican State, the Sixth Louisiana, had been ordered forward from its reserve position. The Louisianans moved into the town and lined up in formation behind a house, waiting for deployment orders.[47]

Trimble's brigade filled the vacancy left by the Sixth Louisiana Infantry on the hill above the village. The Sixteenth Mississippi deployed in line of battle on the western side of the Gooney Manor

Road, and the Fifteenth Alabama moved up in line. There they stood from 3:00 P.M. listening to the harrowing sounds of battle. The anticipation of entering their first fight took its toll on the green troops. As cannons moved past them to the front and wounded soldiers were helped to the rear, the incessant popping of small arms, booming of artillery, and sights of blood and powder-blackened faces broke the resolve of many in the reserve ranks. A Mississippian admitted, "There is not much fun in hearing the shells a coming. We can hear them from the time they leave the cannon until they burst." An Alabama private recalled that the suspense "caused a chill to pervade my system to the extent of causing my knees and teeth to knock together. . . . The hair on my head seemed to rise . . . like the quills of a fretful porcupine, and I had some trouble in keeping my hat pressed down." The soldier took some solace when he looked down the line and noticed the same "chill" had seized many in the rank and file of his regiment. The stress of anticipation would remain with the Alabamans the rest of the day, as they were not called into action.[48]

Shortly after 3:30 P.M., Colonel Kenly received Union reinforcements. Two companies of the Fifth New York Cavalry galloped onto the peninsula between the Shenandoah River branches. General Banks had sent them out earlier that afternoon, not in response to a battle he had no knowledge of, but to fulfill an overdue request of Kenly's. Maj. Phillip Vought brought Companies B and D, one hundred cavalrymen total, to the river branches, and before the horse soldiers clattered across the span, Parham detached two men. Concerned that General Banks had yet to learn of the attack, Parham instructed his handpicked messengers to gallop back to Strasburg, find General Banks, and request immediate aid. The two messengers rode out as Vought reported to Kenly.[49]

Rousing cheers from the First (USA) Maryland greeted the cavalry, but Kenly was well aware that their arrival was several hours too late. Kenly's situation had become critical. Colonel Johnson had taken the initiative to redeploy the First (CSA) Maryland against Kenly. He ordered Company G under Capt. Wilson Nicholas to support Wheat's Tigers on his left, sending them to the elevation dominated by the Richardson home, known locally as "Rose Hill." The Louisianans swarmed over the Rose Hill lands. Realizing that their home had become a focal point of the battle, Sue Richardson and her two sisters carried their frail mother to the basement to protect her against the incessant cannonade. "Our yard was full of our soldiers," she entered in her diary, "Major Wheat gave orders from the yard."

At the same time, Johnson ordered Capt. J. Louis Smith to lead Company F through a skirt of woods on the right. Lieutenant Atwell reoriented his Parrotts toward the flanking maneuver and forced the Southerners to fall back. Kenly realized that the success would only be temporary. As Confederate infantry enveloped both of his flanks, he had arrived at a critical conclusion: "it was painfully apparent that I was being surrounded."[50]

Kenly worked desperately to buy more time. He moved Vought's men onto Richardson's Hill and readied them for a charge. Once they aligned on the pike, Vought ordered his men forward, down the hill toward the center of Johnson's skirmish line. The New Yorkers charged to the base of the hill. The unexpected sight of enemy horse soldiers galloping toward them startled some members of the First (CSA) Maryland. "For God's sake, Lieutenant, don't let them pick us up!" cried an elderly member of Company D to Lt. George Booth. Booth's company held on to their position at the stone wall and awaited support.

Colonel Johnson immediately withdrew Captain Smith's company from a skirt of woods to fall back and reinforce Company I. Meanwhile, Lieutenant Colonel Dushane's Union companies on the western flank forced Wheat's Tigers from Rose Hill and delayed Captain Nicholas from reaching that destination to reinforce the Louisianans. Vought's cavalry charge, however, came to an abrupt halt when he saw the Confederate infantry lined behind the stone wall off to his left and in a small woodlot to his right. Riders quickly reared their mounts to avoid needless casualties from an ill-fated charge. Retracing their steps, the Fifth New York Cavalry regained the crest of Richardson's Hill, where Kenly repositioned them in line behind Atwell's two guns. The four o'clock hour was minutes away, and Kenly stubbornly remained entrenched upon the height.[51]

Colonel Crutchfield found two more rifled pieces in the Baltimore Light Artillery under the command of Capt. John B. Brockenbrough. His four-gun battery was the third to reach the height in ninety minutes. In the meantime, Jackson's orders for more rifled pieces were delivered to the center and tail of his army. Col. William C. Scott, commanding the fourth brigade in the army line, had recently jammed his troops onto Gooney Manor Road when he received the directive. He sent Capt. John Lusk forward with two rifled pieces. As the cannons of the Stonewall Brigade rolled toward Asbury Chapel, Capt. William T. Poague, commanding the Rockbridge Artillery, received the order at 4:00 P.M. He pulled two rifled cannons from his battery and moved forward as fast as his jaded horses could move. But Poague started from too far back to provide any assistance on May 23. Capt. George Wooding of the Danville Artillery also got the order to bring his lone rifled piece to the battle. He, like Poague in front of him, would not reach Front Royal until nightfall.[52]

The other half of Jackson's directive—to bring up the infantry—signified a change in his battle plan. No longer was Jackson as concerned about revealing his strength in numbers to his opponent. A courier was sent to find General Winder to deliver the Stonewall Brigade to Front Royal by continuing northward on the River Road. Stonewall apparently deemed a more direct and forceful approach necessary to dislodge Kenly before nightfall. According to Major Dabney, the cavalryman sent rearward to deliver the order to General Winder got overwhelmed by this his first battle and fled before he completed his mission. It made little difference; considering how spent Jackson's prized brigade was the night before, their chances of contributing to the outcome after having marched twenty miles (and still with five miles to go) were nil.[53]

Front Royal marked Stonewall Jackson's first sustained tactical offensive in the war. In preparation, he had performed masterfully to maneuver and concentrate an overwhelming force, but the battlefield had yet to see those troops. Amazingly, the fight had lasted two hours and Colonel Kenly with his eight hundred Union stalwarts (including his cavalry) and two cannons still outnumbered and outgunned the 450 Confederate infantrymen who fired their weapons in this contest. Bradley Johnson maintained that the sole deployment of his First (CSA) Maryland and the Louisiana battalion was deliberate. "It was evidently General Jackson's intention to make us whip the enemy by ourselves," he opined twenty years later.[54]

This, however, was not Jackson's intention. At 4:00 P.M. on May 23, 1862, the battle of Front Royal dragged on with no clear outcome in sight—an embarrassment for the Confederate high command. The Southern artillery concentration was an ongoing fiasco; the three pieces concentrated were apparently too distant to suppress Kenly's position. Jackson attempted to rectify the problem by detaching

Lieutenant Boswell to find a height closer to Richardson's Hill to place Southern artillery on to dislodge the Union cannons. Boswell immediately rode forward to inspect a height only four hundred yards from the Union cannons.[55]

The infantry deployment vied for equal anonymity with the artillery. The Louisiana brigade clearly had not been handled properly, but the responsible commander was not easy to identify. If General Taylor had been given the orders, the responsibility would fall on him. If General Ewell was apprised of the plan and failed to delegate the authority to Taylor, he would be fingered as Jackson's stumbling block. It was apparent by the disjointed action in and around Front Royal that Jackson's subordinate generals seemed befuddled as to how to counter Kenly's Richardson's Hill defense.[56]

All of this had unfolded while Jackson personally witnessed the action. Finally, after 4:00 P.M., Jackson saw to the deployment of another regiment from Taylor's brigade. The Sixth Louisiana was first to move. Ordered to "attempt the capture of the battery," the Louisianans marched through town to work their way on Kenly's right flank. As soon as they walked into the open meadow north of the town, they received the same artillery "greeting" that Johnson's and Wheat's men met before them. The Sixth Louisiana's commander, Col. Isaac Seymour, directed his men into a patch of woods to protect them against Atwell's menacing rounds as the Maryland and Louisiana infantry lay in the open valley behind the wall. The remaining regiments from Taylor's brigade continued to linger in or close to the village. "[We] did not get to fire a gun," complained a member of the Eighth Louisiana.[57]

Kenly had beaten back everything thrown against him. Always watching his flanks, the Union colonel agonized as the progression of the battle resulted in a widening and massing Confederate front. He had little left to counter it. Parham's command stayed in reserve on the opposite side of the North Branch. The men were needed there to cover the bridges should Kenly be forced to withdraw. Tremendous quantities of supplies and equipment lay scattered around the camp of the First (USA) Maryland. Kenly had no means available to salvage the regimental property. Sunset was still three hours away; unless Banks had sent more men than the two cavalry companies that had already arrived, Kenly had little hope of holding his position long enough to withdraw safely under the cover of darkness.

At 4:15 P.M. a messenger notified Kenly that a cavalry force was rapidly riding in from the west between the two river branches. Could it be the reinforcements vital for his survival? Kenly wheeled from his post on Richardson's Hill and rode out to study what was coming in. The approaching cavalry did not come from Banks's army at Strasburg. These men bore a Confederate flag. At that moment Kenly's greatest fear was realized—he had been flanked.[58]

To avert checkmate, Kenly needed a little time and a lot of luck. He would soon painfully learn that neither was in the offing.

3

A TALE OF
TWO CAVALRY ATTACKS

C ol. John S. Clark struggled in his mission to acquire reinforcements for General Banks. After arriving at the capital late on
Thursday, Clark sought out the President on Friday morning, May 23,
only to learn that Lincoln had already left for Falmouth. When Clark
called upon Secretary of War Stanton, he was informed that he had
gone with Lincoln. Secretary of State Seward was next on Clark's
priority list. Seward agreed to see Clark, but would not take the responsibility to carry out Clark's mission to send General Shields's
division back to the Valley. At 4:00 P.M. Clark met with Peter H.
Watson, the assistant secretary of war, who informed Clark that he
could not act on such a request without Stanton's approval. "Call and
see the Secretary in the morning," suggested Watson. Disappointed,
Clark left the War Department, hoping against hope that his efforts
on Banks's behalf would prevail before it was too late.[1]

Buckton Station sat near the midway point on the Manassas Gap
Railroad between Strasburg and Front Royal. Passage Creek flowed
northward where it skirted the western side of the depot buildings
and emptied into the North Branch of the Shenandoah River behind
them. The Strasburg–Front Royal Road crossed the railroad twice in
the region on each side of Passage Creek: the Buck home and mill
marked the west crossing, while the depot stood inside the east cross-

ing. Another road, halfway between each railroad crossing, led northward from Buckton Station where one could cross the river using a
good ford on the east side of the creek and river junction. From there
the road is picked up immediately and runs down to the Chapel Road
at Providence Church halfway between Middletown and Cedarville.
The railroad bridged the creek fifty yards south of the Strasburg–
Front Royal Road. A wheat field spread out on each side of the bridge
immediately south of the railroad. A thick wood sprawled south of
the field.[2]

The Union force guarding Buckton Station throughout the afternoon of May 23 numbered 150 infantrymen. They had been there
since May 17 with specific instructions to protect the vulnerable
railroad bridge and depot. Company B of the Twenty-seventh Indiana
covered the eastern side of the railroad bridge in the wheat field south
of the depot. Company G of the Third Wisconsin guarded the field on
the western side of the Passage Creek bridge. Edward L. Hubbard of
the Third Wisconsin, the only captain on the field, took charge of the
entire detachment. Hubbard's men were particularly wary since two
members of the Wisconsin company had been captured a day earlier.[3]

Captain Hubbard had good reason to remain especially alert, although he would never have expected what was about to hit him.
After crossing McCoy's Ford late in the morning, Col. Turner Ashby
advanced with two hundred horse soldiers from five companies (A, B,
E, F, and G) of his Seventh Virginia Cavalry on an old road that ran
from the ford to Waterlick Station, one mile west of Buckton. Five
miles from the ford the horsemen trotted past Bell's Mill, where Passage Creek flowed from the mouth of Powell's Fort valley at the northern end of the Massanutten range. Ashby sent four men toward Waterlick Station while he took the remainder on the crossroad that
followed the course of the creek northward toward the Buckton depot.

With their movements concealed by dense woods near the hills,
Ashby's cavalry passed Frederick's Mill and halted near Warren
Springs, one mile from Buckton Station. From there Ashby moved
forward with a handpicked guide, Sergeant J. R. Jenkins of Company
E. The third such member of E Company was chosen for the same
reason as Walter Buck and James Simpson before him—he was most
knowledgeable about the area, for his family owned the home next to
the depot buildings currently under Union control. Ashby and Jenkins inched close enough to realize that the element of surprise

would be imperative here since the Yankees were numerous enough to offer a stiff resistance if afforded time to align.[4]

Ashby rode back to his battalion and fed them their instructions. They aligned in battle formation and trotted forward, moving toward the eastern side of the depot. Ashby's mission was threefold: destroy the railroad and telegraph at the station, block reinforcements from Strasburg, and scoop up retreating soldiers from Front Royal. At 4:00 P.M. Ashby barked out the order to charge.[5]

One hundred tons of horse thundered from the woods into the wheat field, the ground shaking from their pounding hoofbeats. The Indiana company took the brunt of this assault and immediately fell back toward the riverbank. The cavalry captured the outer ring of infantry pickets, but this absorbed some of Ashby's momentum. The Hoosiers quickly aligned under their lieutenant (Capt. William Davis was in Front Royal) while Captain Hubbard brought his Badgers into line of battle across the creek. Meanwhile, Union pickets raced back to their lines to avoid capture. Corporal Henry L. Pittman had taken a circuitous route to return to his Hoosier company. Capt. George Sheetz of Company F, Seventh Virginia Cavalry, caught sight of the fleeing Yankee and galloped after him. The two were isolated from the remainder of the action. Caught up in the thrill of the chase, Sheetz neglected to consider that Pittman carried a loaded weapon as he gained ground on the corporal and demanded his surrender. Pittman wheeled around and killed Sheetz with a shot from point-blank range. As Sheetz toppled from his saddle, Pittman took the dead man's horse and rode it to the Union camp.[6]

Scores of Wisconsin infantrymen scampered across the railroad bridge to assist the Hoosiers. Unable to initiate a panic in the bluecoats, Ashby and his men closed in. Both infantry companies fired, dropping a man from Ashby's command on his left flank as several of the horse soldiers worked their way down the bed of Passage Creek, shielded by its shrub-laden banks. Armed predominantly with long-range rifles, the Virginia horse soldiers peppered the Union infantrymen with an arrhythmic volley as the foot soldiers fell back across the bridge to the west side of Passage Creek. There the infantry watched as a lone and wounded Indiana soldier hobbled toward the bridge as two Virginians closed in on him with sabers drawn. Although the injured U.S. soldier subdued one of the cavalrymen, the other one struck his foe with several merciless blows that crumpled the foot soldier to the ground. On his knees and begging for mercy, the Hoosier received none as the Virginian hacked away at him. Unable to watch the torture, Ance Edwards—a Wisconsin soldier—scaled the embankment from across the bridge and unhorsed the Confederate with a well-aimed rifle shot. But as Edwards turned to descend the embankment, he fell dead with a shot through his brain. One of his company mates noted the "smile of satisfaction beaming over his handsome face" at the instant he died.[7]

With much of his command preoccupied with herding prisoners, Ashby ordered his men back to the shelter of the woods. While he reformed his men for a second charge, the remaining Indiana infantry east of Passage Creek crossed over the trestle bridge to join the Badgers. Captain Hubbard ordered both companies to back up and reform behind the fill of the railroad. Using the embankment as a fortification, they leveled their Belgian rifles on the embankment and awaited Ashby's next move.[8]

They didn't have to wait very long. "All was still for a few moments," remembered one of the Wisconsin soldiers, "then we could hear the tramp of hoofs and the clang of sabres." The Seventh Virginia Cavalry debauched from the woods a second time, minutes after their first assault had been repulsed. This time the wheat field south of the railroad was cleared of troops and the entire region east of Passage Creek lay unprotected, save for a token resistance offered at the depot. Company B of the Seventh Virginia circled in from the east and galloped toward the depot. As Capt. John Q. Winfield neared the building, a rifle shot took his mount out from under him. Recapturing his senses and freeing himself from his downed horse, Winfield shouted while swinging his sword, "Come on, boys!" Several members of Company B dismounted and followed their captain into the depot while the remaining Union infantry scampered across the railroad bridge to the west side of the creek. Winfield emerged from the depot with a flag wrapped around his arm. He seized another horse and mounted it. Winfield's men set fire to the depot and its supplies; they also cut the telegraph lines.[9]

Ashby's other companies charged toward the railroad from south to north, brandishing their sabers and renting the air with demonic shrieks. Twenty-five-year-old Capt. John Fletcher led Company A to the railroad embankment, but when the cavalry approached within one hundred yards, the Union troops loosed a volley at them. "That discharge told upon their ranks, for our aim was a sure one," recounted Van R. Willard of the Third Wisconsin. Saddles emptied and riderless horses meandered in all directions as the momentum carried the Virginians closer to the Union line.

Shot in the arm, Captain Fletcher continued forward with a handful of horse soldiers and recklessly charged up the railroad fill. Sporadic infantry fire thudded into both riders and horses, successfully checking the advance. Fletcher fell dead at the top of the embankment; his body remained in Union hands. His attire attracted curiosity from the Badgers. "His underclothing was silk; he had on long patent leather boots and gray uniform," noted a Wisconsin soldier. "In his pockets was a heavy gold watch, some sixty dollars confederate money, and a miniature of a beautiful girl whom I have no doubt now weeps her dead."[10]

The Union counterfire tore the heart out of the cavalry charge. Union confidence grew as Confederate confidence waned. Harry Hatcher of Company A attempted to ride to the woods after the repulse, but he changed his mind when five Union infantrymen left the protection of the embankment and goaded him into the wheat field. Hatcher sped toward his antagonists. Seconds earlier, Hatcher's friend and company mate, Billy Brent, had his horse shot out from under him near the scene. Brent ran toward his comrade as Hatcher turned toward the bluecoats and engaged in hand-to-hand combat with the quintet of westerners. One of the infantrymen pierced Hatcher with a bayonet. Brent drew a saber and struck the soldier as the other four ran back to the railroad. Alone in the field, Brent and the Union soldier grappled while Hatcher lay wounded nearby. In seconds it was over—the injured Yankee lay in the field as Brent escorted his wounded friend to the woods on foot.[11]

Ashby's second charge ended like the first one: a retreat back to the woods south of the wheat field. Down two captains, both dear friends of his, Ashby refused to give up on his mission. He had rendered the telegraph inoperable, but the little railroad trestle remained intact. Most surprising was the fact that the Union infantry did not flee. Thwarted twice in his effort to destroy the creek bridge, Ashby rode in front of his men. "Forward boys!" he snapped, "We will get every mother's son of them." The Virginians dashed forward again, gracefully jumping fences and managing every natural obstacle as they charged toward the railroad embankment.[12]

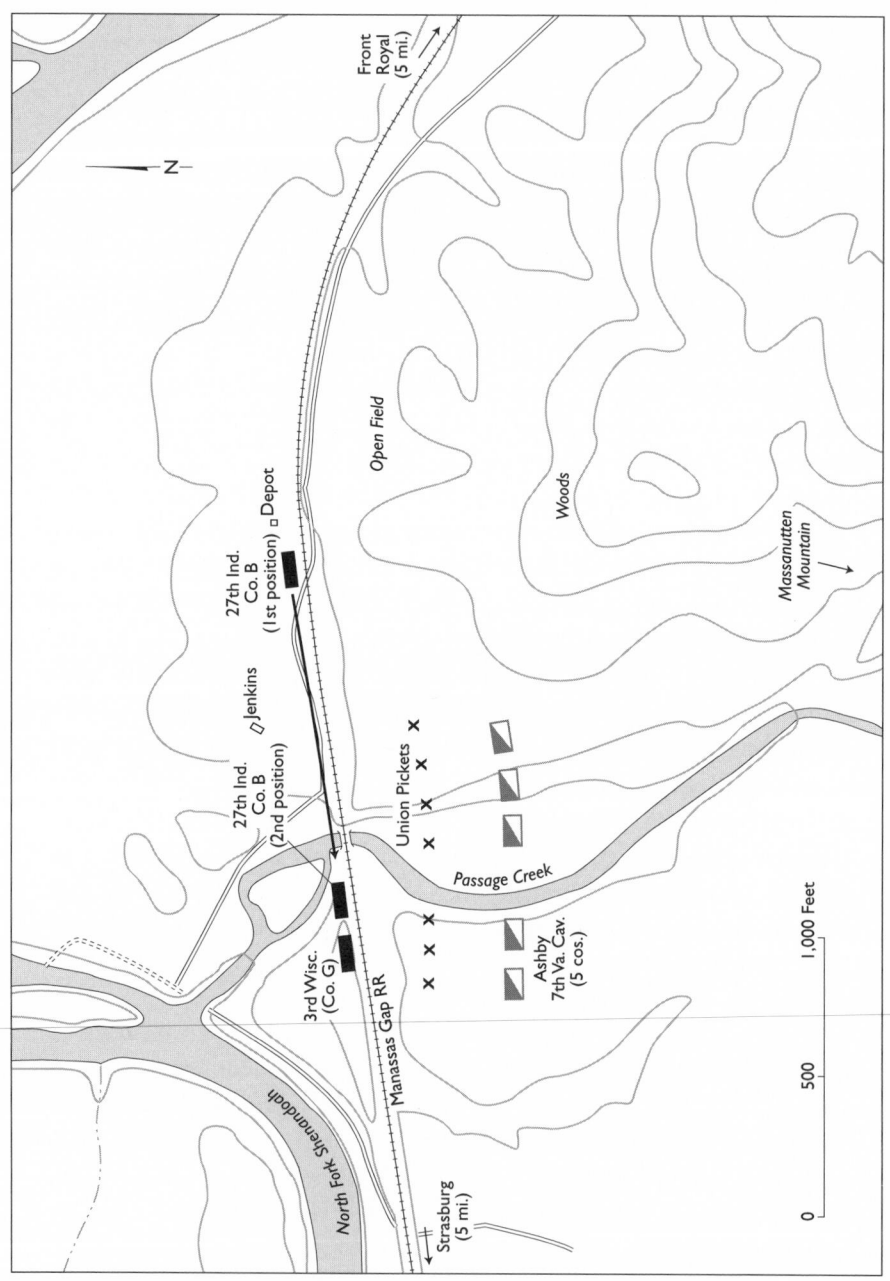

Action at Buckton Station, 4:00 P.M., May 23, 1862

Front Royal (5 mi.)

Open Field

Woods

Massanutten Mountain

27th Ind. Co. B (1st position) □ Depot

◊ Jenkins

27th Ind. Co. B (2nd position)

Union Pickets

Passage Creek

3rd Wisc. (Co. G)

Manassas Gap RR

Ashby 7th Va. Cav. (5 cos.)

North Fork Shenandoah

Strasburg (5 mi.)

0   500   1,000 Feet

–N–

The Badgers and Hoosiers refused to yield. With confidence growing after each successive repulse, the Union infantry lying behind the
railroad fill coolly waited for the Confederate cavalry to close in to
within range of their rifles. At one hundred yards Hubbard barked out
the order to fire. The volley proved too much for the cavalry as they
reeled away from the menacing Union line and again sought the
safety of the woods. No one dared to ride up to the railroad during this
charge.[13]

As his men returned to the woods, Ashby showed no signs of
giving up. Longing for his horse artillery, he muttered, "If my little
Blakely were here, these people should not escape." He rode forward
alone to reconnoiter for a fourth attempt at the railroad trestle. He
scaled a piece of rising ground within rifle range of his opponent. As
expected, his position attracted fire. A bullet tore through the ear of
his black charger. Seemingly undaunted by the close call, Ashby
quieted his injured horse with soothing whispers, assuring a concerned cavalryman nearby that the incident was merely the result of a
stray ball. Indeed, Ashby was fearless, but nerves of iron alone would
not win the day at Buckton Station.

Ashby finally came to the conclusion that many within his command had realized two charges before: he could not dislodge his opponent. Ashby gathered up his prisoners and headed eastward toward
Front Royal, leaving a token force near Buckton Station to check any
attempt at a Union advance. Although only three horse soldiers were
known to have been wounded in the Buckton charges, two dead soldiers served as painful reminders of the consequences of Ashby's
reckless style: the lifeless body of Captain Fletcher lay on the contested ground and that of Captain Sheetz rode in a wagon with his
eastbound column.[14]

Captain Hubbard remained wary behind the railroad embankment near the station. The Indiana company lost seven wounded and
six captured. The Wisconsin men fared better, with one killed and
two wounded. The westerners had held their position and saved the
bridge and still controlled the roads to Strasburg. But no artillery had
been present for either side, reducing the likelihood that General
Banks or anyone at Strasburg heard the skirmish six miles away.
Shortly before 5:00 P.M., Hubbard scrawled a dispatch detailing what
happened at the depot, then recruited a volunteer to ford the North
Branch of the Shenandoah and deliver the news to headquarters,

along with a request for reinforcements. It took the courier two hours to travel the distance on foot.[15]

At the same time that Colonel Ashby attacked Buckton Station, another Confederate cavalry detachment under Lt. Col. Thomas Flournoy closed in on the Union infantry. A fifty-year-old lawyer who had served a term as a U.S. representative in the Thirtieth Congress with Abraham Lincoln, Flournoy had enlisted in the Sixth Virginia Cavalry along with two of his sons. Natural leadership skills enabled him to rise from captain of Company G in August 1861 to command of fourteen companies of horse from the Second and Sixth Virginia Cavalry nine months later. During the midafternoon of May 23, Flournoy's cavalrymen destroyed Manassas Gap Railroad tracks and the telegraph communication halfway between Buckton Station and Front Royal. Once this mission was completed, Flournoy led his command eastward between both Shenandoah River branches toward Front Royal. He halted his horse soldiers on high ground west of the town where he watched Jackson work against Kenly.

It was Flournoy's men whom Kenly spied at 4:15 P.M. Kenly had crossed the South Branch bridge to study the approaching cavalry. In doing so, he observed Capt. David Lane marching his Company B of the Twenty-ninth Pennsylvania away from the rope ferry at the river junction toward the newly constructed Pike Bridge that spanned the North Branch of the Shenandoah. Lieutenant Colonel Parham had issued the orders with the intent that Lane put his men up on Guard Hill on the north side of the North Branch. Kenly changed the plan when he realized that Lane's departure would leave no holding force on the river branches. Lane's men returned to their post with a cheer as Kenly rode back to Richardson's Hill.

Once Kenly ascended the crest of the ridge, he noted Confederate infantry continuing to threaten his position near the base of Richardson's Hill. The approaching Sixth Louisiana Infantry more than doubled the force that had opposed him for two hours. Outnumbered and flanked, and with no response from Strasburg via the couriers he had sent (as it turned out, none of Kenly's couriers reached Banks by this time), Kenly realized that "nothing was now left but to cross the rivers."[16]

The task before him would be a difficult one. Not only did he have two rivers at his back, one thousand yards apart; he also had mass stores of government supplies at the camp on the south bank of the closest river. Kenly instructed his regimental quartermaster to pack up the valuable camp equipment, load it into wagons, and carry it to Winchester. The national flag was taken down, furled, and placed in a wagon with a trunk containing Kenly's personal belongings. Kenly ordered his servant to stay with that particular wagon and escort it to safety.[17]

The supplies could not be saved. Kenly ordered a detachment to torch the camp while he passed orders for his men to withdraw. The First (USA) Maryland Infantry pulled back first and filed over the South Branch bridge. Those troops on the left flank made their way to the railroad bridge and attempted a crossing there. As they crossed and marched briskly toward the Pike Bridge, Lieutenant Atwell limbered his Parrotts, rolled them down the reverse slope of Richardson's Hill, and followed the Maryland infantry over the bridges. Major Vought screened the movement with his one hundred horse soldiers. To this point, Kenly's entire loss on Richardson's Hill (not counting the pickets captured in and south of Front Royal) amounted to fewer than twenty men. The casualty list would grow as the Union troops made their way across the peninsula at 4:30 P.M.[18]

The Confederate infantry opposing Kenly quickly caught on to his planned escape. The Southerners surged forward. Wheat's Tigers and the left flank of the First (CSA) Maryland raided the portion of Kenly's camp not set to the torch while the right flank of Confederate Marylanders chased their Union brethren to the bridge. Several Union Marylanders were trapped on the Front Royal side of the river before they could climb onto the railroad trestle. They surrendered as a small cluster. Pvt. Tom Levering, of Company H, First (CSA) Maryland, proudly marched seven Union captives back to Colonel Johnson.

While their comrades to the east gained some success, the left flank Confederate infantry succumbed to the temptation lying within the unburned portion of the Union camp. The First (CSA) Maryland captains kept their infantrymen from the plunder, but Wheat's Tigers beelined to the Union quartermaster stores at the camp. The hungry soldiers treasured the supplies. The extravagant selection included spiced and pickled oysters, sardines, all types of confectionery, oranges, and lemons. "The fight would have terminated then and there had not the Louisiana battalion stumbled upon the enemy's camp," complained Capt. William W. Goldsborough of the First (CSA) Maryland, "and bent on plunder, the threats and entreaties of their officers were for some time in vain, and when they were at length prevailed upon to move forward, it was found that the enemy in their front, with their artillery and cavalry, had escaped over the bridge."[19]

The left wing of the Confederate Marylanders' line bypassed the camp plunder to chase after the Union forces crossing the wagon bridge, firing as they double-quicked to the river. Pvt. John Gill witnessed a member of the Fifth New York Cavalry fall dead in front of the bridge amidst a swarm of musket balls. As his company mates hastened across the bridge (in the process extinguishing the feeble attempt to burn it), Gill stood over the dead horse soldier, eyeing his boots. Planning on joining the Confederate cavalry when his term was due to expire in June, Gill decided not to waste the opportunity to prepare for that arm of the service. He pulled the cavalry boots off the dead man's feet. "The temptation was too great and I could not let some one else make this important capture," justified Gill.[20]

As the Southern infantry filed across the bridge onto the peninsula, Kenly's Union force deployed on the Winchester side of the Pike Bridge over the North Branch of the Shenandoah. Guard Hill towered over the north bank. Lieutenant Atwell unlimbered his cannons on the height west of the turnpike, near Dr. Kenner's prominent home, while the Union infantry redeployed on each side of the road to contest any attempt at the Pike Bridge. Kenly's force increased as he picked up one hundred Pennsylvanians who had been deployed behind him for most of the afternoon. Captain Mapes's pioneer company, dressed in civilian attire, was also put to use. Kenly ordered Mapes to torch the Pike Bridge after his men had crossed it, the same bridge they had recently constructed. As Mapes waited for the rest of the Northerners to file across the double-span bridge to comply with his instructions, Atwell opened fire toward the South Branch by 5:00 P.M.[21]

Stonewall Jackson spurred his horse Little Sorrell onto Richardson's Hill with his staff working to keep pace with him. Scaling the height, which had been vacated by his opponent less than fifteen minutes earlier, Jackson took in the scene that lay in front (north) of him. To his near left, billowing smoke rose from Kenly's original camp. Farther to the left, across the South Branch, an ascending trail of road dust announced the approach of Flournoy and his cavalry. But Stonewall was most taken by the scene playing out directly below him. At least one-quarter of a mile of Federal infantry marched across the North Branch in excellent order, apparently unopposed. Seized with eagerness tainted with a little frustration, Jackson exclaimed, "Oh, what an opportunity for artillery! Oh that my guns were here!" He turned to an aide and repeated the directive he had dictated an hour before: "[O]rder up every rifled gun and every brigade in the army."[22]

Colonel Crutchfield had been working desperately to comply with his superior's request. He unlimbered three rifled pieces on the commanding height that formed Front Royal's northwestern border. That artillery force had barely fired a shot and was now being rendered useless by the Union withdrawal. The next artillery force to make its way to the front were two rifled pieces from Col. William C. Scott's brigade. Capt. John A.M. Lusk commanded the section. As it rolled past Trimble's brigade on the Gooney Manor Road, Lieutenant Colonel James Shannon of the Sixteenth Mississippi received his orders to provide support. Shannon detached the four right-flank companies of his lined-up regiment and raced with the battery over the hill and into the town. The remaining Mississippi companies soon followed, inhaling clouds of dust and sweating profusely under the late-afternoon sun. Leaving the other cannons on the western height, Crutchfield led Lusk's rifles toward the riverbank.[23]

To this point, only the Sixth Louisiana Infantry had been deployed from Taylor's brigade. They had scaled Richardson's Hill as Kenly's men withdrew from it. General Taylor trotted to the South Branch bank where he met up with General Jackson. Seeing that Atwell's guns commanded their front, Taylor suggested to Jackson that he could flank the position by sending one of his regiments over the railroad bridge. Jackson consented, and the closest Louisiana regiment moved forward.[24]

This was the Eighth Louisiana Infantry, commanded by Col. Henry Kelly. Kelly led his men forward as the time closed in on 5:00 P.M. As Union artillerists lobbed shells in their direction, the Louisianans filed onto the railroad trestle and worked their way across the single-span bridge, adjusting their footwork to negotiate the cross ties. They jumped off the span onto the peninsula and rushed forward, keeping to the east of the Union artillery ensconced one-half mile in front of them.[25]

Confederate soldiers flooded the peninsula from three directions: Flournoy's cavalry from the west, the Eighth Louisiana from the east, and the First Maryland from the south. Two buildings existed on each side of the pike on the peninsula. The River Station depot hugged the east side and Riverside, the home of Maj. James Richards, dominated the west side. Major Richards's mother-in-law recorded in her diary how excited they were to have Jackson's army coming to their rescue. "We were almost frantic with joy," she confessed. "As soon as the Yankees saw them they scampered. I never saw such running in all my life. We were all so excited we screamed with joy, but soon were compelled to go to the basement."[26]

Atwell's cannons attempted to sweep the peninsula as the Southerners rushed to the Pike Bridge. Lusk's guns countered from Richardson's Hill. By this time General Ewell had ridden up near the South Branch with a cluster of aides. Atwell's guns directed their muzzles toward the irresistible target and opened fire. Ewell quickly realized that his clinging couriers were endangering his life. "Clear out, sir, clear out!" he bellowed to Capt. Frank Myers. The aides left Ewell's side and rode to the Union camp looking for abandoned weapons and equipment.[27]

With a total force numbering approximately eight hundred effectives on Guard Hill, Colonel Kenly was determined to hold his position. He quickly noted, however, that an integral duty had not been fulfilled. The Pike Bridge still stretched over the North Branch of the Shenandoah unburned. Mapes's pioneers had attempted to set it afire, but the bridge had been constructed of fairly green timbers and had not kindled. Desperate to complete the job before the Confederates closed in on his position, Kenly ordered Sergeant William Taylor to fire the bridge. Taylor dutifully rushed to the span as bullets whizzed by on all sides of him and rekindled it. Taking a musket ball in the hand, the sergeant returned to Guard Hill. This time the flames spread across the south span and licked the edges of the opposite lane. (Taylor's mission would earn him the Congressional Medal of Honor in 1897.)[28]

Stonewall Jackson trotted across the South Branch Bridge and entered the peninsula between the two branches. Ewell followed behind. Both were guided by the billowing smoke of the burning bridge in front of them. Virginia cavalry had also closed in near the River Railroad Station. Union artillery continued to sweep the peninsula in an attempt to stymie the Southerners' pursuit.

In the meantime, Colonel Kelly rode forward with the Eighth

Louisiana Infantry. Keeping to the right (east), they approached the North Branch of the Shenandoah. Kelly rode at the head of his command and followed a worn set of horse tracks to the bank. Guessing correctly that this was the ford, he plunged in and his men followed him into the waist-deep but rapid current. As he climbed the opposite bank, Kelly saw the burning bridge and acted immediately. He sent Lt. Nicholas J. Sandlin with a small detachment to extinguish the flames. Kelly continued to lead the rest of his regiment forward. "Come on boys," he shouted. "We will have them."[29]

The time passed 5:00 P.M. as Colonel Kenly perched himself directly in front of the burning Pike Bridge. What he saw forced him to adopt a new battle plan. "I discovered that the river below the bridges was alive with horsemen," he lamented as he watched Sixth Virginia cavalrymen fording at two different places. Directing Capt. George W. Kugler of Company A to hold the daunting Southern force in check, Kenly galloped back to his Guard Hill force and ordered them to withdraw immediately. Atwell relimbered his guns and rolled them down the northern face of the ridge. Kenly ordered Major Vought to protect the rear with his two cavalry companies while Parham's Twenty-ninth Pennsylvania headed down the Front Royal–Winchester Pike directly behind the cannons, followed by the First (USA) Maryland Infantry. Kenly's destination was Middletown. He determined to reach it by turning west off the pike at the hamlet of Cedarville where the Chapel Road would lead them seven miles to the Valley Turnpike at Middletown. But Cedarville was still two miles from Guard Hill.[30]

The race was on, but Jackson's infantry was out of the contest. The First (CSA) Maryland remained on the peninsula. The Eighth Louisiana was the lone Confederate infantry regiment to completely cross both rivers. Colonel Kelly and his men attempted to flank Guard Hill to the east only to discover the height evacuated. A frustrated private noted, "They out run us and could be overtaken only by the cavalry." Kelly's command did capture several members of Company A, First (USA) Maryland, the sacrificial lambs left by Kenly to slow the Confederate onslaught. Colonel Kelly continued the chase with a portion of the Eighth Louisiana.[31]

Jackson's men had finally dislodged Kenly's stronghold more than twelve hours after he began his march to Front Royal. But his sole hope to prevent Kenly's escape rested with Flournoy's cavalry, which was fording the river and crossing single file over the unburned span of the Pike Bridge. After the first four companies of the Sixth Virginia Cavalry had crossed to the north side of the North Branch, Jackson ordered Flournoy to continue the pursuit. Companies A, B, E, and K crossed first and galloped northward. "I never saw such a yell & running of horses," reported an Alabaman to his wife while witnessing the genesis of the pursuit by the Sixth Virginia Cavalry. They charged down the pike after Kenly's men, who were barely one mile north of them. Three more companies (D, F, and I) managed their way across the river branch and followed close behind. They passed a portion of the Eighth Louisiana Infantry a little more than one mile north of the North Branch. The Pelican State soldiers stopped, realizing that only cavalry was able to catch the fleeing Union garrison.[32]

Maj. Aaron Davis rode with the cavalry, an unusual participant given the fact that he was the commissary officer for the Louisiana brigade. Intoxicated with adrenaline (and, suggested some Confederates, too much alcohol), Davis changed roles once he realized that horse soldiers alone could run down the enemy. He rallied some orderlies and couriers and rode with the cortege to join the Sixth Virginia Cavalry.[33]

The horse soldiers trotted northward in sections of fours with Company K, under the command of Capt. George A. Baxter, in the lead. Trying to comply with orders relayed from Lieutenant Colonel Flournoy, Baxter grew impatient at two nonmembers of the cavalry who were riding immediately in front of them. One was notably older than the other; he wore a dingy uniform with an old kepi pulled well forward across his head. The two had slowed the pace of Baxter's trot, and he let them know it with choice language. "Get out of the way of my men," was the gist of his message. The younger of the two men in front of him turned toward Baxter and—motioning to his companion —announced, "This is General Jackson."

Baxter was stunned but recovered quickly enough to order his men to shout, "Three cheers for General Jackson." As the cheers and shouts rippled from front to rear of the cavalry column, Jackson followed the path of the acclamation, riding through the lines bareheaded, the same way he initiated the Front Royal campaign half a day earlier. His presence inspired again. The Sixth Virginia horse soldiers quickened their pace, and Jackson took up the rear where he would not impede their progress. General Ewell and headquarters staff members quickly joined him, including Jed Hotchkiss, who had arrived to the battle from Luray less than one hour earlier. Jackson's attacking force numbered fewer than three hundred cavalrymen.[34]

Kenly's force had been disintegrating throughout the day. Atwell's artillerists and Parham's Twenty-ninth Pennsylvania companies had been reduced slightly through casualties and capture. But the First (USA) Maryland had borne the brunt of Jackson's assaults. With few battle casualties but scores of lost men to capture, Kenly's regiment did not exceed 700 men participating in the retreat. A total force of 850 Union infantry, artillery, and cavalrymen scurried northward to escape Jackson. Kenly was desperate for reinforcements to meet him on the route.[35]

Ten miles to the west of Kenly, Banks's languid army lolled in and around their Tom's Brook and Strasburg camps, oblivious of what had transpired at Buckton Station and Front Royal. The stillness was broken by Charley H. Greenleaf, the first of two Fifth New York Cavalry messengers sent by Lieutenant Colonel Parham from Front Royal. Greenleaf galloped up to the brigade headquarters tent of Col. George H. Gordon. Gen. John P. Hatch and Gordon sat under canvas when Greenleaf entered and frantically asked for General Banks's whereabouts. The two commanders sent Greenleaf to Hupp's Hill.

Greenleaf entered the Hupp house at 5:45 P.M. and fed General Banks the first news of the hours-long attack at Front Royal. Greenleaf was unable to provide Banks with the Confederate strength or the numbers of reinforcements needed. Banks quickly scribbled a dispatch to send back, informing Kenly that "a regiment of infantry and a section of artillery is on the road to aid you." He ordered up a fresh horse for Greenleaf to ride with the return message. Banks then ordered Colonel Gordon to detach infantry and artillery from his brigade for Kenly's aid. Gordon complied by sending Lt. John D. Woodbury's section of Battery M, First New York Light Artillery, down the Chapel Road toward Cedarville. Gordon ordered the Third Wisconsin off to Front Royal as well, but he sent them on the route that would pass Buckton Station, and not the Chapel Road from where Kenly expected help to arrive.[36]

It was too late to make any difference. Kenly's troops reached the Cedarville crossroads at the same time that Banks first learned he was under attack. "I commenced to indulge a hope that I might yet save my command," he admitted and ordered his force to halt. Lieutenant

Colonel Parham, riding on a caisson after losing his horse in the initial confusion preceding the withdrawal, jumped off his seat and implored Kenly to keep advancing down the turnpike toward Winchester. Kenly overruled him and ordered the men to turn to the left on the Chapel Road. Middletown was less than seven miles away, and reinforcements were likely heading in their direction on the same road. Flournoy's Virginia cavalry settled the issue. As horsemen from the four pursuing Confederate companies galloped through the fields and woods on the west side of the pike, Kenly realized that his planned retreat route was cut off. "The sudden appearance of cavalry galloping . . . on my left convinced me that I was lost," lamented Kenly as the last vestiges of hope fled his thoughts.[37]

Kenly directed his men forward, and they continued northward on the pike as Flournoy's horse soldiers drew in closer for the kill. One and one-half miles north of Cedarville, the turnpike ascended to a flat plateau. Crooked Creek hugged the west side of the pike here as the height abruptly descended to its valley. The east side was cleared, save for an orchard, and was occupied by the Thomas McKay stone homestead known as "Fairview." As Kenly began his ascent, Major Vought rode up to him from the rear of the column to inform him that the Southern cavalry was now upon them. Kenly ordered Vought to check the enemy by charging them while he deployed his men off to the side of the pike and also halted the artillery.

Kenly made his stand on the plateau. He sent his adjutant, Lt. Frederick Tarr, to communicate his order to the artillery. He then sent the left wing of his force to the east toward Fairview while directing the right wing to tear down the plank fence that lined the western side of the pike and align in the fields. Lieutenant Colonel Dushane took charge of this wing while Major Wilson attempted to direct the eastern defense.[38] The time passed 6:15 P.M.

Flournoy deployed his front four companies as Kenly attempted to make his stand. Company B stayed in the fence-lined turnpike while Company E deployed to the left and Companies K and A pulled off to the right and headed toward Fairview. As they deployed they clashed with Major Vought's New York cavalrymen. Not only did the New Yorkers offer no resistance; they thundered northward in a panic, running over and through Kenly's men who were attempting to deploy in line of battle. As a result, some of the Union Marylanders, equally panicked, mistook Vought's men for the Southern cavalry and fired into their ranks. Major Wilson's left wing managed a hasty line in the field while Lieutenant Dushane's wing pulled off to the right. Kenly rode toward the front to watch his last hope in action.[39]

Capt. Daniel Grimsley and his thirty-five horse soldiers of Company B, recruited as the "Rappahannock Cavalry," led the Sixth Virginia Cavalry against Kenly's men. The Virginians charged down the pike four abreast with an eighteen-year-old flag bearer named James H. "Dallas" Brown riding conspicuously in front. They galloped toward the unorganized center of Kenly's line, but the wings had deployed as the horse soldiers closed within one hundred yards. Unfortunately for Grimsley's men, the other three companies lagged well behind them in the fields on each side of the pike. This left the three dozen Rappahannock recruits as the focus of attention. As they crested the plateau, Union guns pointed at them from right and left.

On command, the Union Maryland and Pennsylvanian line exploded with a ragged but devastating volley. The fusillade wrecked the Rappahannock company. Cavalrymen and their whinnying mounts tumbled onto the pike, and riderless horses carried their momentum past the Union line. The dust and gunsmoke lifted to yield a macabre scene. Twenty-one animals and twenty-three Virginians littered the road, nine men killed and fourteen wounded. Among the dead was Dallas Brown, the teenager who had led the Virginians onward. Twenty-one bullets riddled his body; eleven tore up the arm that carried the standard.[40]

Kenly's initial success was short lived. Several of his captains disregarded their duty and galloped away, leaving the regimental officers with the burden of directing all the men. Two more companies of Confederate horse were upon the U.S. soldiers in less than the twenty seconds the Yankees needed to reload their weapons. Companies A and K of the Sixth Virginia Cavalry thundered up the height on the east side of the turnpike; Company E did likewise on the west side. The thrust of the attack was directed from the east where Capt. George A. Baxter led his Loudoun County recruits in Company K. Conspicuous at the head of his company, Baxter charged his men toward an orchard on the McKay grounds where Union Maryland soldiers had arrived seconds earlier. The Southerners drew their sabers and pistols as they closed in on their foes. "Left into line," bellowed Baxter while waving his pistol over his head, "charge!"

Company K slammed into the Union line. One member likened

the charge to a tempest and claimed the Northerners "might as well have tried to stop a tornado." But Captain Baxter was denied the fruits of his labor when a point-blank musket shot ended his life. Retaliating pistol shots found their mark in Kenly's men, some of whom were hit as they attempted to get off the road and into the fields. Kenly became a target as well. On horseback as he tried to keep a line in formation, he was knocked off his mount by a hard-hitting musket ball. Dazed, Kenly slowly picked himself off the ground as Southern cavalryman rode upon his force. Lieutenant Atwell sent one of his cannons north-ward and turned his lone remaining piece toward his foes. In an incredibly desperate maneuver, Atwell ran the gun through the charging cavalry. It failed to slow their momentum one iota.[41]

The next several minutes of action proved surreal, vicious, and remarkable all at the same time. Rarely in the first year of the Civil War had cavalry sustained a clash of hand-to-hand encounters against infantry. The size of the attacking force was disproportionately small. Company E was limited by the deep creek valley west of the pike and was unable to penetrate the line. With Company B destroyed by the lone Union volley, a Virginia cavalry of no more than one hundred horse soldiers defied military doctrine to pour into the front and flank of seven hundred Union infantry. Yet, despite their huge advantage in numbers, the U.S. soldiers had no chance. Tired, panicked, conspic-uously devoid of leadership at the company level, and armed with unloaded weapons, the Northerners were in no condition to defend. Flournoy's force had entered a realm of close warfare with an incred-ible window of advantage. Their success relied on a weapon that had become an accoutrement for display but was rarely used in combat—the saber.

Slashing left and right, the Sixth Virginia Cavalry ripped Kenly's ranks amid a cacophony of snorting and whinnying horses, crackling pistol fire, howling Confederates, and shrieking Federals. Kenly reeled from a blow that slit the top of his head. Some of his men whisked him into an ambulance and sent it northward. Lieutenant Tarr, Kenly's adjutant, fared much worse. A Virginia horseman tow-ered over Tarr and slashed him diagonally across his nose and upper lip. Instinctively, Tarr threw his right arm across his head to shield his face. Another saber stroke tore into his elbow joint while a third swing destroyed the thumb joint on his left hand. Tarr's terrifying ordeal ended without mercy. The cavalier delivered a most devastat-

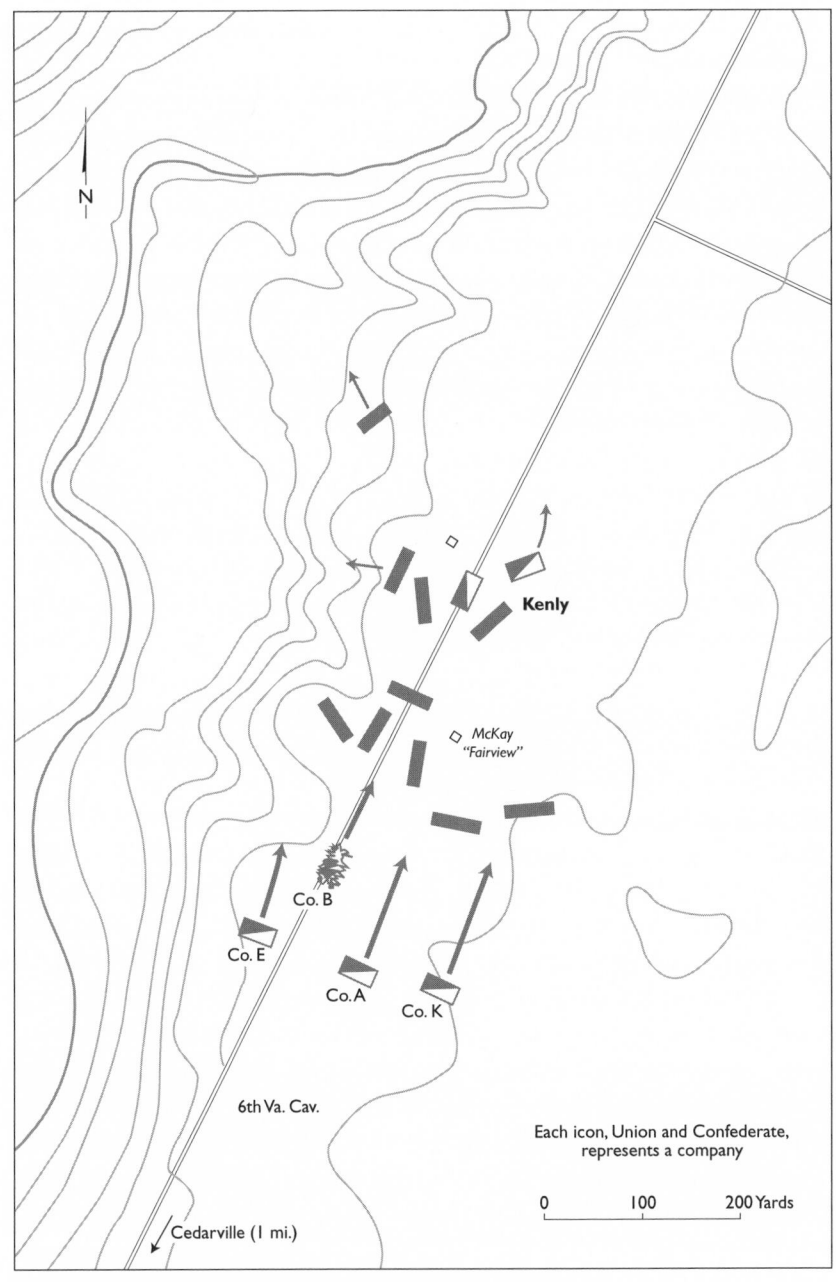

Denouement at Cedarville, 6:30 P.M., May 23, 1862

N

Kenly

McKay
"Fairview"

Co. B

Co. E

Co. A

Co. K

6th Va. Cav.

Each icon, Union and Confederate,
represents a company

0   100   200 Yards

Cedarville (1 mi.)

ing blow that split the soft tissue of his scalp all the way to his skull from the crown to the forehead. Tarr crumpled to the ground. Remarkably, he survived.[42]

With no time to reload their smoothbores, Kenly's Marylanders clubbed their muskets and used their bayonets to fight off the onslaught, thrusting them at both Confederate horse and rider. Lt. George F. Means of Company K lost his horse to savage bayonet wounds. The animal toppled on top of its rider. A sergeant saved the officer's life by pulling him from the maelstrom before the Maryland Unionists could pound him to death with their muskets. Company A at full strength and the remaining dozen men that Captain Grimsley could muster in his Company B continued the momentum of the charge. "I do not believe they could have checked our onset by any volley they could have given us, without killing our horses," raved John Donohue, a Virginian in Company K, "for if the majority of the riders had been shot down the horses would have been carried by their tremendous momentum into the ranks of the enemy."[43]

Unfortunately for the Union Marylanders and Pennsylvanians, the Confederate riders remained in the saddle as they hacked and slashed their way through Kenly's ill-fated defense. Lieutenant Colonel Parham had remained on his caisson when a charging horseman raised his saber to cleave his head. Fortune clung to Parham when the side wheel fell off the caisson at that very moment, throwing the rider aside and pulling Parham underneath his horse. Parham lay still as dozens of pursuing Southerners galloped past him, then he dragged himself to the side of the road. "The fighting here was terrible, as we were shown no mercy," complained artillerist Charles Atwell. "Our infantry stood up to the work, and were most of them cut to pieces."[44]

The members of Kenly's force that were not lying dead or wounded attempted to flee the scene. The Union foot soldiers were captured immediately, while the mounted officers and Fifth New York Cavalry members made a good head start to Winchester. The captains of the two Twenty-ninth Pennsylvania companies hid in the woods; four company commanders of the First (USA) Maryland also escaped the tumult, leaving their men behind. George W. Thompson, the lieutenant commanding Company D of the First (USA) Maryland, continued to lead his unit but realized it was suicide for them to stay in the road. After dodging a saber swipe that tore his sleeve, Thompson took several of his men into the wheat field west of the road where they realized their gummed-up muskets could no longer accept cartridges. Powerless to aid his regiment, Lieutenant Thompson watched the cavalry destroy the Marylanders. "They closed in upon us, literally cutting us up to pieces, the men fighting desperately," he later recounted. Thompson eventually took the Company D soldiers into the woods to escape capture.[45]

With Colonel Kenly incapacitated in an ambulance and more than half of the company officers fleeing the battlefield, the three remaining regimental officers presided over a hopeless situation. Lieutenant Colonel Parham had narrowly escaped death when the caisson he was fleeing in had broken down at a fortuitous moment. Pulling his spent body to the side of the road, Parham found himself surrounded by four Virginia horse soldiers. His luck would continue. Parham gave up his pistol and empty scabbard and was engaging his captors in a brief discussion when he abruptly sprang to his feet and shouted, "Here come our reinforcements, boys; we're good for another fight!" The ruse worked to perfection. The quartet spurred their horses toward the fabricated threat. Parham grabbed a free horse and rode it to freedom. Several other captives also benefited from Parham's trick by escaping to the woods before the Confederates realized they had been duped.[46]

Lieutenant Colonel Dushane and Major Wilson were not blessed with Parham's serendipity. Wilson was captured as he attempted to escape after the left wing of the regiment crumbled from the cavalry charge. This left Dushane as the only remaining regimental commander, leading the western wing of the regiment in the wheat field. Watching the other wing destroyed near the orchard with his men now completely surrounded, Dushane realized that any further resistance was suicide. He ordered his men to surrender to escape slaughter.[47]

Kenly remained in the ambulance as it headed northward. A cavalryman rode up to the two-wheeled vehicle, lifted the curtain that covered the back of it, and fired a shot. The bullet missed the wounded colonel. A few miles north of the scene, near the hamlet of Nineveh, Flournoy's men overtook the ambulance and brought Kenly away as the most prized capture of the day. Adding further to Kenly's woes, the national flag that he had furled and ordered away hours before was also captured.

The Sixth Virginia Cavalry compiled an impressive tally of captures. The three rearward companies had ridden up to aid their comrades who were involved in the initial attack. Close to 650 members of the First (USA) Maryland Infantry, Twenty-ninth Pennsylvania Infantry, Fifth New York Cavalry, and Atwell's battery surrendered to the cavalry north of Cedarville; another 150 members of the First (USA) Maryland surrendered to Confederate infantry at Front Royal. Confederate cavalry killed and wounded fifty others at the cost of twenty-six men. The Sixth Virginia Cavalry also captured both of Atwell's cannons. Of the 975 members of Kenly's force who resisted Jackson's attack, fewer than 100 escaped death, injury, or capture.[48]

The battlefield on the heights north of Cedarville presented a grisly sight immediately after it was all over. "Blankets [and] overcoats were strewed promiscuously in every direction," observed an overawed cavalryman. "I galoped over dead bodies so covered with durt and dust that you could hardly tell that they were human. Dead horses [lay] scatered all along the road." One of the Confederate bodies found was not a designated horse soldier. Maj. Aaron Davis, the impetuous brigade commissary officer, met his fate when a Union rearguard resisted his approach. Davis was killed with a shot through his right breast.[49]

Lt. Col. Thomas Flournoy salvaged Jackson's objective by maneuvering the Sixth Virginia Cavalry to prevent the escape of the Union Front Royal garrison. Without his available cavalry, Jackson had still captured the vast government stores in the depot and had planted himself firmly on Banks's left flank. Still, Flournoy's destruction of 90-percent of the garrison force prevented a military embarrassment for the general. Had Kenly escaped, Jackson's mission objective would not have been impeded, but he would at some time have had to explain why he allowed it to happen. His failure to beat Kenly in nearly five hours when Jackson outnumbered him by at least twelve thousand men would have fallen under greater scrutiny by the Confederate War Department. Flournoy and the Sixth Virginia Cavalry wiped away the need to question the performance.

Jackson and Ewell and members of their respective staffs trotted beyond Cedarville in time to witness the cavalry's remarkable performance. So impressed was Jackson that he confessed to Major Dabney that never in all his experience of warfare had he seen a cavalry charge performed with such efficiency and gallantry. Ewell later told one of his staffers that the Sixth Virginia Cavalry conducted "one of the most gallant affairs" he had ever witnessed. Jed Hotchkiss reached Front Royal too late to aid General Jackson, but early enough to witness Kenly's annihilation. "There was no halt, but with uplifted sabres our men . . . scattered them to the four winds, causing many of them to bite the dust, and inflicting horrible wounds upon others," he raved. Assured of a complete victory this day, the generals and their respective staffs turned around and rode back to the village of Cedarville. Leaving the staff there to secure a place to stay for the night, General Jackson rode on to Front Royal. The sun had already set as the time passed 7:15 P.M.[50]

Front Royal bustled with activity throughout the evening of May 23. Most remarkable was the reaction of the opposing First Maryland Infantries, particularly the prewar acquaintances from Baltimore. "We were gathered around fires, engaged in making coffee, when the cavalry came in with their prisoners," recalled George Booth of the First (CSA) Maryland. "Then ensued a strange scene, as the antagonists of a few hours back now freely mingled, acquaintances were renewed and enquiries made for absent ones." Men from Trimble's brigade saw the strange reunion between family members. An Alabaman noted a doleful Union Marylander riding on the same horse as his jubilant Confederate brother. David Holt of the Sixteenth Mississippi claimed to witness a Confederate Marylander capture his brother near the South Branch late in the afternoon. That night the two brothers shared a campfire and talked about home and reminisced about their lives together before the national strife tore their country and family apart.[51]

The citizens were animated in the joy of their liberation. The Confederate soldiers coming into town from the south were the happy recipients of their fervor. "Regiment after regiment filed past all looking pale and haggard, dusty and ragged," noted Lucy Buck, "and yet when we saluted the battle flag when they were going by, their countenances brightened, their step grew elastic and cheer after cheer rent the air as they seemed to forget suffering and danger in their enthusiasm." According to young Tom Ashby, "The return of the Confederates so cheered our people that they opened their hearts and homes to the soldiers with joyful welcome and dispensed lavish hospitality." Dr. Charles Eckardt spoke for the majority of the townspeople when he gushed, "Everyone was now rejoicing in Front Royal, that we were free of the damned Yankees."[52]

Soldiers marched into and through the town well into the night. Those that arrived before darkness enveloped the region bore witness to what three hundred thousand dollars' worth of U.S. property looked like, including two captured trains that Lieutenant Colonel Parham had tried to send out to Strasburg. "Everyone in high spirits," a Mississippi soldier succinctly entered in his diary. Soldiers encamped in town drew rations from the captured Union commissary. "We ate Yankee food," recalled a member of Trimble's brigade, "We lived on what we had captured in that campaign: coffee, bacon, and hardtack." Those with family ties to the area managed a brief visit with relatives. Capt. Samuel Buck of the Thirteenth Virginia encamped briefly with his regiment near Guard Hill, then took temporary leave to get a home-cooked meal at his cousin's home. He entered Bettie Richards's house near the River Station depot, where he got a good supper. He also received a special treat—an introduction to Maj. Gen. Thomas J. Jackson.[53]

Jackson headquartered himself at Riverside that evening to receive information from his chief subordinates, including Turner Ashby. He diplomatically wrote a dispatch to thank Belle Boyd for her selfless efforts to aid the Confederacy. With her home currently the center of Confederate operations in the Shenandoah Valley, Mrs. Richards stepped up her role as gracious hostess to the general and the slew of officers that entered her home. The bustle of activity outside her house invigorated Mrs. Richards and her neighbors as soldiers marched into the area until midnight. She was taken by the reaction, noting that "such shouting and cheering I never heard before. I did not close my eyes with sleep the whole night."[54]

Jackson did not stay the night at Front Royal. After completing his evening business, he rode back to his staff at Cedarville. What would his next move be on the Shenandoah Valley chessboard? He had destroyed Banks's flank and in doing so had opened the road to Winchester, but he still was unsure of Banks's troop disposition. He learned that Turner Ashby had damaged the telegraph and the tracks, but the Seventh Virginia Cavalry had been unable to disperse the garrison that protected Buckton Station. This prevented him from gaining closer access to the U.S. force at Strasburg. Additionally, he had no knowledge of the existence of any force that lurked in the woods on the Chapel Road that ran westward from Cedarville to Middletown. Jackson did not send any scouting party onto the three crossroads that connected the Front Royal–Winchester Pike with the Valley Pike. No one was ordered to Signal Knob to watch Banks's reaction; no one was sent down the Winchester Pike beyond Cedarville to ascertain the Union reaction at Winchester. All of that would wait until morning's light penetrated the Valley.

The reaction indeed was important. Jackson was still under the impression that Banks numbered twice the six thousand men in his remaining army; therefore, he needed to probe cautiously against him. As soon as Banks learned of the extent of the threat he now faced, he would be forced to do something. Jackson hoped to pull him from his Strasburg trenches and bring him out into the open. Stonewall contemplated what he should do on Saturday morning. "In the event of Banks leaving Strasburg he might escape toward the Potomac," reasoned Jackson, "or if we moved directly to Winchester he might move via Front Royal to Washington City." Jackson eventually decided to close up his army in the morning as they advanced down the Front Royal–Winchester Pike toward Winchester. This would plant him both on Banks's flank and in his rear. As soon as he learned of Banks's decision on May 24, he would strike a decisive blow.[55]

Jackson trotted into Cedarville and found that his staff had fastened their horses to the fence in front of Jacob McKay's home at the southwest corner of the crossroads. Observing that the general had nothing but an overcoat to protect him through the quickly chilling evening, Jed Hotchkiss pulled a rubber-lined blanket off the back of his horse and suggested that Jackson share it with him. Jackson agreed and lay down in McKay's front yard.[56]

Jackson drifted off to sleep knowing that the morning would dawn with the opportunity to achieve something yet to be accomplished by a Confederate force in the war—the complete destruction of a Union army.

4

BANKS'S FOG OF WAR

On Friday evening, May 23, Abraham Lincoln and Edwin Stanton entered Gen. Irvin McDowell's headquarters after completing their review of his thirty-eight-thousand-man army, the Department of the Rappahannock. The condition of Shields's division disconcerted Lincoln. The president recognized that the hard-marching Valley soldiers needed more rest and organization before McDowell marched off to join McClellan at Richmond. Lincoln decided to suspend McDowell's advance by two days. Instead of moving out on Saturday, McDowell's entire army would march on Monday morning.

After completing their business with General McDowell, Lincoln and Stanton entrained at Falmouth and rode to their steamer at Aquia Landing. Their return trip to Washington would consume the entire night. No U.S. War Department news would reach the two until they disembarked at Washington on Saturday morning.[1]

At Strasburg, General Banks sought for missing pieces to his situational puzzle throughout the afternoon and early evening of May 23. The only evidence he had of trouble on his flank was the late-afternoon verbal message supplied by Charley Greenleaf of the Fifth New York Cavalry. Banks had returned Greenleaf to Front Royal at 6:00 P.M. and had ordered out an infantry regiment and a section of artillery to aid Colonel Kenly. The only confirmation of Greenleaf's report came at 6:30 P.M. from a Union citizen who had fled Front Royal late that afternoon. He stated that Kenly indeed was under attack and falling back from the town.[2] But decisions could not be made solely on the report of a cavalry private and a Valley resident. As the light faded with the passing of the seven o'clock hour, Banks remained in the dark to the extent of the catastrophe that transpired within twelve miles of him.

An ominous message clicked over the telegraph at the Hupp house headquarters at 7:15 P.M. An aide handed it to Banks, who read it and immediately turned to Brig. Gen. Samuel Crawford, who had arrived at headquarters in mid-May for future brigade assignment. Banks asked him to consult with him in private. Both generals entered Banks's room, where Banks showed Crawford the troubling dispatch.[3] It was from Lt. Thomas Saville of the First (USA) Maryland Infantry, the Company D commander who fled the battle and galloped down to Winchester as the Southern cavalry annihilated Kenly's force. Saville had reached Winchester at sunset and immediately found the telegraph office, manned by Capt. George A. Flagg, the assistant quartermaster for the Department of the Shenandoah. If found true, Saville's desperate message spelled doom for the Union army in the Valley:

May 23, 1862

Winchester
General Banks:
    Col. Kenly is killed. Lt. Col., adjt., Dr. Mitchell, Major Wilson & all the rest of comd. officers [of] 1st Maryland Regt. Taken prisoners—Regt. cut all to pieces & prisoners 1st Mich Cavalry d[itt]o. The enemy's forces are 15 or 20,000 strong & on the march to Strasburg. If you want me to report in person, telegraph to Capt. Flagg.
                            Lt. Saville
                            Comdg. Co. D, 1st Md. Regt.[4]

Could any or all of this be true? Giving it skeptical but worthy attention, Banks asked General Crawford his opinion. Crawford was ostensibly as troubled and confused about the message as was his superior officer. Lieutenant Saville was obviously panicked and prone to errors (the First Michigan Cavalry was not at Front Royal, for example), but if a mere kernel of his report were true, Banks needed to react immediately. Banks told Crawford to ride to Winchester and interrogate Lieutenant Saville to assess his credibility.

Banks's troubles escalated. At 7:30 P.M. Captain Strother received and analyzed Captain Hubbard's message from Buckton Station. Hubbard's report indicated that a mixed cavalry and infantry force of three hundred to four hundred Southerners assaulted him at 4:00 P.M. Hubbard expected the attack to be renewed in the morning and pleaded for reinforcements. Banks had yet to learn if the same enemy force initiated the Front Royal and Buckton Station assaults. The possibility existed that 15,000–20,000 Confederates were advancing toward Strasburg!

Banks asked his staffers their opinions on the intelligence. Captain Strother all but dismissed it. He insisted to Banks that Saville was a coward who "had ingloriously fled the field and covered his ignominy by monstrous lying." Strother swayed Banks to the point of telegraphing Captain Flagg to interrogate him more carefully. In the meantime, General Crawford left headquarters for Winchester. Minutes after Crawford departed, Col. George H. Gordon entered headquarters.[5]

No member of Banks's department claimed to understand Stonewall Jackson better than George Henry Gordon. A graduate of the famous West Point class of 1846 (twenty of its alumni became Civil War generals North and South), Gordon had been Jackson's roommate at the academy, where he graduated forty-sixth out of fifty-nine cadets. Gordon, like many of his classmates, had distinguished himself in the Mexican-American War, earning a brevet promotion for gallantry for his performance at Cerro Gordo. After serving his country in Mexico, Gordon returned to his native state of Massachusetts, where he studied law at Harvard. He recruited the Second Massachusetts Infantry in 1861 and was immediately awarded its colonelcy. Gordon rose in responsibility to brigade command in August 1861, and he continued to lead when Banks's army entered the Shenandoah Valley the following March. By May 1862 the forty-year-old continued to seek military promotion. Gordon was true to his Bay State roots. As opinionated as he was ambitious, Gordon felt no qualms about airing his views to superior officers.

Unlike Banks, Gordon had been convinced that General Jackson had somehow gained the Union flank with a superior force. Gordon pleaded with Banks to retreat to Winchester under the cover of darkness. Gordon reminded Banks of his earlier observations that suggested an ever-enlarging enemy force near the Blue Ridge Mountains. Even if he had overestimated the threat, Gordon claimed Winchester still served as a better location than Strasburg to keep Jackson in front of Banks rather than on his flank or rear. Banks listened to every word uttered by his brigade commander, but quietly told him that the army would not move. Banks's orders were to protect the railroad; unless the threat against him was confirmed, he could not jeopardize his mission. Realizing that the information was merely one hour old, Banks rebuffed Gordon's entreaties, persisting and repeating the phrase "I must develop the force of the enemy." Disappointed, Gordon exited headquarters and rode back to his tent.[6]

By 8:30 P.M. no other intelligence had come in to help Banks "develop the force" of his opponent. Relying on the minimal information at hand, Banks decided to cover the roads approaching Strasburg. Learning that Colonel Gordon had sent the Third Wisconsin to Front Royal on the road from Strasburg, Banks sent orders to the Badger commander, Col. Thomas H. Ruger, not to advance to Front Royal by his earlier orders. Instead, Banks had him halt at Buckton Station. Not only did this prevent another one of his regiments from meeting a disastrous end, but it also satisfied Captain Hubbard's request for reinforcements. Banks did allow a smaller reconnaissance to advance closer to Front Royal. Capt. Charles H.T. Collis volunteered to explore the contested area with a small escort He departed with his company of colorful Zouaves at 10:00 P.M.[7]

Back at Washington, Assistant Secretary of War Peter Watson quickly realized that his boss had taken a daylong leave from the capital at the most inopportune time. Brig. Gen. John Geary, stationed east of the Blue Ridge at Rectortown, was the first to inform the War Department about the Front Royal attack. Geary wired three messages between 9:30 and 10:00 P.M. Admitting that no telegraph communication linked Rectortown with Front Royal, Geary still insisted that the Union force there had been engaged in a five-hour battle. A Michigan cavalry scout overlooked the area from Markham, where he saw the smoke from small arms fire emanate from the river branch junction. Geary estimated the attacking force to be at least three thousand rebels and four cannons. Watson realized that General Banks had to fill in the blanks, and he wired an inquiry to him at Strasburg. Not realizing that three hours had passed since Jackson destroyed the Front Royal garrison, Watson replied to Geary, "The Secretary of War not in town. Can you make any movement in time to aid General Banks, either with or without re-enforcements?"[8]

Reinforcements were exactly what General Banks had in mind. Three hours had passed since Lieutenant Saville and Captain Hubbard first informed him of the assaults along the Manassas Gap Railroad lines. Virtually nothing had clicked across the telegraph since then to confirm or add to the dispatches. The telegraph lines from the west had been destroyed to magnify the general's uncertainty. Banks was left guessing at the intention of the attack. Banks clung to the notion that the Confederates were after the rail lines, both the Manassas Gap and the B&O. He wired Col. Dixon S. Miles, commanding a brigade at Harpers Ferry, to inform him of the fight on the Union Valley army's flank. "It is necessary that you should immediately put all your available force in motion toward Winchester as the best protection of the railway," Banks added, predicting that the enemy is "likely to move from [Front Royal] toward Winchester for the purpose of intercepting our forces." In the meantime, Banks intended to stay put until he could learn more about what had happened.[9]

Colonel Gordon could not disagree with Banks more on these intentions. Rebuffed at 7:30 P.M. in his attempt to get Banks to move the army down to Winchester, Gordon hoped the passage of three hours would sway his superior's opinion. He was particularly hopeful when he received a dispatch from Banks at 10:00 P.M. informing him of the decision to halt Colonel Ruger instead of having him continue on to Front Royal. Gordon reentered army headquarters at 10:30 P.M., believing that Banks had now developed the force of the enemy enough to be convinced that it would be suicide to stay at Strasburg. Before he confronted Banks, Gordon learned from Major Perkins that the chief of staff shared Gordon's views about the danger they were in, but Banks could not be persuaded of the same. Gordon then confronted Banks and demanded a few more minutes of his time. He altered his tactic to assure the general that the movement to Winchester should be construed not as a retreat but rather as a necessary military movement to extract himself from a vulnerable position to realign in a stronger one and avert being cut off.

Banks had always welcomed the opinions of staff personnel and continued to listen to Gordon while sitting in his chair. But as Gordon continued to urge the "military movement" to Winchester,

Banks bristled at the connotation that such an endeavor would present. Banks suddenly became animated; he rose from his seat and exclaimed, "By God, sir, I will not retreat! We have more to fear, sir, from the opinions of our friends than the bayonets of the enemies." Exasperated, Gordon took his leave again. It had dawned on him the exact reason why the army was going to stay put: "General Banks was afraid of being thought afraid."[10]

Although Gordon firmly believed that Banks was placing politics over the safety of his command, the general likely relied on more altruistic reasoning for his decision. Banks had yet to understand what actually had happened at Front Royal. A dearth of intelligence on the matter persisted throughout the night of May 23. Banks answered Watson's query (with copies sent to General Frémont and General McDowell) confirming the attack. Likely receiving more reports from fugitives who reached Winchester, Banks informed the War Department that the Confederate force numbered five thousand; they were believed to be advancing on the Chapel Road from Cedarville to Middletown. "No definitive information has yet been received," continued Banks. "Re-enforcements should be sent to us if possible." Immediately after receiving the telegram, Watson ordered transportation to be ready and told General James Wadsworth, who led a division near the capital, to prepare for the same.[11]

Banks realized that he could not defend against an enemy force advancing on the Chapel Road without taking unacceptable losses, particularly if the enemy also advanced from the south. As the midnight hour neared, Banks ordered Gen. Alpheus Williams to send a reconnaissance force to scout the Chapel Road. Banks also prepared to close up his force and prepare to march back to Winchester. "You will with all possible dispatch send all your baggage trains to the rear under charge of the brigade and regimental quartermasters, and with a suitable guard as speedily as possible," wrote Banks to his subordinates at midnight. Additionally, he instructed his officers to keep the troops in readiness, with two days' rations, for immediate movement to Winchester.[12]

Clouds cloaked the midnight sky, blocking the pinpoint starlight and threatening rain at the same time. The Twenty-ninth Pennsylvania Infantry struck their tents south of Strasburg and marched toward Middletown. Joined by three companies of First Michigan Cavalry, Col. John K. Murphy's Pennsylvanians stumbled past Strasburg as brigade and regimental commanders prepared to pack and load all of their property onto the wagons for immediate removal. The Pennsylvania infantry and Michigan cavalry had been chosen to scout the Chapel Road, but it would take them three hours to reach the bisecting avenue at Cedarville.[13]

While his reconnaissance marched to its destination, Banks continued to prepare to evacuate. He couriered a dispatch to Colonel Ruger at Buckton Station to pull back to Strasburg by 7:00 A.M. Banks exposed his ignorance when he instructed Ruger to "communicate immediately if possible with Col. Parham and any other comdg officer on the R. R. line to Front Royal and bring them in to join you without a moment's delay."[14]

Banks's fog about Front Royal thickened almost immediately after sending the dispatch to Ruger. Shortly after 2:00 A.M., General Crawford wired headquarters from Winchester. He had been sent there to personally interrogate Saville, and his message to Banks left the strong impression that Crawford considered Saville to be entirely reliable. David Strother could not fathom why the confirmation "gained audience." He was sure that Saville was guilty of exaggerating the danger. A dispatch received at headquarters within half an hour of Crawford's wire bolstered Strother's opinion. This one came from Maj. Philip Vought, the Fifth New York Cavalry commander who had hidden off the Front Royal–Winchester Pike until 11:00 P.M., then had ridden to Winchester. Vought's estimation reduced the attacking force to a maximum of six thousand men. Vought maintained that Winchester was not under direct threat that night because he had overheard the Southern cavalry reveal that they would all fall back to Front Royal.[15]

Six thousand men seemed more reasonable than twenty thousand, but Banks knew this was still an unexpected and significant threat. Certain for the first time that Front Royal was completely under Confederate control, Banks's decision was complete. He would pull his army back to Winchester in the morning. Banks retired for the night, leaving Strother in charge of transmitting messages to the War Department.

Strother wired the gist of Vought's intelligence, but never mentioned receiving a War Department communiqué that was sent well before 3:00 A.M. Assistant Secretary Watson was still in charge due to Stanton's absence. Concerned that Banks would evacuate Strasburg,

Watson agonized at the thought of giving his assurance to such a movement. Promising timely reinforcements, Watson pleaded, "Do not give up the ship before succor can arrive."[16]

But the ship was sinking. Throughout the night, Banks's army consolidated. The infantry regiments had been spread out the four miles between Strasburg to Maurertown. But by daybreak regiments from Donnelly's and Gordon's brigades trudged into Strasburg. "In the town the utmost state of excitement prevailed," noted a member of the Twenty-eighth New York. All were reacting to the reports of the attack at Buckton Station and the disaster at Front Royal. While many foot soldiers dismissed the news as extravagant rumors, the townspeople firmly believed what turned out to be the truth. The Unionists in Strasburg began to flee the area, while the secessionists could do little to disguise the satisfaction they felt at hearing the welcome news.[17]

Unrefreshed after a trifling amount of sleep, Banks awoke before dawn without new information concerning Confederate disposition. No couriers had returned from the reconnaissance of the Chapel Road. As far as Banks was concerned, no news was good news. Vought's information seemed accurate. The Confederates had returned to Front Royal. "Jackson is still in our front," he insisted. "We have sent our stores to the rear, but troops remain here." He went on to thank the War Department for the reinforcements, but those troops had yet to arrive.

Past the six o'clock hour, Banks had convinced himself that the danger to his army was ameliorated by the passage of night. At 6:30 A.M. he assured Colonel Gordon—his most outspoken and antsy subordinate—that the Southerners returned to Front Royal and would not attempt to gain the rear. "You will make your men as comfortable as our circumstances will permit," Banks directed Gordon, "The Secretary and Assistant Secretary of War both telegraph that ample reinforcements will be sent."[18]

All of that changed at 7:00 A.M. when Charles H.T. Collis reported back to Banks from his overnight mission to Front Royal. The Zouave captain claimed that the enemy force that attacked Front Royal was not a raid but an army already on the road to Winchester. Collis also came across the two company captains of the Twenty-ninth Pennsylvania who fought at Front Royal. The infantry officers had spent the night heading westward through the woods between Cedarville and the Valley Pike. They came out between Middletown and Strasburg, telling Collis that Kenly's force was "cut to pieces" by as many as ten thousand Confederates, that both guns were captured, and that Jackson's objective was to cut Banks off by beating him to Winchester. Nine other Pennsylvanians escaped with their captains. Collis deemed the accounts believable.[19]

Next came Pvt. Charley Greenleaf of the Fifth New York Cavalry, the same young soldier who delivered the first news of the Front Royal attack to Banks late the previous afternoon. Banks had given Greenleaf a fresh horse and sent him back toward Front Royal Friday night to rejoin his company. Greenleaf was back at headquarters again on Saturday morning with a fanciful tale of reaching Cedarville at dark, intermixing with Jackson's staff and the Eighth Louisiana Infantry, and learning the twenty thousand Confederates had seized Front Royal and were already marching down the Front Royal–Winchester Pike.[20]

Could the Southerners be on the road to Winchester? Colonel Strother laughed off Greenleaf's story and doubted the credibility of Collis's discovery, claiming that the Zouave captain could have mistaken a small forage party for a large force. Surprisingly, Banks had yet to hear from the larger reconnaissance he had sent out on the Chapel Road. They could confirm the presence of Confederate soldiers marching on the Front Royal–Winchester Pike. His orders were not to move; reinforcements were supposedly on the way. Repeating the story to the War Department that Collis had relayed to him from the Pennsylvanians, Banks assured Washington: "We shall stand firm."[21]

Within minutes of sending the appeasing telegram to Washington, Banks received a dispatch from Middletown. Authored by Col. John K. Murphy of the Twenty-ninth Pennsylvania, the message informed Banks of the result of the Chapel Road reconnaissance. Murphy admitted that his command did not reach the intersection of the Front Royal–Winchester Pike at Cedarville. He saw no enemy and instead was relaying information gleaned from Unionists in the area. He claimed that the Southerners were demonstrating toward Winchester. "We have returned to this place," closed Murphy from Middletown, "and await further orders."[22]

Murphy failed Banks miserably—not so much for cutting the reconnaissance short of completion but for not sending any information by cavalry courier while he remained on the Chapel Road. Banks should have learned the meat of the message before dawn. Not only did Murphy cost Banks two hours, but by returning his entire force to the Valley Pike he abandoned the most important road that Banks needed to control. A large Confederate force could be advancing toward Middletown on the Chapel Road that very morning, and Banks had no men to slow the movement or even inform him of the threat. Strother seethed at the shoddy reconnaissance. "If this duty had been executed, we should have immediately known our position," he declared, "but the troops sent, through timidity, utterly failed in their duty."[23]

Although late, the information Banks received did confirm intelligence that two other sources had already provided him: the Confederates were heading toward Winchester on the Front Royal–Winchester Pike. Banks had Major Perkins wire Col. Dixon S. Miles in Harpers Ferry the news; Miles responded by promising to divert any reinforcements that reached him to head to the same threatened locale. At Strasburg, Banks was now limited to one option. He had pulled back from Harrisonburg against his wishes ten days earlier; now he would order a retrograde movement to save his army. Banks reversed his original position to stand firm and ordered a withdrawal to Winchester. He informed his division and brigade commanders that the enemy was on the Chapel Road and warned them to look out for this avenue once they reached it.[24]

Prudently, Banks sent his supply train rolling northward before daybreak, but barely half of the wagons had moved out of Strasburg by 7:30 A.M., and these vehicles already stretched the train to seven miles. Because Strasburg had served as an army depot, Banks found himself burdened with more than five hundred supply wagons—five times the number usually associated with a six-thousand-man force.[25]

Adding to the transportation woes was the issue of how to remove all the sick and wounded at Strasburg. When Shields departed the Valley on May 16, he left behind 1,000 sick and wounded soldiers from his hard-marching, hard-fighting division. Fifty soldiers had since died, and another 220 members of Shields's division could be furloughed, returned to duty, or discharged; 65 were too sick to move and would have to be left behind, and 450 others received rations and were ordered out of the hospitals. This left 78 sick and wounded men who required twenty ambulances to cart them to Winchester. Their 450 debilitated comrades marched alongside the ambulances, keeping pace as best as their weakened bodies would allow. The abrupt orders to leave beds and embark on an eighteen-mile march were destined to impede the army's movements.[26]

As if the unusual numbers of government wagons were not trouble enough for Banks, an unexpected influx of civilian vehicles significantly elongated the train. Panicked refugees and antsy sutlers spliced their belongings into the supply line of the Army of the Shenandoah, thus taxing the quartermasters responsible for moving the supplies to safety. The sight of this train startled Banks's infantry who entered Strasburg from their outposts as the civilian wagons rolled out of town. A New York soldier took note of the scene:

> The road in the direction of Winchester was crowded with every kind of vehicle that was ever invented since the days of Noah. Here was the ponderous Virginia market wagon, fashioned after the Ark, drawn by six horses, and loaded with a heterogeneous mass of articles pitched in promiscuously, bureaus and bedsteads, tables, chairs and stoves. . . . There was four-horse teams, two-horse teams, and wagons and carts with only one horse or mule attached, all hurrying in the same direction, all actuated by the same motive—fear. Troops of women and children, black and white, were following the wagons on foot. Some of the loads were "topped out" with children of both races, who were the only ones that showed no symptoms of fear. They were as joyous and gleeful as though the cavalcade of hurriedly loaded teams were racing along for their especial amusement.[27]

The failures of his subordinates and the subsequent vulnerability of his supply line swayed Banks to consider the very likely possibility that neither he nor his army would survive this movement. His column was exposed to attack from two crossroads: the Chapel Road, which terminated at Middletown; and the Millwood–Newtown Road, which terminated at Newtown. If the reports were true that a large Confederate army was heading down the Front Royal–Winchester Pike, then Banks well understood that the only force blocking their passage into Winchester was the 856 white-gloved and inexperienced members of the Tenth Maine Infantry. Once this force was swept away, Banks's wagons would be next, then Banks's army, and Banks himself.[28]

At 8:00 A.M., as the chaotic sounds of a packing army swirled around the Hupp house, Banks sat down to write what he believed to be his final letter home. He addressed it to his wife, whom he affectionately called "Mother" out of respect for her duties in raising his five children during his absence. He was overwhelmed with the longing to be with his family, but these feelings were rivaled by his bitterness over his vulnerable circumstances.

"To day we are very likely to have an encounter with the enemy," he began. He then went on to inform her of what happened at Front Royal, how a much larger Southern army mauled an undersized United States force there. "Thus they mass their men upon us while our govt. separates its forces in little powerless squads without power even to crush the foe—anywhere," he complained, yet without taking any blame for not providing Colonel Kenly with any of his sixteen hundred horse soldiers prior to the Front Royal battle. He continued, "This policy must be changed or our government and people [will be] destroyed." Banks's desperation, frustration, resignation, and anger melded in his next paragraph:

> Kiss the dear children for me. I love them and their mother greatly. Dear Birney—how I should love to hug her once more. And Fremont and Maud. Darling children. How I love them. I want them all to be just. It is the terrible injustice of our people to each other, the terrible lying they indulge in on all sided that has destroyed us. I want our dear children to be just, to be truthful. That embraces everything. Nobody is wise who is not just. Teach them to be just . . . I have been very fortunate in having so good a friend in my wife and I can never say how dear she is to me. Take good care of our dear children. They are very fine creatures. It would be a pleasure to live if only to watch them; but life is not worth much. Remember me affectionately to my mother, my brothers and sisters. I need not write any more.

But he did write more. He suddenly realized the fatalistic tone of his letter and tried to assure his family of his survival, claiming, "I am in good health and in good spirits—the best. Have perfect confidence in getting through our difficulties." But perhaps Banks understood he was kidding himself. For weeks he had pleaded for attention and direction, but in the midmorning hours of Saturday, May 24, 1862, General Banks had come to the realization that it was too late to save himself or his army. Therefore, he did not sign off his letter assuring his family he would write again soon. Instead, he closed with the definitive words of an already beaten man: "Good Bye."[29]

5

Jackson's Fog of War

The steamer carrying President Lincoln and Secretary Stanton docked at the Navy Yard at 5:00 A.M. on May 24. On their way to the War Department, they met Treasury Secretary Chase, who, after a brief conversation, noted that the two were "highly gratified by the condition of the troops and anticipating an imposing and successful advance on the Monday following."[1]

That all changed the minute they entered the War Department to be briefed by Assistant Secretary Watson. John S. Clark returned to the War Department at that moment to witness "the great council of wise men with elongated faces just getting the news of [the] attack on Kenly." Stanton immediately wired General John Dix to send off reinforcements to Banks from Baltimore to Harpers Ferry. Informing Banks of the order, Stanton instructed Banks to "please report the present condition of things."[2] He sent the wire at 7:00 A.M. He never received a response.

While Nathaniel Banks predicted impending disaster to his wife, General Jackson labored to fulfill the prophecy. Stonewall had his army moving northward on the Front Royal–Winchester Pike by 6:00 A.M.; two hours later, the vanguard marched through the hamlet of Nineveh, six miles north of the North Branch of the Shenandoah. The advance not only put Jackson's army on Banks's flank; he also had gained his rear. Winchester was thirteen miles away with fewer than nine hundred infantrymen guarding it against Jackson's thirteen thousand to fourteen thousand effectives.

But Jackson could go no farther that morning without vital information. He worked cautiously on Banks's flank, unaware that his infantry outnumbered that of his opponent by nearly three to one. Twenty hours earlier, Lieutenant Boswell had misinformed Jackson that Banks had three divisions of twelve thousand men rather than a lone six-thousand-man division. There was no reason for Jackson to doubt Boswell's report (after all, Boswell had spent several hours on Signal Knob studying the Federal deployment). Banks could have received reinforcements from Harpers Ferry over the past week. The possibility left Jackson with a perceived three-to-two advantage in numbers, not overwhelming enough to charge inward against Banks without cautiously sniffing out his flanks first.

Winchester must also be approached cautiously. No available intelligence ruled out the very real possibility that Union reinforcements had marched into the town from Harpers Ferry or through Snickers Gap. Since Jackson was under the false impression that Banks's numbers were double their actual strength, then Winchester could have also seen significant numbers of blue-clad troops. Banks's decision, of course, would direct Jackson's objective. Jackson reasoned that Banks, upon learning of the Confederate presence on his flank, would react in one of three ways: he could stay put; he could head eastward to get to Washington; or he could head northward toward Winchester and the Potomac River.[3]

The latter seemed to be Banks's most likely course since he could make use of the best road. Winchester, therefore, was the key destination point for the Confederate army. Even if the town was not Banks's destination as he retreated northward, it still was an ideal location for Jackson's men to converge on Banks's harried troops. But Jackson could not commit to countering any movement without confirming that it actually was taking place. If the Confederates moved directly toward Winchester, Banks could head eastward from Strasburg to Front Royal, destroy the bridges over the forks of the Shenandoah, and cut off Jackson from his supplies. Stonewall also had to cover his own exposed flank whenever he committed to a direction.

Banks's wagons had been rolling down the Valley Pike toward

Winchester for more than three hours. At 8:00 A.M., the leading wagons entered Newtown, but the trailing wagon had yet to budge from
its Strasburg depot. The ten-mile-long train would lengthen even
more when all seven hundred government and civilian vehicles had
begun to roll from Strasburg. Unfortunately for Jackson, he stood five
miles east of that inviting target and had no idea that it existed. Inex-
plicably, he had sent no scouts on any of the three roads that bisected
the Valley Pike. Nobody was ordered onto Signal Knob overnight,
from where one might have watched the first wagons roll northward
at first nautical light. Uncontroverted proof that Banks had chosen to
retreat to Winchester at 5:00 A.M. remained absent from Stonewall
three hours later.

Jackson decided to correct the oversight at Nineveh. The Richmond Road, a colonial-era road, ran from this hamlet six miles northwestward to Newtown. Leading the army toward Winchester were
the Sixth Virginia Cavalry—the saviors of the previous day—and four
companies of the Second Virginia Cavalry. Jackson ordered their commander to strike the Valley Pike at Newtown to observe Union movements. Approximately three hundred horse soldiers galloped away
from the army and took the Richmond Road to Newtown.[4]

Lieutenant Colonel Flournoy no longer led the cavalry force. Although Flournoy's leadership was responsible for the best single-day
effort Jackson had ever seen with the cavalry, Stonewall was apparently uncomfortable with the notion that most of his available cavalry was led by a regimental second in command. After the Cedarville
fight, Jackson had tagged Brig. Gen. George H. Steuart to command
the fourteen horse companies.

Although he had led the Maryland Line for a week, "Maryland"
Steuart's abilities appeared best suited to the cavalry, where he served
in the prewar army. Recently promoted to general, Steuart had essentially been without a command over the past three days. The thirty-
three-year-old Baltimore native and West Pointer had marched to
Front Royal with Colonel Johnson's First (CSA) Maryland Infantry, a
regiment he had previously led as their colonel. While Steuart took
over his new cavalry responsibilities on Saturday morning, Flournoy
returned to his role as commander of the Sixth Virginia Cavalry, a
regiment that Ewell dubbed "The Bloody Sixth" for its astonishing
fight on the heights north of Cedarville.[5]

Jackson's army crept another three miles northward, all the way to "Double Tollgate," the unique intersection formed by the Front Royal–Winchester Pike and the Millwood–Newtown Pike. Jackson ordered his front troops to halt and allow the rear to close up ranks. He could do no more until he was sure of Banks's decision. To bide his time until then, Jackson, Ewell, and their respective staffs rode one and a half miles back to the house of a physician with the surname of Mason, a distinguished dwelling recessed to the west of the pike about five miles north of Cedarville and one and one-half miles south of Double Tollgate. The generals and their staffers rode up Dr. Mason's stonewalled lane to his house, entered it, and were served breakfast. The time passed 8:30 A.M.[6]

Over the next hour, as the front-line Confederate troops halted, the tail of Jackson's army closed ranks. Jackson's original division, including his Stonewall Brigade, crossed the Shenandoah forks north of Front Royal and neared Cedarville. In the meantime, stores of captured supplies and the hundreds of Union prisoners remained under guard in Front Royal.

Banks's leading wagons methodically rolled on their slow journey to Winchester. Except for wagon guards, Banks's entire army waited for the last wagon to roll off before they began to move. "You cannot appreciate the difficulties of moving these long mule trains or the impediments they make," explained Gen. Alpheus Williams, "especially in retreat, when hurry and confusion, frightened teamsters and disordered teams, breakdowns and collisions and ten thousand nameless things conspire to make up the turmoil and increase the disorder." As the first of Banks's wagons rolled toward the southern outskirts of Winchester, the regimental band of the Forty-sixth Pennsylvania in Strasburg appropriately struck up their rendition of "Oh Dear, What Can the Matter Be?" With that, at a quarter past nine o'clock, the army began its march, following a wagon train that stretched fifteen miles on the Valley Pike.[7]

Forty-five minutes later and five miles east of the wagon train, Stonewall Jackson and his officers and aides stepped out of the Mason house. Totally unaware of the inviting target west of him, Jackson discussed the situation with General Ewell. For the second straight day, Stonewall was forced to hold his men in an hours-long respite before he could commit the troops in movement or battle. Uneasy about not knowing what Banks was doing, Jackson had to aggressively seek out his opponent. He took Jed Hotchkiss and escorted him back five miles to the Cedarville crossroads where they had slept the previous night. Ewell stayed with the van to await orders. Ten o'clock came and went with no new information.[8]

General Steuart and his cavalry approached the Newtown crossroads from the east just before 10:00 A.M. There they watched what must have seemed to them a savory opportunity. Miles and miles of the Valley Pike were lined, as far as the eye could see, with Banks's wagons. Without question, Banks was attempting to pull back from Strasburg. Steuart and his horse soldiers were the only obstacles to that movement. Banks's infantry and artillery would be hours behind those wagons. The general quickly detached a courier to ride back and inform Jackson of the movement.

Considering the time required for the information to reach Jackson and then for the commander to react, it would be impossible for Confederate infantry to strike the Valley Pike until at least 1:00 P.M. Still, if infantry troops moved from the van and marched to Newtown from Double Tollgate, they could feasibly intersect the Valley Pike in time to smash into Banks's rear wagons and completely cut off the Union infantry from its supplies. Steuart realized that his role must change from observer to aggressor. Until infantry arrived to support him, he could disrupt the wagon train with his cavalry. He gathered up his horse soldiers, and at 10:00 A.M. he charged his men upon the unsuspecting wagoners.[9]

The Confederates happened upon the portion of the train carting the scores of sick and injured soldiers along with the 450 wounded men who had been deemed strong enough to walk with the ambulances. Most of the men were the former hospitalized members of Shields's division. They were in the midst of transferring to the hospital at Winchester when their wagons had stopped temporarily at Newtown so they could get some water. This is when and where the Virginians entered the scene.

"The whole regiment charged with a tremendous yell," raved a member of the Sixth Virginia Cavalry, working on his second attack in sixteen hours. Shocked at the assault, many of the infirm Union soldiers scattered for cover. The Virginia horsemen approached a stone wall already lined with Yankees on the opposite side. Aiming pistols at the unarmed men, the cavalry quickly claimed the surrender of more than two hundred soldiers.[10]

Helpless to defend themselves, most of the sick and injured

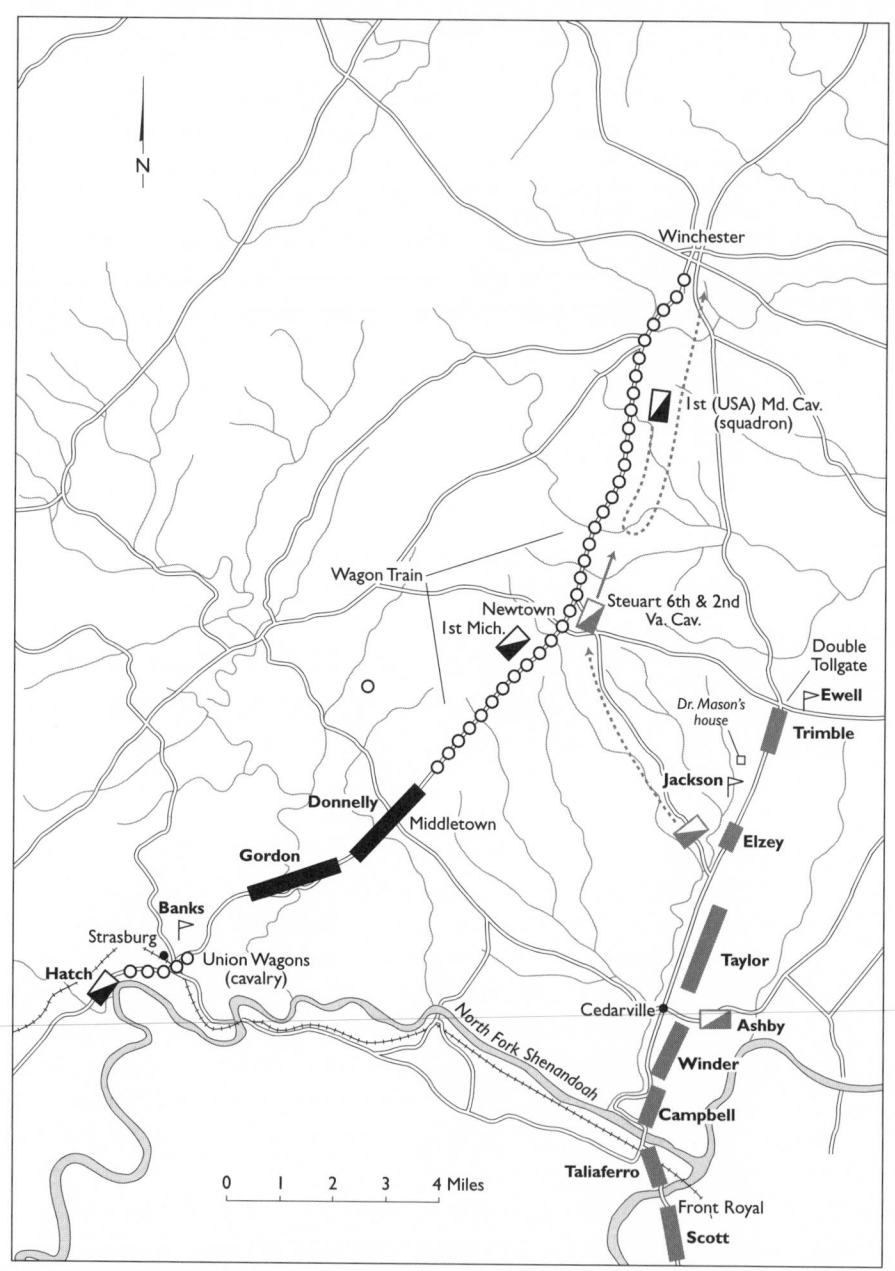

N

Winchester

1st (USA) Md. Cav.
(squadron)

Wagon Train

Newtown
1st Mich.

Steuart 6th & 2nd
Va. Cav.

Double
Tollgate
▷ **Ewell**

Dr. Mason's
house

Trimble

Jackson ▷

Donnelly

Middletown

Elzey

Gordon

Banks ▷

Taylor

Strasburg

Union Wagons
(cavalry)

Cedarville

Hatch

Ashby

North Fork Shenandoah

Winder

Campbell

0   1   2   3   4 Miles

Taliaferro

Front Royal

Scott

Position of forces at 10:00 A.M., May 24, 1862

Northerners offered no resistance. Only one shot was reportedly fired during the melee. Daniel Derrickson, a forty-six-year-old private in Company B of the Sixty-sixth Ohio, was the unfortunate recipient of the bullet. The pistol ball struck him square in the face. A woman living in Newtown, aided by some of her neighbors, carried Derrickson into her house. Knowing his wound was mortal, Derrickson motioned for a paper, then wrote his name and regiment to make sure his family was informed of his demise. He died minutes after scrawling the message.[11]

Steuart's attack initially accomplished much more than capturing sick soldiers. Black teamsters manned most of the wagons directly behind the ambulances. They feared the consequences of being captured by the Confederates. The minute they saw Steuart's men emerge from the woods east of the village, they panicked. Several jumped from their wagons and fled rearward. Others attempted to wheel their wagons around, tipping them over in the process. The panic rippled southward, completely halting the train and jamming the pike with toppled and unmanned wagons. A *New York World* reporter—the only newsman to witness the action—equated the scene to "a miniature Bull Run stampede."[12]

If Steuart could continue the chaos, the result would be devastating. However, many in his command were now tied up with the sick soldiers from Shields's division. The remainder, now fewer than one hundred cavalrymen, soon met swift resistance from opposing horse soldiers. Maj. Angelo Paldi of the First Michigan Cavalry had kept his squadron near Middletown after his men had returned with Colonel Murphy and his Twenty-ninth Pennsylvania from their early morning reconnaissance on the Chapel Road. The Union horsemen became the first witnesses to the wagon panic as it flowed rearward. Without orders, Paldi charged his men northward to meet the source of the problem.

At the same time, several Southern cavalrymen headed northward on the pike from Newtown, but they were checked by a squadron of the First Maryland Cavalry, commanded by Col. Charles Wetschky, who had led his command southward from Winchester after receiving word that Banks's wagon train was threatened. The Marylanders well outnumbered Steuart's men. As the Virginians fled back to Newtown, the Maryland squadron reclaimed one of the hospital wagons, but not before the Confederates had cut loose and rode away with the horses.[13]

Steuart saw Paldi and his men heading toward them as he had led his Virginians south of Newtown. The Confederates immediately pulled back to the cover of woods on the eastern side of the pike, joined by the horse soldiers who were repelled north of Newtown. Knowing he could not move without greater numbers, Steuart dispatched a second courier toward Nineveh with a request for infantry and more cavalry support.[14]

Col. Dudley Donnelly's brigade had begun to march into Middletown at 10:15 A.M. when the rippling wagon panic greeted them. Donnelly expediently ordered the wagons to clear the road and led his brigade at the double-quick north through the village. One-half mile beyond the outskirts, Donnelly spied the rebel cavalry in the woods to the right of the pike. The brigade commander ordered out two companies of skirmishers followed up by two guns from Battery M of the First New York Light Artillery and the Forty-sixth Pennsylvania. The force filed off toward the woods southeast of Newtown and drove Steuart's men back, capturing a member of the Sixth Virginia Cavalry in the process. Overwhelmed by the Union thrust, the Confederates pulled back eastward.[15]

At about 10:45 A.M. General Banks had just reached the Cedar Creek bridge when he nearly collided with a panicked teamster. Banks stopped him and learned about the chaos created miles ahead of him. Taking David Hunter Strother with him, Banks rode northward to scout out the situation. Strother recalled, "We met sutlers wagons, mounted teamsters, and bummers rushing frantically back toward Strasburg, while the regular army train stood still in the road, many of the teams deserted by their drivers." Strother was mortified at the obvious conclusion that Confederates were indeed in force in the Lower Valley and that his own persistence to the contrary may have influenced Banks's delay in leaving Strasburg. Banks, resolute about his fate, took the opportunity to twist the knife into the pride of his opinionated aide. "It seems we were mistaken in our calculations," he reproached Strother. "It seems so," came Strother's reply.[16]

Had Banks witnessed the events near Middletown, he would have realized that the assault was too small to have serious consequences. He had been concerned that Confederates had been closing in on Middletown on the Chapel Road, and what he saw at Cedar Creek confirmed, in his eyes, that this had in fact occurred. Initial reports also informed him that the attack originated from Middletown, even though the Chapel Road was Confederate-free for its entire seven-mile length. Soon all the troops south of Middletown were equally fatalistic. A Massachusetts soldier between Cedar Creek and Middle-town concluded that "being cut off from the rest of the forces our only chance to get away was to say the least doubtful."[17]

So convinced that his worst fears had come to fruition, Banks altered his formation. He halted his wagons explaining, "It being apparent now that our immediate danger was in front, the troops were ordered to the head of the column and the train to the rear." Toppled wagons and those without mule or horse teams were emptied of their supplies, as were the thirty or forty wagons that had reversed direction and stalled north of the creek bridge. The stores were piled and set ablaze. Several troops crossed back into Strasburg and Banks sent orders back to Captain James W. Abert of the Topographical Engineers to keep Collis's Zouaves at the Cedar Creek bridge. Banks determined that if he were forced to fall back again to Strasburg *en masse*, the Zouaves could burn the bridge to buy them more time for a last stand.

Relief soon followed when Banks learned that only isolated and understrength enemy cavalry had caused the temporary panic. "Men were now seen flocking back," reported the *New York World* correspondent, "and the baggage train was again supplied with teamsters." Order was soon restored, and the column proceeded forward with infantry in front, followed by the wagons. Union cavalry and reserve artillery waited near Strasburg to form the rear of the column. Strother felt assuaged but puzzled. "It seemed impossible," he later noted, "that Jackson, with the force attributed to him, having opened the campaign with so vigorous and successful a blow, should permit our weak column, encumbered with so much coveted and needful spoil, to walk away, intact and at its leisure."[18]

Stonewall Jackson had yet to learn about the direction of Banks's column. He, Major Dabney, Lieutenant Boswell, and Jed Hotchkiss trotted past five miles of his halted army from the Mason farmhouse back to the Cedarville crossroads. They turned west on the Chapel Road at 11:00 A.M. and passed the McKay house, where they had slept in the open air the night before. They halted and Jackson fed his aide instructions. Not knowing Banks's destination or if he had yet moved at all, Jackson ordered Hotchkiss "to take 16 cavalry[men] and go and find where Banks was, and report to him every half hour." Hotchkiss adhered to duty, grabbed his escorts from the Seventh Virginia Cavalry, and started up the road.[19]

Jackson and the other aides returned to the crossroads, where the Louisiana brigade had halted. His attention immediately diverted to a lone rider galloping from Nineveh. This was General Steuart's first courier; he reined up and informed Jackson that the Sixth Virginia Cavalry had seen wagons moving northward at Newtown. Thus, at 11:15 A.M., the commanding general of the Confederate Valley army had finally possessed the information he needed to commit his command.[20]

Minutes later, the second courier arrived on a foaming horse. This one revealed the initial attack at Newtown and the request for reinforcements. Jackson's options still weighed heavily to his advantage. Ewell was within ten miles of Winchester and could reach the town in a three-hour march, four hours maximum from the time that orders left Jackson. The bisecting roads from Cedarville, Nineveh, and White Post offered more attack avenues for Jackson to exploit. At least two of these options could be used simultaneously, affording Jackson the opportunity to cut off Banks at Winchester while harassing his flank at the same time.

Jackson turned to Dabney and dictated his decision, an order to be carried to General Ewell north of Nineveh. Jackson briefly explained that two messages arrived from Steuart and that cavalry needed to be freed up to support him. To do this, the prisoners they guarded must be detailed to the infantry. Oddly, Jackson must have known that the remaining Second and Sixth Virginia Cavalry were guarding the prisoners in Front Royal; therefore, considerable time would be lost in carrying the orders first to Ewell, only to have them relayed back to Front Royal. Orders would have to travel five miles northward, then ten miles southward to detach cavalry to move fifteen miles to Newtown, consuming more than three hours for the completion of thirty miles of horse travel necessary for this portion of Steuart's request to be granted.

As for infantry support, Jackson acknowledged Steuart's desire to have foot soldiers aid him at Newtown. Stonewall told Dabney to instruct Ewell to have his "infantry be prepared to march at once . . . but the general commanding does not wish any infantry to actually move till further orders from him." Jackson still was unsure if those men should march directly to Winchester or to Newtown. The final sentence of this key dispatch was advice for Ewell: "Please instruct General Steuart to use his own discretion as to advancing, but if he advances toward Winchester to picket well to his left, and guard against a heavy force of the enemy on that quarter." Dabney immediately handed the note to a courier, who galloped away at 11:30 A.M. Ewell would not receive the note until noon.[21]

At the same time that Jackson interrogated Steuart's couriers, his topographical engineer stirred up a Union force on the Chapel Road. It happened one and one-half miles from the Cedarville crossroads, where the Chapel Road climbed uphill onto rolling tableland after crossing the ravine dominated by Crooked Run. Jed Hotchkiss, with sixteen escorts from the Seventh Virginia Cavalry, were riding over this portion of the road when their advance was suddenly arrested by carbine fire from Union cavalry. Hotchkiss sent a horse soldier back to inform Jackson to send more men.[22]

Lieutenant John Goddard of the First Maine Cavalry fired the first shots at Hotchkiss and the knot of horse soldiers supporting him. He had ridden in advance of his regiment, then returned to the reconnaissance party. The Union force consisted of five companies of the First Maine Cavalry (A, B, C, H, and M), under the command of Lt. Col. Calvin S. Douty, buttressed with two companies of the First Vermont Cavalry (A and G), commanded by Maj. William D. Collins. Armed with pistols and sabers, the Maine cavalry held the advance. They had dismounted; three out of every four men took cover behind a makeshift breastwork of fence rails while the fourth man watched the horses.[23]

The Union force on the Chapel Road overwhelmed Hotchkiss, and Jackson learned of it shortly after 11:30 A.M. He immediately detached a portion of the closest infantry to him—Company H of the Seventh Louisiana—to support Hotchkiss. Now that Banks's movement had been defined, Jackson was faced with a new decision. He could send Ewell to Winchester, but he still had no perception of the size of the Union force there. He could send him to Newtown via the crossroad, or he could hold him in place while he advanced an attacking force to intercept the Valley Pike from the Chapel Road. Jackson chose the latter; he ordered Ashby's remaining companies of the Seventh Virginia Cavalry, Chew's horse artillery, and Poague's section of the Rockbridge Artillery to head westward on the Chapel Road. Min-

utes afterward, General Taylor received his orders to send his large
Louisiana brigade onto the road.[24]

Temperatures that had peaked by midafternoon of the twenty-
third had fallen consistently ever since, relieving the hard-marching
soldiers from both armies. Noontime in the Lower Valley was marked
by annoying rain (it hailed earlier in the morning) falling through a sky
cooled to the mid-fifties, thirty degrees colder than the previous day.
Confederate cavalry, artillery, and infantry deployed in columns of
four and took turns advancing on the westbound road. Ashby, un-
knowingly commissioned brigadier general in Richmond the day previous, now led the advance. Middletown was five miles from the van
at noon, as the Stonewall Brigade began to file onto the road directly
behind Taylor's Louisianans.[25]

The only obstructions to Jackson's movement were the seven
companies of Maine and Vermont cavalry patrolling the road. After
Lieutenant Goddard returned from his encounter, Lt. Col. Calvin S.
Douty and Maj. Jonathan Cilley of the First Maine Cavalry rode up
with a handful of men and studied the Confederates advancing toward them. They returned to their command, and Douty announced,
"Boys, there are too many of them after us; I can see infantry, artillery,
and cavalry, all headed this way." He then ordered the horse soldiers
to mount and draw back to Middletown. They proceeded to do so,
keeping their formation of columns of fours on the road.[26]

Following on their heels was Jed Hotchkiss and his small cavalry
detachment. More Southerners galloped to the van, but Hotchkiss's
progress was impeded. "I could do but little with cavalry on such a
narrow winding road in the woods," he later complained with justifi-
cation. By the time his infantry support arrived, several companies of
the Eighth Louisiana Infantry, the one o'clock hour had passed with
Hotchkiss no more than two and one-half miles west of Cedarville.[27]

The Confederates crawled along the road to Middletown. A good
mile behind Hotchkiss marched Confederate infantry, led by Taylor's
Louisianans, and followed by the Stonewall Brigade. They pulled to
the side of the road briefly to allow one hundred horse soldiers from
the Seventh Virginia Cavalry to pass, as well as six guns, four belonging to Chew's horse artillery, and two belonging to the Rockbridge
Artillery. Capt. William Poague, whose rifled pieces arrived too late
at Front Royal on the twenty-third to be of service, was determined to
see action this day.

The artillery and cavalry caught up with Hotchkiss at the half-way point of the seven-mile road. One of the guns unlimbered on the road and fired at the trailing Union cavalry. The cavalry vedettes fell back to the only inhabited spot along the Chapel Road, the hamlet of Providence, marked by the church after which the road was named. There they returned to the remainder of the seven companies that were halted near the church. Lieutenant Colonel Douty of the First Maine, Maj. William D. Collins of the First Vermont, and their respective detachments had been covering the crossroads when they heard the skirmish fire. Douty's pickets rode out of the woods and joined the seven companies at Providence Church. Determined to stand his ground and gain time for the moving Union column three miles behind him, Douty kept his men in line of battle as a growing Confederate force exited the woods east of them and also formed a battle line. Union couriers galloped to the signal station two and one-half miles away to apprise headquarters that their worst fears had become a reality.

The stalemate was broken at 2:30 P.M. when Chew's battery un-limbered and began sending rounds into the Union force. The first shell struck a tree on the southern flank of the Maine cavalry and cut it off about twenty feet from the ground. It was the first time the horse soldiers had ever come under fire. "I won't say that I was not scared, for I was," frankly admitted Pvt. Charles Gardner of Company A, "and I contend that no man, unless he is a fool can withstand shells shrieking and bursting around him without feeling some scared and for a moment wishing he were at home."[28]

"We fired on them, and at the first fire they ran like wild men," gleefully noted George Neese of the horse artillery. Major Dabney concurred by calling the brief action "a novel instance of a charge effected by field artillery." Douty and Collins quickly sent their men toward Middletown. Another Confederate shell followed them, this one plowing into the road behind them and resurfacing on the left flank. The trotting pace quickened as the seven Union companies wasted no time returning to Middletown.[29]

At the U.S. War Department in Washington, messages had continued to click away since noon. Still reeling from General Geary's preposterous claims of the morning, Lincoln considered them reliable enough to transmit to another general at 1:00 P.M. Then the War

Department was disoriented from an erroneous telegraph. Sent by Gen. Dixon Miles at Harpers Ferry, the message repeated what Banks had already told the War Department—that six thousand to ten thousand rebels were passing Middletown on the turnpike and heading for Winchester. Miles closed his message by stating that Banks will telegraph again, prompting Stanton to ask Miles, "If the enemy is on the line between Banks and you, how is Banks able to telegraph you?" At 2:15 P.M., almost two hours after he asked the question, Stanton received his answer: "I gave this morning what Major Perkins telegraphed to me. He also said he should do so again at noon. I have not heard from him since. The wire has ceased to work within the last two hours."[30]

The ominous message seemed to confirm that Banks was indeed cut off from Winchester. But the intelligence was inaccurate, likely due to the haste in which it was wired from Major Perkins to Colonel Miles. Banks's aide meant that the Confederates were heading to Winchester by the Front Royal–Winchester Pike, passing Middletown on a route seven miles east of the Valley Pike. But he never identified the turnpike, leading to the wrong conclusion at the War Department that the Confederate turnpike route to Winchester was the Valley Pike; in other words, Lincoln and Stanton must have believed that the Southerners were passing *through* Middletown instead of passing *by* it on another road seven miles to the east.

Contributing to this misdiagnosis was the brief Confederate cannonade near Providence Church on the Chapel Road. Lincoln learned about the action at 3:00 P.M. from General Geary at Rectortown: "We can distinctly hear cannonading in the direction of Winchester from this point," transmitted Geary. Geary's message—obviously hearing this artillery fire as there was no other occurring since 10:30 A.M.—was the first confirmation of battle that Lincoln received after being misinformed from Dixon Miles (through Banks's chief of staff Major Perkins) that the enemy was between Banks and Winchester. Concerned that enemy forces were approaching on each of his flanks (a threat that did not exist), Geary notified Secretary Stanton that he must withdraw eastward on the Manassas Gap Railroad ten miles to White Plains.[31]

The War Department received another message at 3:00 P.M., this one from General Shields near Falmouth. He provided Lincoln an option: to use Frémont's Mountain Department. "If Jackson and

Ewell have moved against Banks they have placed themselves in a position to be caught by Milroy, Blenker, and Schenck," insisted Shields, suggesting Frémont's men cross through the Valley by way of Waynesboro and Charlottesville to destroy the railroad, thus locking Jackson's forces within the mountain corridor.[32] If Lincoln glanced at the Valley map at his time, he would have seen that the route Frémont would take out of the Alleghenies over to Charlottesville would necessarily pass through Harrisonburg.

During the same time Lincoln and Stanton were reading the messages from Geary and Shields, Turner Ashby led Jackson's vanguard toward Middletown. One mile from the Valley Pike hamlet, Ashby detached Maj. Oliver R. Funsten with the bulk of the available Seventh Virginia Cavalry—one hundred men—and sent them on the back road to Newtown, known locally as the Ridings Mill Road. This byroad led from the Chapel Road northward to Ridings Mill. From there, a traveler could take one of several avenues to the Valley Pike. Funsten's instructions were to strike the Valley Pike between Middletown and Newtown. Funsten and his command trotted away at 3:15 P.M., leaving Ashby and Colonel Crutchfield with a smattering of cavalry and the six artillery pieces. Allowing Funsten several minutes to work his way down the back road, Ashby surged forward as Jackson and his staff kept pace.[33]

The Maine and Vermont cavalry detachment entered Middletown close to 3:30 P.M. The horsemen were disappointed to see the village evacuated of Union regiments. They turned to the left in columns of four onto Church Street on the eastern side of the town. Douty learned that Banks had indeed passed with his army hours before, but he also learned that General Hatch had just left Strasburg and was approaching Middletown from the southwest. So Douty decided to wait.[34] He would regret the decision.

Ashby charged his men from the woods against an enemy for the second straight day. Douty ordered the rear guard drawn in as Confederate horse soldiers, artillerymen, Louisiana infantry, and staff officers advanced rapidly to the eastern heights overlooking the town. Jed Hotchkiss quickly saw the Maine and Vermont soldiers on Church Street. More savory to the Confederate warriors was the macadamized Valley Pike. For miles, it seemed, wagons rolled through Middletown toward Newtown. Almost instinctively, Captain Poague and Captain

Chew unlimbered their six cannons while members of the Seventh and Eighth Louisiana Infantry (spliced with members of Wheat's battalion) crept along the open fields until they gained the crest of the ridge east of town.

As the Confederate artillery opened fire, some of the Union cavalry slipped from their horses and took refuge in houses or behind stone walls. Those that remained on their horses scattered toward the pike. A lone Union officer refused to yield. He left his command, jumped his horse over a fence directly in front of the Louisianans, brandished his saber, and exhorted his command to follow him. His ostentation failed to impress the Louisianans. They gunned him down within seconds. "That will do him," yelled one of the Southerners, "Fire at the others in the road."[35]

The Confederates soon had more targets to fire at. As his detachment worked its way southwestward, Lieutenant Colonel Douty spied another cavalry column heading toward Middletown from Strasburg. This was Brig. Gen. John P. Hatch with six companies of the Fifth New York Cavalry. Hatch rode up to Douty on the side street and ordered his command to align in fours on the Valley Pike in an effort to escape the danger as a unified command.[36]

As the thirteen companies of Union horse clattered onto Middletown's main street, the Confederates moved toward the pike at the northern section of town to disrupt the wagon train rolling out in front of the Union cavalry. This train was not General Banks's supply wagons, but rather a mix of sutler and cavalry wagons, close to one hundred of them moving between Middletown and Newtown. In addition, several abandoned supply wagons—most of them emptied after Steuart's cavalry strike—lay strewn on the sides of the Valley Pike for at least one mile above and below Middletown. Major Funsten, commanding one hundred cavaliers on the Newtown back road, struck the pike at a point one mile from the north end of town. His command created instant mayhem on the wagon train as the cavalrymen steered their mounts southward.

Ashby's plan had thus far worked to perfection with the Valley Pike now plugged up with wagons. The Louisiana infantry scurried closer to their opponent, right where the pike sharply turned to the left, from east to north. On the eastern side of the bend a stone wall lined the road. To the right of the infantry rolled Poague's two guns, under the overall command of Colonel Crutchfield. Crutchfield ordered the cannons unlimbered on the western side of the Ridings's graveyard, within one hundred yards of the pike. Chew's four guns continued to fire from a half mile away into the confused mass of horse soldiers in the town.[37]

All of this transpired in a few minutes, but to the Federal cavalry, it seemed much longer, especially to Douty's detachment. Unable to fire back with their short-range revolvers, they were forced to wait in formation on the pike as Hatch's six companies moved forward ahead of them. Chew's gunners mercilessly raked the road around them. "We were actually a stationary target for them to practice upon," complained Capt. G.M. Brown of the First Maine. He and the other company officers rode up and down their commands, encouraging their men to keep their formations. Major Cilley of the First Maine remained to the right of his regiment, studying the movement of the Confederates to the east and facing toward them. A shell quickly arched in his direction, and Cilley could not escape its destructive path. The round exploded; a large shell fragment tore off his left arm from the shoulder. Without making a sound, Cilley toppled from his mount onto the road, terrifying those near him who had witnessed their first battle casualty in the Valley.[38]

It was only the first of many. General Hatch started the cavalry forward to get out of Middletown, but he quickly noted that his route was blocked by both Union wagons and Confederate soldiers. The bend in the road gave some the impression that Southern infantry aligned across it. Not willing to risk running the gauntlet, Hatch escaped the pending doom by turning his companies due west. They rode off the Valley Pike and onto the Capon Springs Road (an extension of the Chapel Road that ended at Middletown's Main Street as First Street. Hatch and his 250 followers left a tremendous dust cloud in their wake at the intersection as they galloped westward from it.[39]

Charging up behind Hatch was Douty's detachment of the First Maine—without Douty. He was in the rear, tending to Major Cilley, and could not return to his command in time to direct his regiment. Without leadership, the five companies rode through the blinding dust cloud followed by Collins's detachment of the First Vermont. With sabers drawn and gazes fixed, they galloped through the northern portion of the village—into the waiting trap set by Ashby, Hotchkiss, and Crutchfield, who readied their men near the bend in the road.[40]

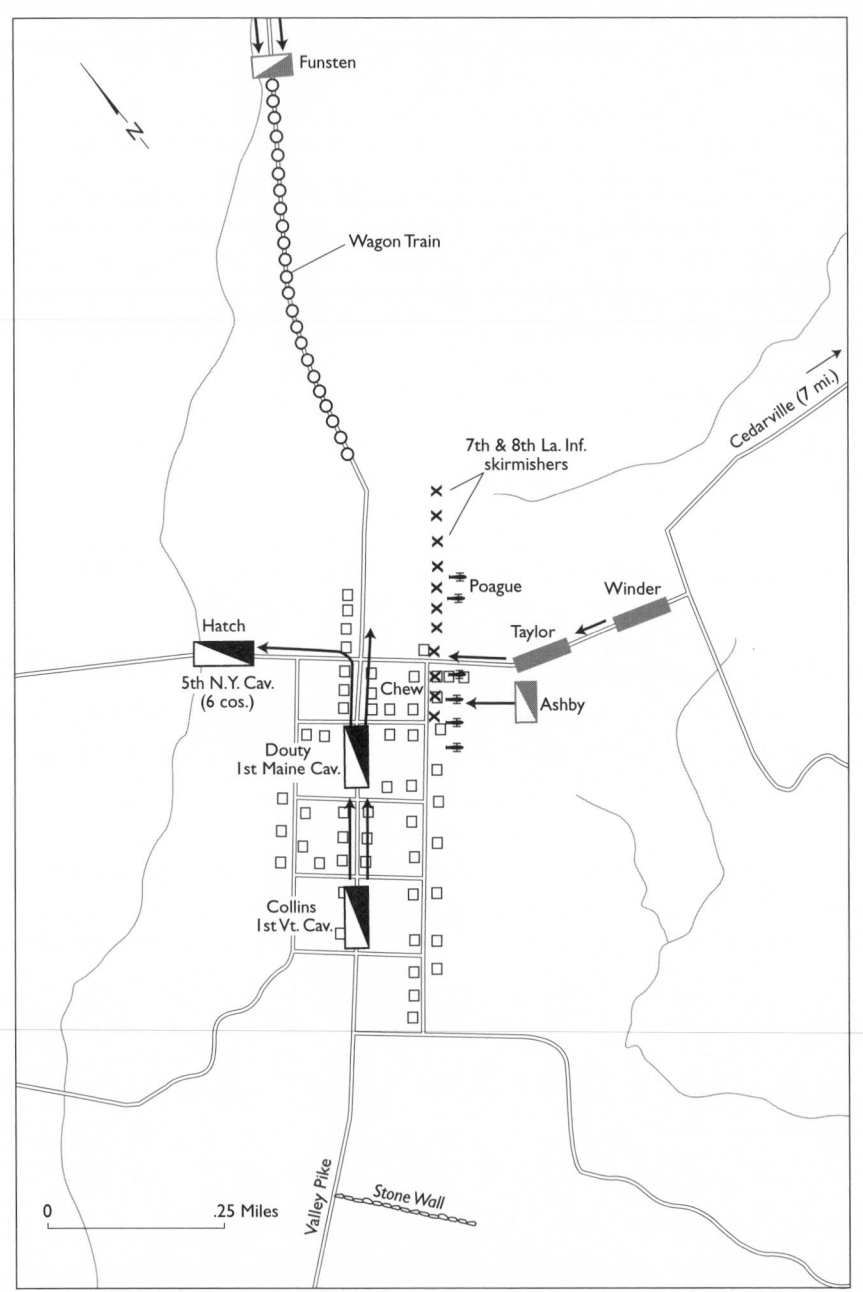

Action at Middletown, 3:30–4:00 P.M., May 24, 1862

Funsten

Wagon Train

7th & 8th La. Inf.
skirmishers

Poague

Winder

Taylor

Hatch

Chew

Ashby

5th N.Y. Cav.
(6 cos.)

Douty
1st Maine Cav.

Collins
1st Vt. Cav.

Cedarville (7 mi.)

0   .25 Miles

Valley Pike

Stone Wall

Chew's gunners initiated the Union disaster that followed. "At a half mile range we opened on the flying mixture with all four of our guns," noted a member of the horse artillery, "and as our shells plowed gap after gap through the serried column, it caused consternation confounded, and vastly increased the speed of the hurrying mixed fugitive mass." Captain Brown of the First Maine watched one of Chew's solid shots annihilate a section of four in front of him while another round took out his horse from under him. "Those behind could not see for dust and smoke," Brown explained, "and in an instant the whole company were piling one on the other—Company A following, and adding to the horror.[41] Pvt. Charles Gardner became one of forty victims in Company A:

> It was a terrible moment . . . for we had not gone very far when the horses in front were down, and we in the rear fell over them. As for myself, I was urging my horse to the utmost, when like a flash he stumbled and threw me over his head and landed on the pike face down. My horse must have turned a summersault for he landed on top of me, his body laying across my back and legs. . . . I was bound down and could move only my head. I heard oaths and groans ahead of me; raising my head as high as I could, I saw a pile of men and horses apparently in about the same condition as myself.[42]

The pile was destined to grow, for more cavalry galloped haphazardly toward the heap. The Louisianans perched themselves next to the pile, waiting to fire at the remaining cavalry to approach. They need not wait long. The Vermont companies charged next, led by the pretentious Major Collins. Reaching full speed, Company A galloped into the cauldron. The Louisianans emptied their rifles into the horse soldiers and sent them careening onto the pike and into the walls that bordered it.[43] The horror had now begun for cavalryman Charles Blinn of Company A:

> I fell into the dense cloud of dust. Thank God I lived after that fall. Stunned as I was I laid beside my dead charger knowing that the whole of Company G was yet to pass over that mass of living and dying men piled up in a heap in the road. On, on they came, and lying on my back with feet and hands raised, I await the tramp of the horse which should send me to a sol-

dier's home. But I was spared and when I arose from among that mass of dead and dying I found that I was only a prisoner in the rebels' hands. Father in Heaven.[44]

The scene was macabre, and it elicited a mixed reaction from General Jackson and his staff. The Reverend Dabney epitomized the sentiments of Middletown's citizens in his fire-and-brimstone style: "Behold the righteous judgment of God; for these are the miscreants who have been most forward to plunder, insult, and oppress us!" Jed Hotchkiss echoed Dabney's exclamation, remarking how the "superbly mounted cavalry, that had exultingly and insolently rode over our valley, was melted like snow before the sun." "I am not vindicative," reasoned Hotchkiss to his wife two days later, "but I really did not feel sorry to see the horse and his insolent rider laid low, it seemed a just retribution for the evils they had inflicted on an innocent people." Lt. H. Kyd Douglas disagreed—he considered the slaughter on the pike as murder. When he uttered this conclusion loud enough for General Jackson to hear, Stonewall responded, "Let them alone."[45]

Jackson knew the work was not complete. Much of Company G of the First Vermont met a similar fate as their comrades in front of them. Those that escaped adding to the pile could go little farther, because the stalled line of cavalry baggage wagons in front of them created a barrier to their escape. Some of the fallen Maine and Vermont cavalrymen recovered their senses enough to work an escape, crawling over fallen horses to reach the safety of the western side of the Valley Pike. Company B and H of the First Maine never charged; they followed Hatch's route to safety by the back road and eventually linked with Hatch's command. Through the dust, Colonel Crutchfield saw the escaped Union cavalry west of town, but believed them to be Virginia cavaliers. Unsure, he asked Colonel Ashby, who assured Crutchfield they were Union horse soldiers. Crutchfield turned his pieces toward them, but the poor quality of the ammunition resulted in the rounds exploding but fifty feet from the muzzles of their guns.[46]

While Crutchfield met with temporary failure, Ashby refused to let the fallen Union cavalrymen escape. Brandishing his saber, he impetuously spurred his black stallion toward a gate and cleared it smoothly. "Charge them, boys! Charge them!" Ashby exhorted while galloping toward the fleeing mass of Union cavalry turned foot soldiers. Returning with scores of captured men, Ashby's ostentatious display electrified his command to pull in two hundred prisoners.[47]

Jackson's rout of the Union rear guard at Middletown lasted less than half an hour. Stonewall now possessed two hundred more horses along with an equal number of prisoners. Ahead of him, strewn along the Valley Pike toward Newtown, were dozens of captured supply wagons to add to his impressive booty. More importantly, the opportunity to destroy Banks's army was still viable, though waning. Jackson dictated new orders for General Ewell, fourteen miles away from Middletown at Double Tollgate. The dispatch instructed Ewell to "move on Winchester with all the force you have as promptly as possible." Dabney handed the note to a courier, who galloped away with it at 4:00 P.M.[48]

Once he received the order, Ewell could march the two brigades with him to Winchester by 8:00 P.M. While Ewell headed toward a strike at Banks's vanguard, Jackson planned to harass the tail of his army. At the least, Jackson expected to prevent Banks from digging in and defending the high ground surrounding Winchester. But Stonewall expected to accomplish much more than that. He insisted that "every opposition had been borne down, and there was reason to believe, if Banks reached Winchester, it would be without a train, if not without an army."[49]

Unlike his opponent, Jackson had overcome his own oversights and his own fog of war to place himself in a position in the midafternoon of May 24 to annihilate an army. But a new fog of uncertainty enveloped Jackson just as he planned to face his infantry northward from the Chapel Road to continue the pursuit on the Valley Pike to Winchester. Desultory artillery fire emanated from the direction of Strasburg. Why would Union artillery come in behind cavalry in the tail of an army? Could Jackson have stricken the middle or front of Banks's column? Decisiveness had directed Jackson to this state of the campaign. Rapid-fire decisions, made with little or no consultation with staffers and subordinates, had been the hallmark of Jackson's generalship. This moment would be no different.

Jackson immediately ordered the vanguard of his army to turn southward. Taylor's brigade dutifully complied; the Louisianans wheeled to the left in fours as they stepped onto the pike. All headed toward the sound of the artillery fire south of Middletown. Jackson had no idea that he had just committed his army in the direction of a Union force that amounted to a mere five cannons, fifty artillerists, seventy-five infantrymen, and scattered companies of cavalry. Indeed, this was Banks's rear guard.

Jackson had just made his costliest decision of the campaign.

6

OPPORTUNITY LOST

S ecretary of the Treasury Salmon P. Chase naturally viewed the war through a fiscal lens. The sloth of McClellan's movement to Richmond had been costly to the government, not yet in lives but in expense. Pointing this out to a newspaper editor, Chase sarcastically surmised, "McClellan is a dear luxury—fifty days—fifty miles—fifty millions of dollars—easy arithmetic but not satisfactory." With only six miles between McClellan and Richmond on May 24, Chase may have felt some relief that his million-dollars-per-mile calculation was not as detrimental as it was one month earlier.[1]

When Secretary Chase stepped into the War Department at 4:00 P.M. on Saturday, May 24, 1862, he no longer saw the sanguine signs of Union success on the dour faces of Abraham Lincoln and Secretary of War Stanton. Lincoln was convinced that the enemy had cut off Banks's retreat at Middletown. Forced to apply grand strategy in the theater of Virginia, President Lincoln appears to have taken Shields's suggestion about using the Mountain Department to trap Jackson and modified it.

"The exposed condition of General Banks makes his immediate relief a point of paramount importance," Lincoln wired Maj. Gen. John C. Frémont, ordering him "to move against Jackson at Harrisonburg and operate against the enemy in such [a] way to relieve Banks.

This movement must be made immediately." No sooner had that message left the telegraph office at 4:00 P.M. than two others came through, both sent by Colonel Miles at Harpers Ferry. Dread dripped from the ominous words that "the rebels have cut the wires between Winchester and Strasburg . . . also just been informed rebel cavalry have arrived at Berryville. . . . A battalion of rebels could take this place [Harpers Ferry]. . . . The telegraph operator reports fighting within 8 miles of Winchester. No arrival of troops yet."[2]

Lincoln's fears were now confirmed. In his opinion, Frémont would not be strong enough to take care of matters by himself in the Shenandoah Valley. He needed support, and Lincoln was determined to send a larger body of troops to assure the security of Union interests in western Virginia. He dictated another message to the telegrapher, this one directed to Maj. Gen. George B. McClellan. "In consequence of Gen. Banks' critical position," instructed the president, "I have been compelled to suspend Gen. McDowell's movement to join you. The enemy are making a desperate rush upon Harper's Ferry, and we are trying to throw Fremont's force & part of McDowell's in their rear."[3]

To make certain that McDowell followed his new instructions, Lincoln ordered Secretary Chase to depart the capital immediately and go to Falmouth to explain the circumstances. Shortly after Chase left, Lincoln wired McDowell the new plan. "This is a crushing blow to us," came McDowell's dispirited reply. The president understood McDowell's disappointment. He was stripping McClellan of the thirty-eight thousand men and eighty-six guns he deemed essential to take Richmond. Indeed, if his gamble failed, Lincoln's decision would deal the Union a crushing blow.[4]

Capt. Charles H.T. Collis never envisioned his eighty Zouaves would be involved in the duties of a common soldier. Since reuniting with Banks, the Corps d'Afrique had performed only specialized duties, such as the overnight reconnaissance toward Front Royal, and currently were waiting at the Cedar Creek bridge to burn it. Capt. James Abert, Banks's topographical engineer, had the fire ready by lighting a concoction of straw, tar, commissary pork, and other inflammables. When Abert realized that the ford nearby was in better condition than the bridge for crossing the creek, he abandoned the plan and led the Zouaves toward Middletown.[5]

They never got there. Abert rode up to the southern outskirts of Middletown just in time to watch the Union cavalry disaster unfold on Main Street. He sent Collis to the top of a ridge to the east to see where the enemy was coming from. Collis came back to report hordes of Southerners advancing from the east, but Abert was now more concerned with what lay in front of him. The Federal Zouaves hustled forward just as the Ninth Louisiana Infantry from Taylor's brigade entered the Valley Pike from the east. Collis's men managed to fire the first volley. Lt. Harry Handerson, a native Ohioan serving in the Louisiana regiment, recalled, "As we jumped over the stone wall into the pike . . . a vicious volley of bullets whistled through our disordered ranks, splintering the rails of a neighboring fence and wounding several of my comrades."[6]

The Louisianans quickly left the pike for the cover of Middletown's buildings as other units in Taylor's brigade, wheeling left to add reinforcements, headed directly toward them in column by company. The only object separating Collis from destruction was a shoulder-high stone wall running perpendicular eastward from the Valley Pike. Without hesitation, the Zouaves peeled off the road and raced to the wall.

Collis's men lined up behind the wall as Louisianans poured onto the pike facing toward Strasburg. The Ninth Louisiana Infantry and Wheat's Battalion led Taylor's brigade south of Strasburg. At a distance of one hundred yards, the opposing forces exchanged volleys. Zouave fired on Zouave as the red legged Union company held its ground against the striped-legged Tiger Zouaves of Wheat's command. Members of the Ninth Louisiana cleared the pike to find cover behind houses and rail fences on each side of the road. Collis ordered his men to reload and fire two more volleys, but in a couple of minutes he was flanked and therefore ordered his men to withdraw.

As the Pennsylvanians headed southward, the Louisianans reformed on the pike, sent out their skirmishers, and began to chase after the Union rear guard. Collis's Zouaves scampered past the Belle Grove mansion, Captain Collis and Captain Abert urging them on. Relief came into view on the hill south of the mansion. Across the pike on the rise of ground stretched five cannons in battery. One was a twelve-pounder howitzer from Battery F, Fourth U.S. Artillery. The other four guns—all ten-pounder Parrotts—belonged to Capt. R.B. Hampton, commanding Battery F, First Pennsylvania Light Artillery. The guns were positioned one mile north of Cedar Creek. No one was

happier to see the show of strength than Captains Abert and Collis;
Abert reflected on the sight as "the greatest good fortune," while
Collis deemed the presence of an artillery line as "an intervention of a
generous God."[7]

The new defense, according to Collis, lasted about half an hour.
As the Zouaves rallied behind the artillery pieces, Hampton's gunners opened upon the Louisiana skirmishers carefully approaching
them. Screaming rounds forced the Pelican State soldiers to hesitate.
"[Union] numbers were unknown, and for a moment they seemed
threatening," remembered General Taylor. He had good reason to
display some caution. One of the Union shells struck the earth at his
horse's feet and exploded. Terra firma flew in all directions, some
covering the general, and the saddlecloth was torn away, but according to Taylor, "neither man nor horse received a scratch." Although
Taylor was spared, he maintained that several Louisianans near him
were wounded in the explosion. This turned out to be the only destructive round; immediately after it exploded, Taylor's men wormed
their way into a battle line nearly one mile across.[8]

The time approached 4:30 P.M. General Jackson studied the defense arrayed on the high ground. The presence of so much artillery
was uncharacteristic of a rear guard. Hopeful but confused, Jackson
firmly believed he had split Banks's force and had the singular opportunity to wreak havoc on a significant portion of it. So convinced was
Stonewall that—with the stroke of Dabney's pen—he changed his operational approach to the theater within the triangle of roads between
Strasburg, Front Royal, and Winchester:

> Middletown, May 24, 1862—4:30 o'clock
>
> Major-General Ewell:
>
> General: the major-general commanding requests that you
> will forward General Elzey to us at this place, and by the route
> we marched, as rapidly as possible, and that you will not ad-
> vance any nearer Winchester with the remainder of your com-
> mand till further orders. There seems to be still a considerable
> body of the enemy advancing on us from Strasburg.
>
> Respectfully,
> R. L. Dabney[9]

By sending the message Jackson committed himself to the southward advance, and in so doing he left Ewell with a stripped force of

barely one brigade. Jackson's request also showed strong evidence that he had a blurred perception of time and distance. Reason dictates that Jackson would have disregarded the sounds between Strasburg and Middletown had he understood that six and one-half hours had passed since General Steuart struck the wagon train at Newtown. Factoring in Boswell's intelligence that mistakenly swelled Banks's ranks to twelve thousand effectives, even those phantom troops would have cleared Middletown and not abandoned the wagon train by late afternoon. More evidence for Jackson's fog exists in the meat of his message to Ewell. Thirteen miles separated Ewell from Jackson; therefore, the time required to deliver the 4:30 P.M. message and bring Elzey over to Middletown would take a minimum of five and one-half hours. It would be ten o'clock by the time Elzey wheeled his men onto the Valley Turnpike at Middletown. So unless Jackson intended to extend his efforts into the following morning south of Middletown, his request for Elzey's troops was a wasted one.

Confederate pursuit northward proved to be feeble and disorganized. From the northern portion of Middletown rode General Ashby with forty horse soldiers. He was followed by Chew's guns and a section of the Rockbridge Artillery. No infantry supported this pursuit. Leadership existed in the form of Colonel Ashby, Captain Chew, Colonel Crutchfield, and Jedediah Hotchkiss. They maneuvered past the Union cavalry wagons captured and plundered by Major Funsten and his men. The Confederates met no resistance in the first mile north of Middletown.

That would soon change. Lt. William Rowley, acting signal officer for Banks's army, had set up five signal stations between Strasburg and Newtown. The Confederates disrupted all but two of those stations when they pierced Middletown in midafternoon. Signals were instantly waved northward between the two stations closest to Newtown. General Williams, overseeing his division's march between Newtown and Bartonsville, reacted immediately upon receiving the news that the column was pierced. He sent a directive to his subordinate Col. George H. Gordon: "Keep the enemy back, and protect all the train that's left." Gordon looked for the closest infantry force to give immediate succor to the threatened wagons. He found the Twenty-seventh Indiana.[10]

The Hoosiers had never felt like they fit in Banks's army. Indeed, they were the only westerners in what could generally be considered a Northeast force. Apparent friction had been sparking between the western recruits and their New England comrades. "The Yankeys and Hoosiers dont harmonise," opined a member of the Twenty-seventh Indiana. One month earlier, General Shields had offered to rectify the situation with a trade of two of his regiments for the Twenty-seventh Indiana, which he proposed to place with another Indiana regiment in a brigade commanded by the popular Hoosier, Brig. Gen. Nathan Kimball. Banks nixed this idea; his decision was justified by one Hoosier company at Buckton Station. Now the remaining Indiana soldiers would be seeing their first action of the Civil War.[11]

Union colonel Silas Colgrove received the orders for his regiment as they approached Newtown. Colgrove directed his men to file off into a field on the west side of the pike where they unslung their knapsacks, haversacks, and canteens and piled them by companies. This accomplished, the Hoosiers ran southward past the wagons squeezing by them as they rolled northward toward safety. The second panic put to the teamsters was not as pronounced as the morning threat, but it provided a grand spectacle for the citizens of Newtown who took pleasure in watching frantic drivers racing their wagons northward or abandoning their responsibilities and running pell-mell through the town. Riderless vehicles were set afire to prevent the plunder of supplies, but some Newtown residents became beneficiaries of the Union commissary department. Buckets laden with sugar, coffee, rice, and tea were carried to the houses of Newtown. "One man threw a sack of bacon in my yard," recalled Mollie Hansford Walls, "and another threw a gum blanket over my fence."[12]

Reaching a break in the wagon train one mile south of Newtown, Colonel Colgrove filed his men into a field on the east side of the road and ordered them to form a line of battle behind a paling fence. Moving with the Twenty-seventh Indiana was a section of Battery F, Fourth U.S. Artillery, under the command of Lt. Henry Cushing. Cushing fired his guns at the mass of Funsten's cavalry sacking stalled wagons, but the rounds fell well short of their mark. After the remaining wagons rolled past the rear guard toward Newtown, Cushing moved one of his guns into the middle of the pike and waited.[13]

Their wait could be counted in mere seconds. "Soon we heard the rebel yell across the ridge which lay in front of us," recalled Lewis King of the Twenty-seventh Indiana. Ashby, with forty horse soldiers, had organized for another charge, complete with bugle call. "I had hardly got my gun in position on the road when down came a whole company of rebel cavalry . . . whooping and yelling like demons," witnessed Lieutenant Cushing. But Ashby broke this charge off two hundred yards short of the Union line, and all of his followers stopped the pursuit—all but one lone horseman. The Virginian, name unknown, was either unaware or unconcerned that no one charged with him. Galloping at a steady pace with his sword aloft and cheering, the rebel rushed toward the cannons in the road and the waiting line of Indiana infantry in the fields to the east. The cavalryman closed within ten yards of Cushing's gun when the Hoosiers loosed a volley upon him at point-blank range. "At the volley, his head seemed lifted from his shoulders. However, it was only his cap," recalled a member of the Twenty-seventh Indiana. "When the smoke arose, I saw him lying all blown to pieces—his horse limping away and his company flying for dear life," wrote Cushing. "Poor man! His was a bloody sacrifice," remembered another Hoosier infantryman as he saw the quivering corpse riddled with bullet holes.[14]

No interval of respite was afforded the Union rear guard, however, for Confederate artillery immediately came up. Capt. William Poague had been working his guns furiously since the attack at Middletown. Pursuing the Union tail and "firing as often as I could," Poague brought his guns to the top of a gentle rise near the Chrisman house. "We soon struck the rear guard of Banks' army and simultaneously it struck us," assessed one of the Confederate gunners. Unlimbering on the higher ground opposite the house, the Southern artillerists sent round after round into the Union line. The Indianans instantly and instinctively flattened themselves behind the rail fence, while Cushing returned fire. The U.S. soldiers were gone in less than ten minutes, scampering to the rear and completely forgetting their piled knapsacks on the other side of the road.[15]

The Union troops fled northward into the village of Newtown, Confederate gunners nipping at their heels. As this occurred, more assistance was on the way. After sending the Twenty-seventh Indiana back, Colonel Gordon had proceeded down the pike with his command until he came to Bartonsville, one and one-half miles north of Newtown. Here Gordon saw General Banks escorting the Twenty-eighth New York southward. Banks had received the message near Kernstown about his line being split. Banks reined up to Gordon and told him to take the Twenty-eighth back and to support it with his own Second Massachusetts and include a battery. Like the Indiana troops before them, the Massachusetts men unslung their knapsacks and reversed their steps toward Newtown.[16]

Chew's horse artillery led the Southerners toward the village. They passed by the discarded knapsacks of the Indiana infantry, realizing that a rearward force would capture the booty. Chew's men entered Newtown and fed their horses on the street. Ashby rode with them, dismounted on Main Street, and led his horse to a pile of corn placed at the doorstep of one of the residents.[17] The Confederates took a respite waiting for the rest of the strung-out force to catch up. It was now 5:00 P.M.

Six miles up the Valley Pike from Chew's battery fought General Jackson with more Confederate troops, but they were facing in the opposite direction (southward), toward the Union defense arrayed on the hill between Cedar Creek and Middletown. More Union troops joined the Zouaves and artillerymen on the ridge. Col. Charles H. Tompkins of the First Vermont Cavalry came up with the remaining five companies of his regiment (F, H, I, K, and L). A Virginia native, the thirty-one-year-old Tompkins was a celebrity of sorts for his courageous but reckless charge at Fairfax Court House in the war's first clash on June 1, 1861 (a feat that won him the Congressional Medal of Honor in 1893). Becoming the third commander for his regiment in six months, Tompkins was a solid appointment , for he brought the experience and stability of a regular army officer. He took the helm of the First Vermont Cavalry on May 23, merely one day before he was tested on the Valley Pike.[18]

Tompkins had his force formed in columns of squadrons, ready to charge, but he had a change of heart as soon as he saw the Confederates stretched out in front of him, enveloping the flanks. "Before us along the pike as far as the eye could reach arose a cloud of dust . . . while in front, in the village of Middletown and to the right, shots sounded," claimed one of the Vermont horsemen. Tompkins "deemed it advisable" to withdraw from the position. Indeed, this was a sound conclusion, but a decision that did not go over well with the artillerists who expected the cavalry to conduct a more aggressive mission. ("The cavalry refused to charge," complained one of the gunners.) As the Southern line inched toward the guns, the batterymen switched to canister, then discharged one ineffective round. As the Confederates closed in to within one hundred yards, "their balls flying thick and fast," the Union stalwarts pulled back toward Cedar Creek.[19]

Tompkins's quick decision caused a huge problem with his baggage wagons. As the cavalry and artillery crossed over to the Strasburg side of the creek, a detail of twenty men from Company D of the First Vermont Cavalry took charge of the nineteen regimental wagons. Southern skirmishers closed in within pistol range. Wagon horses fell into the creek, downed by the Confederates. The horse carcasses jammed the ford after a mere four wagons crossed to safety. This left fifteen wagons and scores of horses unprotected. They, and the bountiful stores they held, quickly fell into Confederate hands. The wagon fiasco drew some attention away from the rear guard as they escaped across the creek.[20]

Ten miles down the pike at Newtown, Chew's artillery horses never got to finish their meal. Less than a half hour after Banks ordered him to the rear, Col. George H. Gordon led a rearguard force into the village from the north in response to his earlier instructions to react to the assault on General Hatch's command at Middletown. With him double-quicked the Second Massachusetts Infantry from his brigade, the Twenty-eighth New York Infantry from Donnelly's brigade, and a section of Battery M, First New York Light Artillery, under the command of Lt. Thomas Hodgkins. Gordon's men reversed their steps from Kernstown and passed by several overturned wagons on the side of the pike as they approached the town. These were the relics of the Confederate cavalry attack made seven hours earlier. Lieutenant Cushing's two guns and the Twenty-seventh Indiana had come back from their efforts south of Newtown and now took up position on a height near the northeast corner of the town.[21] Gordon's force approached fifteen hundred infantrymen to support the four guns.

The Twenty-seventh Indiana stayed north of Newtown in reserve. The guns commanded by Hodgkins mirrored Cushing's deployment by unlimbering on a dominant height on the northwest corner of town. Cushing's men shelled the woods off to the east of Newtown to drive out Ashby's cavalry while the Second Massachusetts was ordered forward. In addition, Four companies of the Twenty-eighth New York and two companies of the Twenty-seventh Indiana fanned out as they marched into Newtown, one hundred yards south of the batteries. They immediately came under fire from Chew's lone gun in the road. Hodgkins's section instinctively replied by sending their rounds over the heads of the Union infantry. The Bay Staters negotiated the fences and homes in the northern part of the village and flanked the Southern battery.[22]

"I do not know just where our cavalry was at that time," complained artillerist George Neese, citing an oft-repeated refrain about Southern cavalry in the late afternoon. The Southern gunners pulled back south of the town (one of them admitted that this was "a narrow escape") as more New England soldiers crept in. Maj. Wilder Dwight of the Second Massachusetts led his skirmish line to the southern edge of town. Noting a half-eaten pile of corn at the doorstep of a house, Dwight directed his horse to the feed. "The man of the house said Ashby's horse was eating there," noted Dwight. "I fed my horse with what was left." Lt. Col. George L. Andrews ordered five members of the color guard to climb onto the roof of the highest house they could find. Believing General Hatch was still held up at Middletown, the quintet waved the U.S. flag from the rooftop as a signal.[23]

Ashby rallied Chew's men on a commanding height across Stephen's Run to the west of Dr. McLeod's elegant stone house, which straddled the western side of the pike. Poague brought up his section and deployed next to Chew. Now six Southern guns were in place, but there was no infantry support for them. Ashby had kept fifty cavalrymen in order, but no other help was immediately available.

Crutchfield rode up the pike to find the Louisianans he had begun the pursuit with. He found approximately one hundred members of the Seventh Louisiana pacing themselves because of fatigue. Crutchfield hurried them forward but could acquire no other infantry support. He found other infantry, but they, along with scores of cavalrymen, were left plundering the stalled sutler wagons north of Middletown. Those wagons consisted of the segment of the Union cavalry train that Major Funsten captured ninety minutes earlier, intermixed with some supply wagons that were abandoned during the panic caused by Steuart's cavalry strike at Newtown six hours before that (the wagoners rode off with the mules and horses that had been pulling them). When Crutchfield returned to the McLeod house at 5:15 P.M., he found his cannons engaged in a spirited artillery duel with four Union cannons ensconced on the northern heights of Newtown.[24] Without support, the Confederates would stay where they were.

Five miles east of Newtown, near Double Tollgate, General Ewell distinctly heard the rumble of cannon fire trace northward for nearly an hour. At 5:15 P.M., after holding his place for nine hours, Ewell agonized over not receiving any orders. If Jackson's first courier—the one sent off from Middletown with the 4:00 P.M. message to march toward Winchester—ever found Ewell, no evidence exists that Ewell acted on the instructions. Jackson's second courier most certainly did arrive with instructions to hold his place and send Elzey's brigade back to him. Ewell complied, stripped of his entire command except for Trimble's brigade and the Maryland Line. Ewell was well aware that daytime was waning in the Valley. In two hours, it would be completely dark.[25]

By 5:15 P.M. Jackson also had to be aware of the diminishing time to complete his operation. But he was still facing southward against what he had believed to be the main body of Banks's army. By this time, however, he must have entertained some doubts. From across Cedar Creek, the Union rear guard still offered some resistance. Tompkins and Hampton briefly reformed on the height just south of Cedar Creek, joined by infantrymen who had fallen back to Strasburg after they had feared the worst near Middletown in the midmorning. The hill was deemed untenable, and they fell back again, this time to Hupp's Hill, directly north of the town of Strasburg. There they held while activity swirled behind them. Billowing smoke could be seen from the south side of Strasburg, and panic pervaded the air. Realizing the size of the force that opposed them, a Massachusetts soldier claimed, "Each and every man was aware that nothing that he could do would prevent our capture, but we were anxious to make a show of resistance and so we organized for action by unanimously choosing the ranking officer for our commander."[26]

They chose Col. Othneil De Forest, who had a busy hour before joining the force on Hupp's Hill. After halting his remaining companies of the Fifth New York Cavalry at the church there that held the ordnance stores, he emptied the church of the stores, then set them afire. He loaded thirteen wagons with clothing but realized there was no time to save any supplies. De Forest ordered the torch to be applied to all the remaining depot stores. All of the tents belonging to Banks's army went up in flames in the buildings above Strasburg as De Forest moved his command northward through town.

De Forest and his companies rode up to the summit of Hupp's

Hill, where they found Hampton's guns, the Zouaves, and Tompkins's command in position. But according to De Forest, they were far from organized. "Infantry, cavalry, and wagons were streaming back in wild confusion along the road and the fields on either side as far as the eye could reach," he noted. As the artillerist checked the Confederate advance across the creek with a few rounds, De Forest, Hampton, and Tompkins huddled together to find an escape route. De Forest's wife aided her husband by encouraging the more panicked members of the force with optimistic words.

A black civilian pointed out the road to freedom that lay in front of them, at the summit of Hupp's Hill. This simple dirt road led the way to the Capon Road, which broadly skirted the Valley Pike to the west. All agreed to head in that direction. Colonel De Forest led the only supply train south of Cedar Creek not put to the flame—thirty-five wagons full. They started moving westward at 5:30 P.M.[27]

Across Cedar Creek, Stonewall Jackson had finally become convinced that he opposed Banks's rear guard. More than ninety minutes had elapsed since he left Middletown, and only ninety minutes of daylight remained. His decision to chase after the rear guard netted him fifteen more wagons, but nothing else. Unfortunately for Jackson, it did buy Banks precious hours to complete his escape. Leaving one regiment at Cedar Creek, Jackson wheeled around and, with staff in tow, headed toward Middletown as Taylor's Louisianans retraced their steps from Cedar Creek. At 5:45 P.M. Jackson dictated a dispatch to Major Dabney. The note, once again, was addressed to General Ewell: "Major-General Jackson requests that you will at once move with all your force on Winchester." This note was handed to Lieutenant Boswell, who galloped northward to Middletown, wheeled onto the Chapel Road, and rode eastward on his mission to find Ewell.[28]

Boswell's fifteen-mile mission would require close to ninety minutes to deliver the dispatch. Unaware that instructions to advance to Winchester would come after sunset, Ewell languished near Double Tollgate. The time passed 6:00 P.M. It was ten hours since Ewell halted his division on the Front Royal–Winchester Pike, and that division had been reduced to five regiments and one battalion—fewer than two thousand effectives. Ewell fumed that "without instructions my situation became embarrassing." He discussed his predicament with General Trimble and Campbell Brown. He decided to advance to Winchester without orders. Brown wrote out an explanation to Jackson, providing notice of the decision and an option to stop it if he wished, also proposing to come by the Millwood–Newtown Road if it was necessary for him to cross over to the Valley Pike. Brown gave the dispatch to a courier, who carried it to find Jackson.[29]

Jackson's army realigned at Middletown. No longer would Taylor's Louisianans spearhead the march as they had done for the past thirty-six hours. Because they had followed Jackson south, they would bring up the rear. This left the next brigade in line to spearhead the movement. It was propitious for Jackson, for the next unit was the Stonewall Brigade, his Valley-bred soldiers who knew this region well enough to move through it in darkness. Three of General Winder's regiments (the Second, Fourth, and Fifth Virginia Infantry) had also turned southward at Middletown but had not advanced far from the intersection of the pike and the Chapel Road. This left the Thirty-third and Twenty-seventh Virginia Infantry to march in the brigade van beginning shortly after 6:00 P.M. Jed Hotchkiss was struck at how "lustily did the Regiments from that part of the state cheer when they were ordered toward their home."[30]

Across the line, Stonewall Jackson found nothing to cheer. The sight of the road segment between Middletown and Newtown fed Jackson's fury for months. The captured wagons had proved to be too irresistible to the undisciplined cavalry and many in the Louisiana infantry that had originally turned northward before 4:30 P.M. Ninety minutes later, this portion of Jackson's army had still taken themselves out of the hunt. Jackson still believed that he had the opportunity to destroy Banks. "[B]ut in the midst of these hopes I was pained to see," seethed Jackson with eleven months of hindsight, "that so many of Ashby's command, both cavalry and infantry, forgetful of their high trust as the advance of a pursuing army, deserted their colors, and abandoned themselves to pillage to such an extent as to make it necessary for that gallant officer [Ashby] to discontinue farther pursuit."[31]

Jackson's castigation of Ashby's command was clearly justified, for the utter lack of discipline was unacceptable. But Stonewall's ire was exaggerated in his insistence that the vagrancy of a force numbering no more than two hundred men prevented a crushing blow to Banks's army on May 24, 1862. Even if no men plundered wagons, the Confederates would still have been outnumbered by more than a three-to-one ratio at Newtown.

The opportunity existed at several points in time to accomplish that objective. Had Jackson sent out a reconnaissance at daybreak, rather than waiting until 8:00 A.M., he would have learned of Banks's direction three hours before he first was apprised of the Union northward retreat. Even with the late intelligence, had Jackson sent Ewell along the Millwood–Newtown Road, he could have smacked into the flank of Banks's retreating infantry as early as 1:30 P.M. But Jackson chose the Chapel Road and intercepted the pike five miles south and two hours later. And the diminishing hope of wreaking significant havoc upon Banks at this point was destroyed when Jackson turned his vanguard south. Jackson also had held Ewell in place for the entire daylight hours of May 24, thus squandering the availability of any reliable force.

These four points share one commonality: Stonewall Jackson. His misdirection, mistiming, and misjudgments were the costliest reasons for the lost opportunity to destroy an army, not Turner Ashby and his wayward command. "All of these things necessarily consume time, no mater how energetically they are pressed," Jed Hotchkiss concluded in recounting the events of May 24. He recognized that when Jackson was satisfied with his deployments, "it was quite late in the day before he was ready to push on and devote all his energies to the pursuit." Nevertheless, Jed Hotchkiss raved to his wife that from this point he bore witness to "one of the movements in which Gen. Jackson shows his iron will[:] he wished to reach Winchester, or the hills west of it, before the next morning, and he was now off."[32]

Also interfering with Jackson's plans was the dogged resistance kept up by the Union rear guard at Newtown. The cannonade had thus far extended into its second hour with no sign that the Federals would leave. Casualties began to mount, with the artillery on both sides taking the brunt of the duel. Lieutenant Hodgkins, heading up the section of New York artillery on the northwestern height, was helpless as he watched a Confederate shell arch toward him. The round exploded right in front of him, and a fragment spewed from the impact site and tore off his left thumb and bruised his side. A nearby surgeon dressed the severe wound, and Hodgkins resumed command. "This was all the injury I received," Hodgkins matter-of-factly explained to his mother, adding that he was ready for duty again, "with the exception of not being able to use my left hand."[33]

One mile south of Hodgkins, Poague's and Chew's batteries suf-

fered casualties. Three members of the Rockbridge Artillery went
down with injuries. The cannonade and infantry fire was so heated
that Chew decided to abandon the hill for a safer position. As the
Massachusetts infantry continued to harass the Southern gunners, an
infantryman's shot from several hundred yards away cut down the
lead driver of one of the cannon teams. The injured man was carried
to the McLeod house while the rest of the battery headed to the next
line of hills. Furious at the effectiveness of the Union sharpshooters
on the Confederate batteries, Ashby ordered Captain Poague to halt
while he charged toward the town with a squadron of cavalry.[34]

The five Union color guard members continued to wave the flag
from a rooftop amid the artillery duel. "It was quite fine in the sunset
light," raved one of the signal men, "to see the stars and stripes waving a signal to all left behind that in spite of thundering batteries,
Yankee Doodle was still in that village." They all must have been
surprised to see Union general Hatch gallop into Newtown from the
Capon Road to the west.[35]

Jackson rode up to the southern outskirts of Newtown at 6:45
P.M. and witnessed the stiff resistance offered by the Union rear
guard. Ewell's courier soon galloped down to Jackson (from Middletown) and handed him the dispatch Ewell had dictated at 6:00 P.M.—
the one offering to cross over from Double Tollgate to Newtown. As
Dabney scribbled, Jackson dictated an order to Ewell to come to Newtown "as you propose. . . . Our infantry is up." A courier galloped off
with the message as the clock ticked past 7:00 P.M.[36]

The dispatch was significant, for it showed Jackson's willingness
to abandon the two-pronged approach to Winchester that he originally ordered three hours earlier. But Stonewall's fog had thickened
again, for the courier's distance—from the southern outskirts of Newtown to Middletown, over to Cedarville and down past Double Tollgate (Ewell would presumably be marching toward Winchester by
Jackson's 5:45 P.M. directive)—exceeded eighteen miles. It would be
impossible for Ewell to reach Newtown directly from Double Tollgate before 11:00 P.M.; his arrival would more likely be closer to
midnight.[37]

In the meantime, Jackson's infantry closed in toward Newtown
to counter the two thousand Union infantry, cavalry, and artillery
defending the village. The sun appeared to hover near the ridgeline of
Little North Mountain to the west; indeed, in twenty minutes it

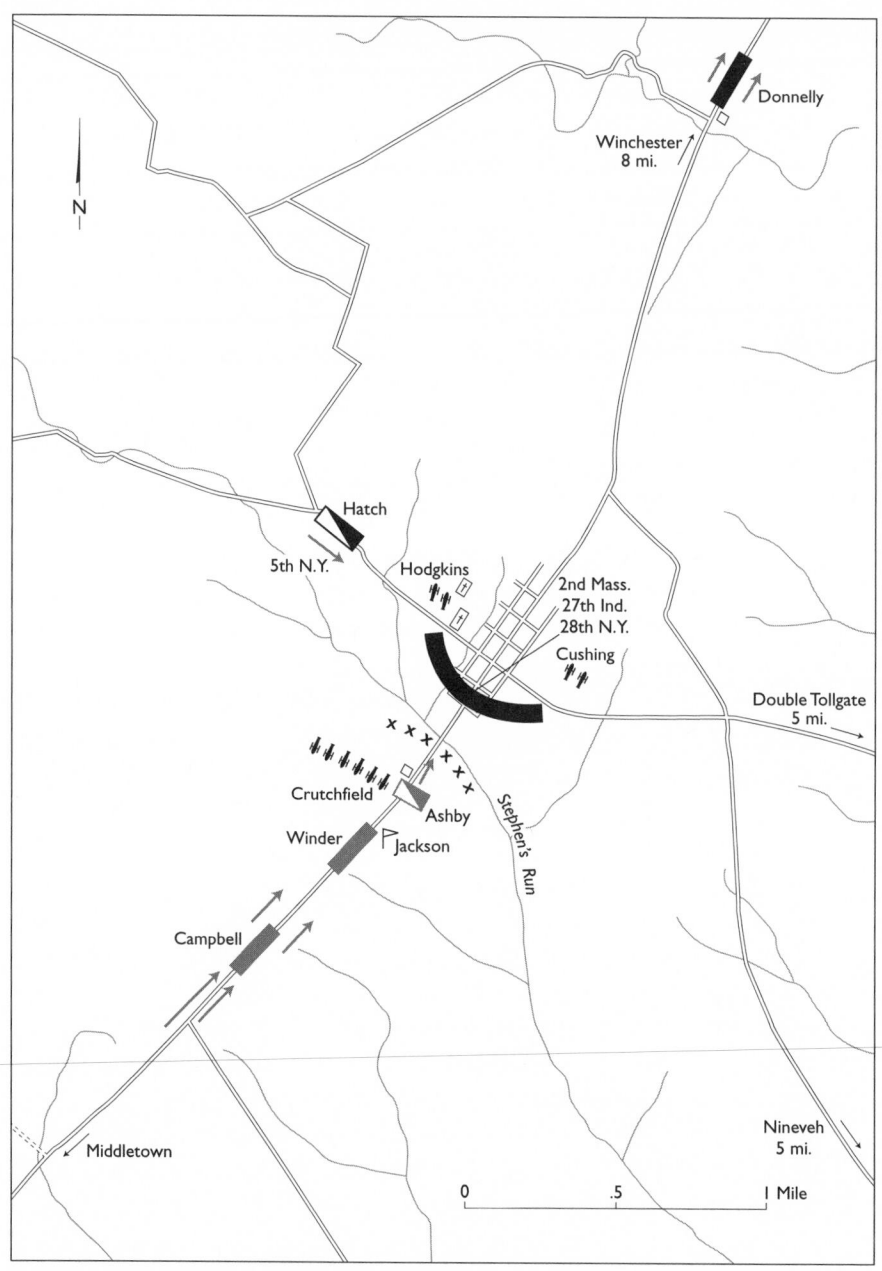

Position of forces at Newtown, 7:00 P.M., May 24, 1862

would set. Unlike the day previous, Jackson refused to rest his army when the skies darkened. Instead, he would continue to apply pressure until he caught up with Banks and destroyed him.

Jackson and his men did not realize it, but they had a very long night ahead of them.

7

CULMINATION POINT

Have you heard anything from Banks or the result of the firing heard this afternoon?" asked Secretary Stanton in a dispatch to Colonel Miles at 6:45 P.M. on May 24, 1862. "Have any troops reached Harper's Ferry? Answer immediately." To General Dix, Stanton wired, "Please send all of your forces to re-enforce Banks, speedily as possible." Receiving news that an eight-hundred-man regiment was leaving Baltimore for Harpers Ferry, Stanton remained unappeased. He wired a message to the governor of Pennsylvania, insisting that reserve units be organized and sent to block the Confederate advance toward Harpers Ferry. The problem for Stanton was his uncertainty of General Banks's fate. No message had come from him for nearly twelve hours.[1]

Stanton was clearly rattled by the drastic change of fortunes for the Union war effort. Just twenty-four hours earlier, he had expected nothing but success as he and President Lincoln finished their review of McDowell's troops at Falmouth. Now those troops—originally earmarked for McClellan—were no longer heading to the Peninsula. Instead, President Lincoln was sending them to the Valley—destination point: unclear.

Lincoln did not specify exactly where McDowell's troops would go, but he did pinpoint Frémont's destination as Harrisonburg. "Much

—perhaps all—depends on the celerity with which you can execute it," wired Lincoln to "The Pathfinder" at 7:15 P.M. "Put the utmost speed into it," emphasized the president. "Do not lose a minute." Although not as overtly unnerved as Stanton by all that had happened as a result of Jackson's presence in the northern Valley, Lincoln still revealed his concern over the safety of General Banks, the general whose troop strength he had stripped and who by doing so he had inadvertently set up for a disaster. Proof of the president's perception of guilt sped along the telegraph minutes after prodding on Frémont. Responding to Maj. Gen. Henry W. Halleck's request for reinforcements at Corinth, Lincoln revealed, "I tell you each of our commanders along our line from Richmond to Corinth supposes himself to be confronted by numbers superior to his own. Under this pressure we thinned the line on the upper Potomac, until yesterday it was broken with heavy loss to us, and General Banks put in great peril, out of which he is not yet extricated, and may be actually captured."[2]

Lincoln and Stanton entertained the notion of Banks's capture and his army's destruction, because in the midevening hours they still had not received positive information that he and his army were safe. In fact, Banks was safe—at least for the rest of May 24—for four reasons. First, all of his supply wagons and most of his command were eight miles ahead of Jackson, rolling and marching into Winchester since 10:00 A.M. Second, Jackson's infantry strength, though nearly three times Banks's numbers, was hampered by the disposition of the Confederate troops. Approximately thirteen thousand infantry, cavalry, and artillery soldiers comprised Jackson's army at 7:30 P.M. on May 24, but they formed three sides of a box with an open top. The troops on the sides of the box moved northward, the western side formed along the Valley Pike with cavalry, infantry, and artillery occupying five miles of road from Middletown to Newtown and inching forward. On the eastern side of the box, General Ewell had made better progress, as the Front Royal–Winchester Pike angled toward Winchester, but he was stripped down to perhaps eighteen hundred soldiers; Banks's reinforcements in Winchester in addition to the regiments on the march doubled Ewell's strength and grew by the hour.

The bottom of the box was formed by the Chapel Road. On it marched reinforcements for Jackson, heading westward to Middletown and using all seven miles of the road. Elzey's brigade was the

Maj. Gen. Thomas J. Jackson. Despite his own mistakes and those of his subordinates, "Stonewall" conquered his opponent to accomplish the mission dictated to him by the Confederate High Command. Courtesy of the Library of Congress.

Maj. Gen. Nathaniel P. Banks. Commanding the Union Department of the Shenandoah, Banks proved ill prepared and woefully outmanned to fend off the three-day assault launched by the Confederates in the Lower Shenandoah Valley. Courtesy of the USAMHI, Carlisle Barracks, Pa.

Maj. Gen. Richard S. Ewell. A peer of Stonewall Jackson as an independent division commander in April 1862, Ewell led his troops as a subordinate in Jackson's army during the heart of the Shenandoah Valley Campaign. Courtesy of the USAMHI, Carlisle Barracks, Pa.

Brig. Gen. Alpheus S. Williams. He handled the tactical deployment of General Banks's two infantry brigades in May 1862, eventually rising to corps command in both eastern and western theaters later in the war. Courtesy of the USAMHI, Carlisle Barracks, Pa.

Maj. Wilder Dwight. As second in command of the Second Massachusetts Infantry, Dwight led several companies of the regiment in a rearguard action that slowed Jackson's army to a crawl during the night of May 24, 1862. Courtesy of the USAMHI, Carlisle Barracks, Pa.

Massanutten Mountain, from high ground west of Strasburg, ca. 1892. This fifty-five-mile range, which divides the Shenandoah Valley into two smaller ones, shielded Jackson's approach to Front Royal on May 22, 1862. Courtesy of the Library of Congress.

Distant view of Union troops entering Front Royal on May 20, 1862, sketched by Edwin Forbes. These troops, commanded by Col. John R. Kenly of the First (USA) Maryland Infantry, were routed by Jackson after a five-hour battle on May 23. Courtesy of the Library of Congress.

Confederate prisoners captured at Woodstock, Virginia, sketched by Edwin Forbes in April 1862. These downtrodden members of Ashby's cavalry (incorrectly identified by Forbes as the Third Virginia Cavalry) provide a visual clue to the discipline problems confronting Stonewall Jackson in his attempt to manage this arm of his Valley army. Note the nonuniformity of their uniforms. Courtesy of the Library of Congress.

The Valley Turnpike north of Middletown, photographed in 1885. Twenty-three years earlier, on May 24, 1862, this portion of the pike teemed with disabled wagons attempting to retreat from Strasburg as they were plundered by Virginia cavalry and Louisiana infantry. Note the stone walls on each side of the road, which locked fleeing Union soldiers in the roadbed. Courtesy of the USAMHI, Carlisle Barracks, Pa.

Bowers Hill, a southward-facing view from high ground to the north, photographed in 1885. On the hill beyond the fence line, visible above and between the midground trees, five brigades of Stonewall Jackson's army overwhelmed four Union regiments and drove them northeastward into Winchester (visible on the left) after a four-hour battle on May 25, 1862. Jackson's victory at the Battle of Winchester capped three days of action that significantly altered military strategy in Virginia. Courtesy of the USAMHI, Carlisle Barracks, Pa.

final unit of troops to enter the road, moving southward from Double Tollgate. All the troops on this road were between thirteen to twenty miles from Winchester. Even at a brisk marching pace of three miles per hour it was impossible for them to reach the town by midnight.

But such a brisk pace was no longer feasible for Jackson's soldiers, leading to the fourth reason for Banks's safety. Much of Jackson's army was approaching the fifty-mile mark in marching over the past three days—two of those in temperatures exceeding eighty degrees. Lt. Col. Lawson Botts of the Second Virginia had feared for the health of his command when the regiment rested in Luray. Exactly forty-eight hours later, the regiment marched through Newtown, logging its forty-fifth mile during that time frame—hardly the rest that Botts thought essential for his men.

The Stonewall Brigade had yet to be engaged with its enemy, making it one of the more rested units in Jackson's command. The Louisianans began this portion of the campaign with much fresher legs than the Stonewall Brigade, but Taylor's men were unquestionably the most exhausted in terms of marching and fighting at Front Royal and Middletown throughout May 23–24. By the time Jackson turned them around at the banks of Cedar Creek late in the afternoon of May 24, most of Taylor's men had marched thirty-five miles over the past day and a half. Fifteen miles separated them from the center of Winchester. Confessing how "footsore and faint" he felt, a Pelican State soldier did not look forward to the miles upon miles of Valley Pike that lay ahead: "The excitement of the battle had begun to wear off, and we soon felt the fatigue and hunger of men who had been marching all day with little or no food."[3]

The sun had set at 7:10 P.M.; twenty minutes later, an ever-widening and darkening shadow seeped from east to west. The dusk bode ill tidings for Jackson. Determination alone could not dislodge the two-thousand-man, four-gun Union resistance that opposed him at Newtown. Behind that huge rear guard—nearly one-third of Banks's army—lay seven miles of Valley Pike. It would require more than an hour to concentrate enough infantry and artillery for Jackson to muscle past the rear guard, or to flank the force and roll it up to open the road to Winchester.

Fortunately for Jackson, he had to do neither. Col. George Gordon, commanding the rear guard, concluded that he did not need to stay in position at Newtown. He could not push Jackson's force any further, and he feared the flanking movement against him that Jackson may have been preparing. "General Hatch was safe; the enemy driven from Newtown; all our train in advance of the center protected from further assault," reasoned Gordon as he ordered his troops to pull back and withdraw toward Winchester.[4]

His immediate problem was the abandoned wagons overturned on the Valley Pike. Gordon counted "7 or 8" of them. (Based on other conflicting eyewitness accounts, there were as few as five and as many as fifty of them.) These were the vehicles struck by General Steuart and his Virginia cavalry that morning. Gordon had no horses or mules available to remove them, so he ordered a detachment of the Twenty-seventh Indiana to put them to the torch. As the Hoosiers complied with the directive, the remaining force had to hold until the job was completed. By 8:00 P.M. Union artillery, cavalry, and infantry were filing past the blazing wreckage and marching northward. As the infantry passed by the wagon fire, they were enticed by the smell of hams cooking within the blaze, a treat for famished soldiers. Several infantrymen poked their bayonets into the flames and pulled out the smoking delicacy—"a kind of meat private soldiers only got, when they were lucky enough to get them by foraging"—then they continued northward.[5]

General Banks had personally superintended his rear guard to harass Jackson's van, but he no longer could be found near Newtown. Satisfied that his subordinates could slow Jackson's movement, Banks rode on to Winchester, where he was informed that Confederate troops were closing in on the pike from Front Royal. He quartered himself in the house of George Seevers, his March headquarters, and for the first time in twelve hours, he wrote a dispatch to be carried to Washington. Addressing it directly to President Lincoln, he absent-mindedly headed his location as "Strasburg." For the first time he documented that Jackson and Ewell were operating against him, inferring that Jackson had been pressing from the Valley Pike and that Ewell had crossed over to Middletown. Banks further reported that he decided to retreat to save his trains, claiming that this was accomplished and that troops had been marching into the city since 5:00 P.M. Surprisingly, Banks entertained the notion that he would immediately return his command to Strasburg, but he never indicated how and why he intended to do this. The dispatch, begun at 8:00 P.M., would not be received at the War Department for nearly two hours.[6]

By 8:30 P.M. the War Department was satisfied that Banks and his command were safe for the evening in Winchester, well before Banks's dispatch clicked off the telegraph in Washington. Even the panicked secretary of war felt more comfortable about Banks's disposition and the efforts to reinforce him. Stanton notified General Geary, who had fallen back ten miles to White Plains, that Banks "has probably secured himself" and that supporting troops were on their way. Informing Geary that he would be reinforced by McDowell heading his way on his mission to the Valley, Stanton ordered Geary to "hold your line, if possible, until he comes up."[7]

Banks was ignorant of how close to Winchester the opposing forces were. When he initiated his dispatch at 8:00 P.M., he had no organized force in the town. His infantry had just begun to enter from the Valley Pike, while the Tenth Maine Infantry and isolated cavalry squadrons represented the only reinforcing soldiers in the town. Col. George L. Beal of the Tenth Maine Infantry had forwarded companies C and I to assist a detachment of First Michigan Cavalry, commanded by Maj. Charles H. Town, in patrolling the turnpike to Front Royal. Four miles from Winchester, the pickets caught sight of approaching Confederates and pulled back closer to approximately half that distance, between a house owned by a resident surnamed Bowles and Buffalo Lick Road, two miles south of Winchester.[8]

Onward marched the Confederates. This was General Ewell's command. Ewell had received confirmation of his decision to head toward Winchester when Lieutenant Boswell from Jackson's staff trotted to his side during that march shortly after 7:00 P.M. Another courier from Jackson came up close to 8:00 P.M., requesting Ewell to support him by marching across to Newtown. Ewell ignored this order, correctly considering it outdated as he no longer heard the cannonading near Newtown, ten miles southwest of him. Ewell later explained that "as circumstances had in every case changed the condition of things before their arrival, I was forced to follow my own judgement as to Genl Jackson's intentions."[9]

Upon first contact with the Union pickets, Ewell ordered Col. William W. Kirkland of the Twenty-first North Carolina Infantry to drive back the Maine infantry and Michigan cavalry. Kirkland detached three companies, two to support Courtney's Battery rolling in the van, and one company to fight it out as they advanced. Kirkland moved with the lead company. They drove back the Union foot and horse soldiers. Passing Buffalo Lick Road on his right, Kirkland wisely ordered up another company to guard this junction to prevent a flank attack.

By Kirkland's next request, the remaining seven Tarheel companies came forward. Lieutenant Boswell also rode up and, with the eye of an engineer, studied the terrain advantages as they advanced. Boswell explained the importance of possessing the woods two hundred yards away, to prevent Union pickets for using it as cover for sharpshooters. Kirkland succeeded in driving back the Union occupants and took possession of the woods. The Union pickets, however, refused to yield completely to Ewell's men. The Carolinians remained constantly under skirmishing fire while Ewell's troops bivouacked behind them by 10:00 P.M. Two miles from Winchester, Ewell decided to wait for dawn's light to initiate a push toward the town.[10]

Immediately after the Union soldiers evacuated Newtown, Stonewall Jackson led his men into the contested Valley Pike hamlet. They were greeted by lusty cheers from the citizens; one Southerner described it as "the most violent demonstrations of joy on the part of the ladies"—just as the Southern soldiers had experienced four miles back at Middletown. But that was four hours ago, and now it was twilight. Jackson would ignore any effort to stop for the evening. The blood was in the water as far as he was concerned, and to stop now would waste the opportunity to destroy or capture an opposing army, a feat achieved only once during the first year of the war—by Maj. Gen. Ulysses S. Grant at Fort Donelson.[11]

The infantry in Jackson's van was Brig. Gen. Charles Winder's Stonewall Brigade—specifically (in order), the Thirty-third Virginia Volunteers, the Twenty-seventh Virginia, the Second Virginia, the Fifth Virginia, and the Fourth Virginia. In front of the foot soldiers trotted General Ashby with fifty cavalrymen and the horses pulling Poague's section of the Rockbridge Artillery and Carpenter's four-gun battery. The remaining batteries were through for the day. Captain Chew's gunners received permission to pilfer wagons abandoned near Newtown. Allotted a twenty-minute spree, the artillerists made the most of it, coming away with clothing, pistols, and other supplies including whiskey. They remained at Newtown, perhaps wishing that soft bedding was in the wagons. One of Chew's cannoneers told his diary that he "slept on a board" at Newtown that night.[12]

On the Valley Pike, the troops under Jackson's direct command would not be turning in as early as those under Ewell's. As some of the artillerists plundered wagons south of Newtown, the head of Jackson's column passed the burning vehicles north of Newtown. "I well recollect," wrote Jed Hotchkiss thirty-three years later, "how peculiar the streets of that town were lighted up by the burning of the commissary train, especially by the flames from burning bacon and from wagon loads of rice." The burning wagons instilled élan and urgency into the horse soldiers leading the van. The spectacle induced the rebel yell as they galloped down the pike in an attempt to run down the rearward infantry attempting to get to safety.[13]

Ashby's cavalry found what it was looking for, but they were wholly unprepared for it. Lieutenant Colonel Andrews placed Maj. Wilder Dwight of the Second Massachusetts in charge of the rear guard. A Harvard-trained lawyer and scholar with a mere six months of training at a private military school, the compact major exuded intelligence, confidence, and patience in his twenty-nine years that exceeded the faculties of equally educated and more experienced commanders. Dwight's friends expressed the utmost confidence in him. "He has just the temperament for standing fire," insisted a fellow Bay State major serving in the Army of the Potomac. "A great many men, you know, are brave under fire without being cool. He is both."[14]

Notwithstanding the accolades, Major Dwight and the Second Massachusetts Infantry had completed the first year of the war with no battle experience, and a minimal skirmishing record. A more formidable task could not be found than the one charged to Dwight that night: hold back the Confederate army as long as possible with three infantry companies. Dwight's command consisted of Companies A, B, and C. He could hear the demonical shouts of the rebel cavalry as he distanced his men from Newtown. "Expecting an attack by their cavalry upon our rear-guard, I prepared for it," he explained.

On the gentle downslope of a hill just south of the hamlet of Bartonsville, Major Dwight halted and called in his skirmishers. There his command, not more than 150 rifles, could now hear the rhythmic beating of hooves, intensifying as they neared the Bay State soldiers. He had Company A form a hollow square one hundred feet from the eastern side of the road; Company C did likewise on the western side. Company B formed their square in the road. Warning his men to fire only upon his command, Dwight waited for his prey to clear the horizon of the hillcrest and fall into his ambush.

Ashby's men complied. Flying up the hill beyond Newtown, the horse soldiers cleared the top and descended toward the creek be-yond, the glare of the fires behind them no longer aiding their sight. The Seventh Virginia cavalry had enjoyed a field day at Middletown with General Ashby at the helm (his commission has been made official the previous day in Richmond, but he would be unaware of it for two more days). Although no one ever confirmed it, Ashby was likely leading his band in this charge; he had been at the front with Crutchfield when they contested for Newtown since the late afternoon. He had with him men who were repelled three times by two infantry companies of western soldiers at Buckton Station on May 23.

North of Newtown, the New Englanders repeated the performance of their Indiana and Wisconsin comrades at Buckton. "The rebels came thundering down the road, literally making the ground shake," claimed a member of Dwight's rear guard. One of the Massachusetts men panicked and fired. Ashby's men reined up from their dash to halt within fifty yards of the Massachusetts defense when Dwight ordered the men to fire. A disciplined volley flashed from their rifles. Surprisingly, only a horse was struck and slightly wounded. Dwight ordered his men to fix bayonets, but this proved unnecessary. The cavalry reared, reversed, and retreated back over the hilltop and back toward Newtown. They had approached so close that the Massachusetts men heard the officers barking orders to their men right before the infantry volleys, then epithets to them as they fell back. Dwight personally followed them to the hilltop and carefully listened for any sign of their return. Hearing none, he went back to the base of the hill and ordered his men across the creek bridge.[15]

The force crossed Opequon Creek and found themselves in Bartonsville, a small collection of a mill, barns, a 110-year-old stately home called "Springdale," and the ruins of Hite's Fort, a former colonial tavern that once sheltered sixteen-year-old George Washington during his first surveying trip to the Shenandoah Valley. Dwight took the opportunity during the respite to replace his skirmishing companies with fresh units from the same regiment, allowing the original pickets to retrieve the knapsacks they had left behind when they passed through Bartonsville on their way toward Newtown four hours earlier. Ahead of them Lieutenant Colonel Andrews received six companies of the Fifth New York Cavalry to watch the flanks of the Twenty-seventh Indiana and Twenty-eighth New York Infantry, as well as the remaining battalion of the Second Massachusetts. They tarried north but close enough to Dwight's men to lend support if it was needed.[16]

General Jackson was equally as disgusted with the cavalry as the officers who could not prevent their retreat. Watching the cavalry fly back toward the head of the infantry column just north of Newtown, Jackson's ire painted the tone of his voice. "Shameful!" he declared as he turned to members of his staff; "Did you see anybody struck, sir? Did you see anybody struck?" Incredulous that his men showed timidity without any discernible casualties, Jackson rectified the formation of his vanguard. Soon, topping the hill south of Newtown was Ashby's cavalry again, but they no longer advanced alone. Poague's section of Rockbridge Artillery followed, as did the entire component of Carpenter's Battery—the Allegheny Roughs—formerly Company A of the Twenty-seventh Virginia Infantry. Next came the Stonewall Brigade regiments, led by the Thirty-third Virginia Infantry. Taliaferro's brigade hustled in behind Winder's infantry. General Jackson and his staff advanced between the infantry column and Ashby's men.[17]

Near the crest of the ridge, Poague's two cannons unlimbered and fired some rounds toward the woods surrounding Bartonsville. The solid shot flew harmlessly over Dwight's rear guard, but it did wreak havoc upon Colonel Andrews's command. Shells apparently landed close enough to the horses of the Fifth New York Cavalry flankers to spook them.[18] A small stampede resulted, putting more terror in both the skirmishers and the rearward Union regiments than Jackson's army could impose. "They went right over us," wrote Capt. Richard Carey of the Second Massachusetts. A member of the Twenty-seventh Indiana limned a vivid scene of chaos created by the New Yorkers:

> We were in mortal terror of our lives "Look out!" someone would shout, and the word would be passed along the line of the tired, sleepy men, followed by the clatter of horses' hoofs and the clink and rattle of sabers and accoutrements. Men crowded each other into ditches, or over stones or logs, in their efforts to get out of the way. . . . Many emphatic words were fired at the fleeing, cowardly scamps, and many adjec-

tives and epithets were used, some of them not popular with the churches.[19]

Apparently, more than "emphatic words" were fired by Union infantry at the Fifth New York Cavalry. Several Union infantrymen, mistaking the thundering approach as a rebel charge, fired blindly at them. "It was a terrible moment," remembered Julius Rhodes, a cavalryman in Company F. "Officers and men shouted, 'You are firing upon your own men,' and for a time it seemed the firing would not cease until we were annihilated." Clearly, the Union cavalry lent more confusion than succor to the rearward regiments, although one claimed the capture of some of Ashby's wayward command during the night. After suffering the pain and horror of having a horse fall on him during this melee, a Massachusetts soldier assessed the cavalry as "worse than nothing" that night.[20]

After Jackson received word that enemy troops may be lurking at Bartonsville, he ordered Col. John F. Neff to provide skirmishers from his Thirty-third Virginia. Neff complied by sending Companies A and F to scour the blackened region near Opequon Creek. Discerning soldiers standing in the road near the bridge, a Virginian declared, "There they are! There they are! In the road!"

Major Dwight was ready for them again. Prewarned of the pursuit by the rounds fired by Poague, Dwight prepared his resistance. With men in position on each side of the road, he had a second blow in store for Jackson's advance, but the Virginians loosed their muskets before he could bellow his order. "A galling and severe infantry fire opened on us," confessed Dwight, but the Massachusetts men from Company I quickly returned the hostile greeting. Flashes of exchanged gunfire were the only source of light for the skirmishing troops on both sides of the creek. Within ten minutes, Company I of the Second Massachusetts had ten men killed and wounded, perhaps a quarter of its strength. Major Dwight quickly sent word down to Lieutenant Colonel Andrews for aid. Companies B and C hustled into platoon formation on each side of the road and attempted to scatter Jackson's infantry. But they could not dislodge it, sacrificing ten more casualties within their ranks.[21]

Colonel Neff's Thirty-third Virginia skirmishing companies had performed well, but they had lost eight members in the brief fight. Behind them, General Jackson personally escorted Ashby's shaky cavalry and Poague's section of artillery. Neff closed this advance with the remaining portion of his regiment. Jackson ordered the cavalry forward: "Charge them!" barked Stonewall. "Charge them!"

It turned out to be a costly order. Dwight's men panicked the Seventh Virginia Cavalry with a menacing volley. Confederate horse soldiers scattered rearward again, careening chaotically into fellow infantrymen and artillerymen and inflicting casualties. General Jackson and his staff were also temporarily caught up in the melee and were forced rearward up the hill. Southern soldiers scampered off the center of the road and hugged the stone walls buttressing its sides to escape a trampling from the frightened cavalry.

Captain Poague reported two artillerists were injured who could not get out of the way quick enough. Colonel Neff claimed two lieutenants and four privates "run over by our cavalry and badly bruised." This was close to the same number the Thirty-third Virginia skirmishers lost in their clash with the Second Massachusetts. Although they reported no casualties, the Stonewall Brigade regiments directly behind the Thirty-third Virginia were temporarily misaligned by the frightened horses and Virginia riders, particularly the Twenty-seventh Virginia.[22]

Dwight's men performed well under the pressure, not fully aware that Confederate cavalry had aided them as much as they did. Taking a moment to size up the situation, the major judiciously concluded that his rear guard had done all it could at Bartonsville. He had casualties to remove: seventeen men wounded and three dead. Having made several requests for ambulances, Dwight was frustrated—as was Lieutenant Colonel Andrews—that none came. Healthy skirmishers carried off their comrades and Dwight withdrew the rest from Bartonsville, as noted by one, "leaving the yelling & the light of the fire in the distance."[23]

Without Ashby present to guide them, the Seventh Virginia Cavalry had performed miserably four times over the past two months. But even with their intrepid leader at the helm, the cavalry demonstrated for the second time in an hour that they were too unruly and unreliable to perform the functions expected of horse soldiers. This, at least, was General Jackson's conclusion. He was forced to consume more valuable time to realign his vanguard. He ordered the artillery to the rear; for them, the night of fighting was over, as it also was for the Thirty-third Virginia Infantry. Jackson called for the rest of the

Stonewall Brigade. General Winder ordered up Col. James W. Allen's Second Virginia and Twenty-seventh Virginia under Col. Andrew Jackson Grigsby.[24]

Directed to clear out the Bartonsville ambuscade, Colonel Allen led his Virginians off the pike in an attempt to flank on the east. But the Second Virginia could not complete the task; the ground was too marshy for them to advance. Colonel Grigsby sent out two of his companies to cross the Opequon Creek bridge and drive the Yankees away. They did just that, followed closely by the remaining battalion of Grigsby's regiment close behind them. Enough of Major Dwight's command was still in the vicinity to inflict two casualties on Grigsby's regiment, but not before a Virginia private walked away with a stand of colors. The Massachusetts soldiers were completely gone by the time Jackson rode Little Sorrel across the bridge and into the hamlet. The time approached midnight as Confederates finally claimed Bartonsville. Three miles remained between Jackson and the outskirts of Winchester.[25]

Jackson made one more adjustment to his vanguard. He sent for Lt. George W. Kurtz, commanding Company K of the Fifth Virginia Infantry. The general knew that Kurtz, a Winchester resident, knew this region better than most and felt confident that he could move his men blindly into the dark beyond. By request, Kurtz also ordered up Company A, a unit recruited in the Winchester area. Colonel Allen sent up Company F of the Second Virginia to provide more Frederick County natives in the front. The skirmishers straddled their flanks on opposite sides of the Valley Pike as they marched through the terrain right and left of it. The northern Valley natives led the column northward out of Bartonsville, with Generals Jackson and Winder walking on the Valley Pike a short distance behind them. To prevent future ambushes, Jackson admonished Lieutenant Kurtz to march slowly. According to Kurtz, Stonewall said, "[Y]ou can drive in all their Pickets if you move cautiously."[26]

Jackson's directive rendered "the advance . . . necessarily slow," admitted Col. William Baylor of the Fifth Virginia. But the march was constant for more than a mile, until the Confederates inched toward the outskirts of Kernstown. There, just before the Valley Pike bent from north to northwest, the Virginia skirmishers clashed with Massachusetts pickets.

Behind those pickets, on the west side of the turnpike, stood one of the only buildings between Bartonsville and Kernstown. This was the brick house of Joseph P. Mahaney. Two months before, the Battle of Kernstown began in Mahaney's yard when Captain Chew unlimbered his horse artillery and fired at Pritchard's Hill. During the first hour of May 25, 1862, Major Dwight was using the home as a temporary hospital, to dress the wounds of his casualties until ambulances arrived to cart them into Winchester. He had not chosen the ground for rearguard action, but the sudden appearance of the Virginia skirmishers on each side of the road forced him to deploy. Within ten minutes he placed portions of four companies into position. They could not hold on to Kernstown for even half the time they battled for Bartonsville. Forced to pull back by the strength of the Virginia skirmishers' fire, Dwight was forced to leave his wounded in the Mahaney house, along with the physician charged to care for them.[27]

The healthy members of the Second Massachusetts Infantry passed Hillman's Tollgate and entered Winchester shortly after 1:00 A.M. They stopped in an open field at the edge of town, where they lamented the loss of a score of comrades. But the New Englanders earned respect and praise for their performance. Major Dwight's tactical deployment of 150 men against an enemy column of thousands yielded unforeseen benefits that night. His leadership forced Jackson to crawl and halt, crawl and halt, and crawl to cover a mere six miles in six arduous hours. Colonel Gordon proclaimed that his regiment would never forget "his gallant services on the night of the 24th." One of his men lauded Dwight's display of "the most perfect bravery and coolness." When reports of the exploits of Dwight's rear guard made it in the newspapers, Massachusetts soldiers in other theaters of operation expressed their pride. "But what a glorious thing the 2nd have done," raved Maj. Henry L. Abbott of the Fifteenth Massachusetts, reading about their exploits while in camp east of Richmond. "Their cheeky little major, they say, was as cool as a cucumber; I have no doubt of it."[28]

Major Dwight took leave of his bone-weary command. Together with Colonel Gordon, he rode into town to report to General Banks. Gordon also took a Confederate with him—a surgeon from Jackson's army captured at Newtown. They reined up at the George Seevers house on the corner of Stewart and Boscowen Streets on the west side of Winchester. Entering the home, they found Banks awake in the bedroom. Gordon—never one to shy from an opportunity to paint his

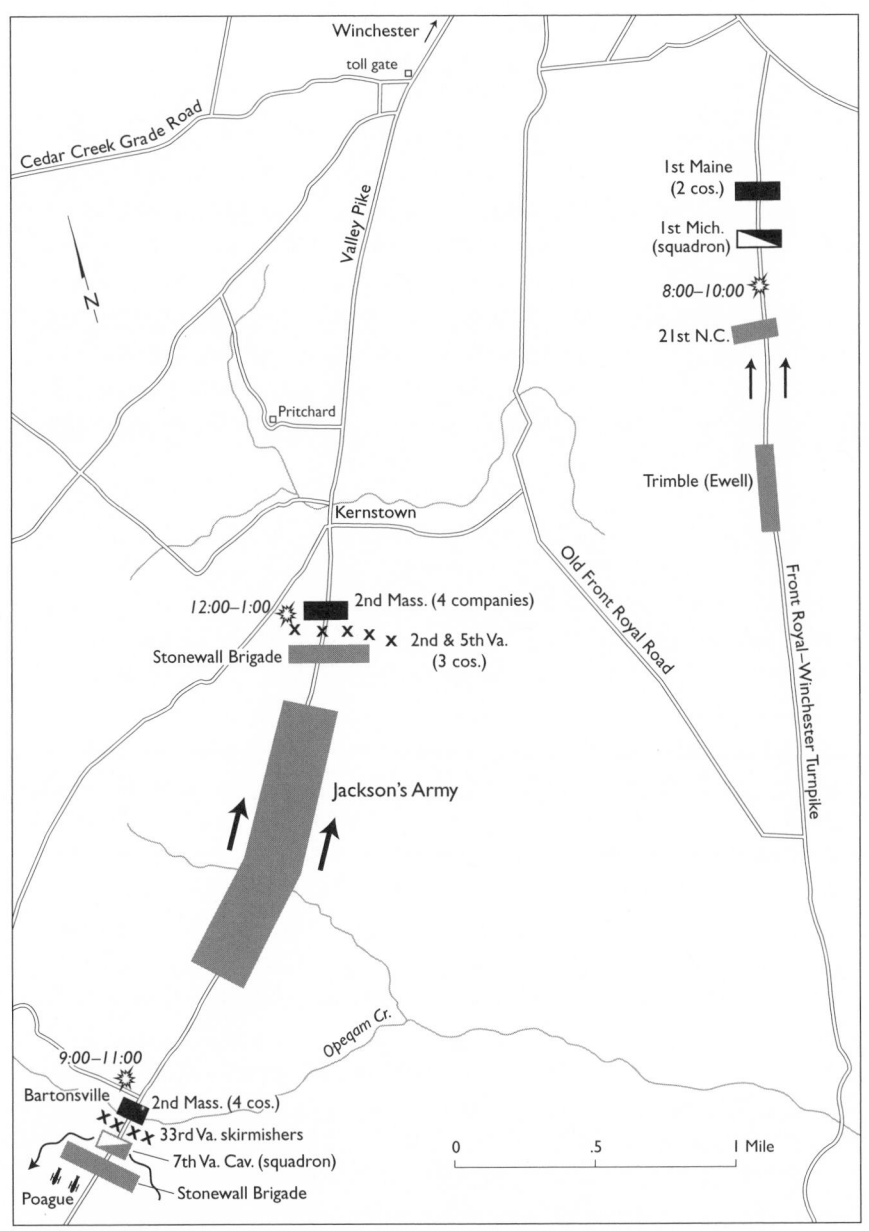

Rearguard action: 8:00 P.M.–1:00 A.M., May 24–25, 1862

superior in the worst light—noted that Banks had found the time to enjoy a bath while Gordon's command were enduring their toughest travail of the war.

Using his prisoner, Gordon tried to make clear what Banks already knew and had reported to the War Department—Jackson vastly outnumbered him. Dwight chimed in his account of what he accomplished and witnessed during the night and predicted that Jackson would attack at daylight. Gordon pressed his belief that they should all be retreating toward the Potomac as soon as possible. He noted that Banks responded with no response, "the same or a more unintelligible silence than had met me at Strasburg." Gordon and Dwight departed with disappointment, both seemingly surprised that Banks had chosen not to reveal his plans to them.[29]

Gordon would not let the matter rest. While Dwight returned to the bivouac of the Second Massachusetts, Gordon rode into the center of the town to the Taylor Hotel. Three generals were sleeping there in the early hours of May 25—Alpheus Williams, Samuel Crawford, and George S. Greene (the latter two without commands). He woke them to press his desire to retreat. Satisfied that he had done what he could, but dissatisfied at the lack of confirmation, Gordon returned to his headquarters to get some sleep himself.

General Banks remained awake through the dark hours of the morning. Despite Gordon's and Dwight's expectations, the army general felt no obligation to reveal a plan to a brigade colonel and a regimental major. These were not the subordinates in his chain of command with which to discuss options. But Banks did listen to their reports. Here at 2:00 A.M., he was finally getting a complete picture of what had happened within his department, what he had available, and what was opposing him.

The muddiest of the three was what was available to him. He had saved most of his wagons as more than five hundred army supply vehicles flooded the fairgrounds north of Winchester. They had completed a twenty-five-mile odyssey begun the previous midnight. Since Banks necessarily changed his alignment on the retreat, at least ten miles of separation impeded his train. The first wagons rolled into Winchester at 10:00 A.M.; the last wagons reached the fairgrounds twelve hours later. They would begin to roll again as a unified train, one that was easier to protect on the road. But Banks needed to buy time for the wagons to move again in safety.

Having occupied Winchester for more than two months, Banks well understood the importance of holding the city. Eight roads spoked into Winchester from all directions. Although this would increase the susceptibility for assault, Banks knew that only rebel cavalry could quickly access the roads entering Winchester from the east, west, and north. He expressed no concern that Confederate infantry would threaten him on these avenues in the morning. He also knew that reinforcements could feed him on the roads north of Winchester, and if necessary, he had more than one escape route from the town. The most important feature favoring Banks was the terrain. He possessed the high ground that surrounded the southern half of the city like the lip of a bowl. Artillery and infantry judiciously posted on these hills not only could effectively block Jackson's attempt to enter Winchester; they could also expose the Confederate strength to confirm or disavow the intelligence he had at hand.

The road networks also provided the best opportunity for cut-off forces to concentrate. This was Banks's quandary at 3:00 A.M. on May 25. He had a mere eight infantry regiments available in Winchester, fewer than forty-five hundred officers and men. Seven of those regiments comprised the two brigades of Williams's division that had marched twenty-five miles from above Strasburg. Only five companies of that force—all from the Second Massachusetts—had thus far been involved in close gunfire exchange with opposing infantry in the Civil War. Two other companies at Buckton Station had stood their ground in a protracted engagement, but the remainder was essentially untested. The same held true for the lone regiment of reinforcement. The size of the Tenth Maine—more than eight hundred officers and men—belied its inexperience. The companies engaged on the Front Royal–Winchester Pike were the only Maine infantry to have fired their weapons at something other than targets.

The Union cavalry, although numerous, was also raw with regiments like the First Maryland and the Eighth New York; they added weapons, but untested ability to use them. The Fifth New York had failed in its first mission supporting troops on the pike, although horses tend to scare easier in the dark. Several of the Michigan troops fought at Kernstown two months earlier and performed well there, but they were the exception to the norm. At best, Banks needed cavalry on the defense as scouts and escorts, but it would take time to organize them. General Hatch likely informed Banks that Union cavalrymen were scattered throughout the town that night seeking forage and shelter for the horses. Precious hours were necessary to organize them to perform even the most rudimentary functions. Although more than 1,000 horse soldiers existed in Winchester, more than 300 were casualties from the preceding twenty hours. Lieutenant Colonel Douty of the First Maine lost three of the four companies engaged near Middletown—more than 120 men and all their horses.[30]

No cannons fell into Confederate hands on May 24, but an entire battery was still unaccounted for in Winchester. Hampton's Pennsylvania Battery was negotiating the western back roads of the Lower Valley in an attempt to get to Winchester; however, Confederate pickets along the roads into town prevented them from uniting with Banks's force. This left Banks with a mere two batteries of twelve cannons, only half of which were rifled. Battery F of the Fourth U.S. Artillery was still saddled with six-pounders, insufficient firepower to match Jackson's fifty cannons (including the two Parrotts he captured near Front Royal on May 23).

General Banks obtained his intelligence from subordinates, reliable Union-supporting citizens, captured Confederates—"Rebel officers who came into our camp with entire unconcern, supposing that their own troops occupied the town as a matter of course"—and secessionists taken prisoner. Banks ascertained correctly that Jackson and Ewell opposed him from the south on the turnpikes from Strasburg and Front Royal. He also was aware of an opposing force due east of him, noting that a party of sixty attacked a Union baggage train at Berryville, but he correctly surmised that this was a small cavalry detachment. As he had demonstrated in his communication to Secretary Stanton on May 22, Banks displayed a sound grasp of the strength of the opposition. Although fielding wild reports of thirty thousand rebels opposing him, Banks believed the number to be half of that, an estimate much closer to reality.[31]

But Banks still had a tinge of doubt whether so many troops opposed him. Embellished opposition-strength estimates were a hallmark of Civil War armies, a tendency of both the North and the South. Despite the reports Banks had obtained claiming more than twenty thousand Confederate infantry opposed him, most of what struck him on May 24 was cavalry and artillery. The only infantry engaged with his men were three regiments from the Stonewall Brigade that fought Dwight's rear guard on the Valley Pike and the

Twenty-first North Carolina that opposed the Maine pickets on the Front Royal–Winchester Pike. Most of the Louisiana brigade, at least two thousand officers and men, deployed against Banks's isolated force at Cedar Creek, but no witness to that deployment had reached Winchester to inform the commanding general of this.

Throughout May 24, the best view offered of the strength of Confederate opposition during daylight hours was achieved in the two-hour fight at Newtown. At no time would the U.S. troops there have been able to see more than three batteries, two hundred cavalrymen, the Stonewall Brigade, and perhaps one hundred members of the Seventh Louisiana approaching from Middletown. It is clear, from what he told his subordinates, that Banks entertained these doubts. After reporting the details of his command to Banks that night, General Hatch revealed to his father, "Gen'l Banks thought he ought not to retire unless he was satisfied that the enemy were in overwhelming numbers."[32]

Banks held no council of war to discuss the options available to him. By 2:30 A.M. he had already concluded that he could not evacuate the town. He needed more time—time for his wayward troops to find him, time to get his wagons rolling to safety, time to evacuate the months-long storage of supplies and the hundreds of sick and wounded in Winchester. The decision was his and his alone. The last dispatch from the War Department informed him that five more regiments were on the way to Harpers Ferry and then to Winchester to his support, and that Frémont had been directed to enter the Valley. Whether these thirty-five hundred reinforcements could arrive before he clashed with the Confederates, Banks entertained the possibility he could avoid having to evacuate at all, hoping against hope that his opponent was not nearly so strong as everyone feared. Since the enemy would hit him from the south, Banks decided to use the high ground to his advantage. "I determined to test the substance and strength of the enemy by actual collision," he reported.[33]

Only one mile south of Banks, Stonewall Jackson was eager to collide with General Banks and reveal his "substance and strength" to him. Driving back the First (USA) Maryland Cavalry pickets at Hillman's Tollgate, Jackson halted at 2:30 A.M. at the collection of mills crowding Abraham's Creek at the southern entrance to Winchester. What started out as a field day at Middletown had soured into an aggravating trek. Ten hours had passed since he first determined to advance the eight miles from Middletown to Winchester. The lost time could not be made up.[34]

Jackson apparently did not spare a moment to take stock of what he had gained. In two days his army had swept all opposition twenty miles northward, thus seizing two bases and a railroad from Union control. For the second straight day he scattered an opponent, collected seemingly countless stores of government materiel, and did so with incredibly few casualties. Not counting the losses in the Thirty-third Virginia inflicted by the Seventh Virginia Cavalry, Jackson suffered fewer than twenty casualties to opposing infantry or artillery fire. The elapsed time also allowed his rearward ranks to close the twenty-mile gap that once separated them from the vanguard. Excluding detachments at Front Royal and near Cedar Creek, Jackson had no reason to doubt he had six brigades of infantry, six batteries, and one regiment of cavalry packed along a six-mile segment of the Valley Pike—close to eleven thousand troops within striking distance of Winchester.[35]

Jackson planned to strike immediately, believing it imperative to do so before his disoriented opponent was reorganized and dug in. "So important did I deem it to occupy before dawn the heights overlooking Winchester," Jackson later recalled, "that the advance continued." He apparently had his sights set on Bowers Hill, the ridge that towered over the west side of Winchester. Claiming this height and planting batteries on it would guarantee suppression upon any opposing artillery, and spelled certain doom for enemy infantry charged with dislodging them. Jackson was unaware that Banks had disregarded the hill. At 2:30 A.M. a cavalry camp and one company of the Twenty-ninth Pennsylvania Infantry lay claim to Bowers Hill.[36]

Although Jackson was determined to continue, his army was not. They grumbled over the lack of sleep with the continuous marching and—except for the cavalry and other vanguard units that were able to plunder sutler and U.S. government wagons—most of Jackson's infantry had no rations. The Confederate wagon train stood on the Front Royal–Winchester Pike, between Cedarville and Nineveh.[37] The combination of these factors produced an army that morning that teetered close to exhaustion. Jackson's command had reached its culmination point.

Jackson may have discerned the fatigue of his sleep-deprived force while observing his staff steal naps by the side of the road. From the south rode up Col. Samuel Vance Fulkerson, of the Thirty-seventh Virginia, who currently led the brigade due to an illness to Brig. Gen. William B. Taliaferro. Fulkerson had taken it upon himself to notify Jackson that the men needed to rest, telling Jackson that the numerical strength of his brigade incrementally dropped with each halt as men fell out of the ranks to sleep at the roadside. Fulkerson pleaded to rest the men for a few hours and move again at daylight.[38]

Jackson did not dress the colonel down. He briefly explained the importance of pushing as far as they had, but the destination had not been reached. The high ground was ahead of them, and Jackson desired it at 3:00 A.M. of May 25 no less than he had at 3:00 P.M. of May 24. Nevertheless, he changed his mind and acceded to Fulkerson's request, first deciding to rest only his brigade. Shortly thereafter, Jackson extended the respite to his entire army. The halt jeopardized his objective to seize Bowers Hill, but his army was in very questionable fighting ability. Horses and men were worn out. "Our regiment had diminished to three companies," claimed a Fourth Virginia soldier. "Many had fallen down in the road and gone to sleep." Other regiments of the Stonewall Brigade were in a similar state. The Thirty-third Virginia was down to 150 officers and men, and Col. Andrew Jackson Grigsby counted a mere 136 rank and file in his Twenty-seventh Virginia. In total, the five regiments of General Winder's Stonewall Brigade could barely muster 1,300 men after midnight, close to one-third the number it boasted on May 3, 1862. In three weeks, nearly twice as many men had deserted or straggled from the brigade than currently stayed within it.[39]

Those still standing greeted Jackson's order to rest as salvation, notwithstanding how short the respite had been intended to be. A member of the Rockbridge Artillery described how fourteen consecutive hours of marching and fighting affected him and his battery mates:

Moving at a snail's pace and halting, and then moving again and halting again, falling asleep at the halts and being suddenly wakened up when motion was resumed, we fairly staggered on, worn almost to exhaustion by the weariness of such a march. When we got a little beyond Kernstown, we turned a little to the left in a field and parked our guns, and as the column came up it formed in sort of line of battle, the men falling down where they stood and going to sleep, for it was then near three o'clock in the morning. I remember how chilly and damp the dewy grass felt to me, but how soon my weariness overcame the thought of cold and I was fast asleep.[40]

Jackson's decision may have resulted from more than Colonel Fulkerson's request. He still was unaware of Banks's strength and position. Did he have twelve thousand men as Boswell reported to him on May 23? The size of the wagon train seemed to suggest so. Did Banks receive reinforcements from Harpers Ferry? Could he be receiving reinforcements from General Frémont?

The ultimate aggressor, Jackson would normally have dismissed the significance of the first two questions, but the latter appears to have weighed on his mind. He received a disconcerting piece of intelligence in the predawn hours. The force he had cut off had been chased over Cedar Creek; that is where Jackson left them at 5:30 P.M. on Saturday, the twenty-fourth. Nine hours had drastically changed the situation there. Jackson was convinced that Federal troops had been reinforced at Strasburg.[41]

A commanding general is always charged with the responsibility to determine the accuracy of each report he receives. The report of reinforcements at Strasburg was erroneous. Not only were there no Union reinforcements there, but the force Jackson chased up to that town was currently negotiating the back roads in an effort to reach Winchester. Encountering rebel cavalry pickets while attempting to enter the Valley Pike near Newtown from the west, the Yankees were forced to retrace their steps.[42] Perhaps pickets uncovered their movement at this point and misinterpreted it as an attempt to fortify a position to threaten the tail of Jackson's army. Regardless, Jackson took no time to confirm it. Showing signs of sleep deprivation himself, Jackson's judgment proved less sharp, but he remained as decisive and resolute as ever.

Stonewall ordered up Col. Stapleton Crutchfield. The chief of artillery had grumbled in the vanguard since Newtown about the late-night march toward Winchester. "This is uncivilized," another staff officer claimed Crutchfield had muttered during the crawl. Jackson gave him something more to fray his nerves. Crutchfield learned he would get no sleep, for Jackson directed him to carry a written order to Dick Ewell. The dispatch instructed Ewell to cross over to

Newtown, then head up to Strasburg to counter the phantom Federal force that loomed there. Jackson had deemed this redeployment crucial to protect the tail of the Valley army.[43]

Ewell and his one-brigade command were bivouacked less than two miles east of General Jackson, but Stonewall had no knowledge of this. Jackson notified Crutchfield that he should find Ewell on the Front Royal–Winchester Pike, about five miles south of Winchester. Jackson was only off by three miles, for Ewell's command was within a mile of the tollgate at the end of the pike. Crutchfield took the dispatch at 3:00 A.M. and rode off. Instead of crossing the twenty-five hundred yards between the pikes and heading toward Front Royal, Crutchfield rode up the Valley Pike to Newtown. He may have taken this route to make sure he was not intercepted by Union pickets, or he was confused about the easiest way to hook into the Front Royal–Winchester Pike. Crutchfield, who had failed Jackson with a lackluster performance at Front Royal, illustrated how fatigue had impaired his sense of judgment at Newtown. Rather than head due east on the Millwood–Newtown Road five miles to Double Tollgate, then north five miles to Ewell's command, Crutchfield chose the Richmond Road. This is the same route Steuart's cavalry used in reverse when they struck the wagon train on May 24. Crutchfield's choice would add five more darkened miles to his mission, which guaranteed a delay of an additional hour in reaching Ewell.[44]

As Jackson paced on the Valley Pike near Parkins Mill, he was oblivious to the route Crutchfield had taken; but even had Crutchfield gone by the shortest route from Newtown, the total trip from Jackson to Ewell was nearly twenty miles and would require more than two hours. By that time, dawn would have already descended into the Valley and General Ewell thus would be responding to the only order he felt justified in following, a laconic directive likely written by Jackson at Bartonsville at midnight—an order Jackson would also follow with his command: "Attack at daylight."[45]

8

THE BATTLE OF WINCHESTER

General Banks's May 25 predawn decision to hold his position near Winchester while his wagons began to roll northward toward the Potomac River initiated the formation of his plan to fight his first battle of the Civil War. Throughout the night, his troops coalesced around the two southern entrances into Winchester. By 4:00 A.M. his available force in town amounted to eight regiments of forty-six hundred infantrymen, perhaps one thousand cavalrymen scattered throughout the town, and—with the late arrival of Lt. J. Presley Fleming's two sections of Hampton's battery—sixteen cannons, only ten of them rifled. Suspecting Jackson's force to total at least fifteen thousand, Banks had a completely overmatched army to "test the substance and strength of the enemy by actual collision."[1]

The troop disparity was offset by the terrain. Banks had the advantage of high ground to defend. He delegated troop deployment on that high ground to his ranking subordinate, Brig. Gen. Alpheus S. Williams. The division commander of Banks's lone division was essentially a supernumerary position, but Banks appropriately left Williams in charge of the tactical handling of his brigades, while Banks oversaw the department with a staff of unusual rank. In addition to his large cortege of headquarters personnel, Banks was also assisted by two brigadier generals, Samuel W. Crawford and George S. Greene, both of whom reported days earlier for brigade commands—but without any brigades to command. Banks chose to leave his two colonels in charge of their respective brigades, relegating Greene and Crawford to staff aides.[2]

After receiving verbal orders from General Banks, Williams made the best use of the ground with the troops at his disposal. After Williams superintended the wagon train, satisfied that it rolled unimpeded toward Martinsburg, he rode toward the southern outskirts. With less than one hour of total sleep since the morning of May 23, Williams was thankful that his brigade and regimental colonels had begun to deploy their respective forces upon the ground nearest their opposition. Col. George Gordon had already begun posting his twenty-one hundred infantrymen in a roadbed angling northwestward off the Valley Pike, two hundred yards south of town. Six hundred yards farther south the skirmishers advanced, two companies of the Twenty-ninth Pennsylvania that climbed a knoll west of the Valley Pike and immediately north of Abraham's Creek, overlooking the mills south of Winchester. Four hundred yards southeast of the left flank of Gordon's brigade, elements of Col. Dudley Donnelly's brigade covered both sides of the road leading into southeast Winchester from the junction of the Millwood Pike and the Front Royal–Winchester Pike.

Conspicuous in the predawn was the commanding position held by the six smoothbore cannons of Battery F, Fourth U.S. Light Artillery, the first guns deployed in Banks's army. Lt. Franklin B. Crosby operated the battery, and at 4:00 A.M. he had them in position on Camp Hill (also known as Potato Hill), the ridge between the Valley Pike and Front Royal–Winchester Pike looming one-half mile south of Winchester. More specifically, Crosby chose a commanding knoll east of a Negro cemetery, pointing his guns southeast to cover General Ewell's approaches into town. Unlike Gordon's brigade, Donnelly's artillery was in position ahead of his infantry. The remaining two Union cannons not attached to Gordon's or Donnelly's brigades occupied a height between the cemetery and the town, protected by several squadrons of cavalry.[3]

Crosby's artillery position caught the attention of the Confederates almost immediately after it unlimbered on the knoll. After resting his men for a mere ninety minutes, Jackson had them moving by 4:00 A.M. His objective was the high ground of Bowers Hill, immediately northwest of his army. Claiming these hills would allow Jackson the ability to place his artillery to counter the Union cannons. Having enjoyed artillery suppression at Kernstown, but failing at Front Royal, Jackson placed a premium on reclaiming dominance from this arm of his army.

The Stonewall Brigade began in the van, exactly where it left off throughout the pursuit of the previous twelve hours. General Winder's brigade, averaging 260 officers and men per regiment, advanced to its skirmish line at Hollingsworth Mill, where two farm lanes ran westward above and below, joining immediately behind the mill to circle around the southern base of Bowers Hill. As the light before dawn exposed the hillocks of the ridge, Winder caught sight of the one hundred Pennsylvanians nestled in the old Union cavalry camp above them. Notifying Jackson of his discovery, Winder received a response from Stonewall that hardly surprised him: "You must occupy that hill."[4]

Occupy he did, but Winder nearly lost his life before he deployed Jackson's namesake brigade. Winder and his staff reconnoitered the fence-lined farm lane that bisected the hollow west of the mill. "As we went on this road," recalled Winder's aide-de-camp, Lt. McHenry Howard, ". . . there suddenly came several shots down from a small hollow or break in the high ground on our right which rattled like stones against the plank fence." The staff put spurs to their horses to escape the fire of the Twenty-ninth Pennsylvania skirmishers. No human casualties were tallied in the brief fury of lead, but the cream-colored tail of a staffman's horse dripped crimson when struck at the root.[5]

While General Jackson observed in the road, Winder rapidly deployed more than one thousand infantrymen to sweep and storm the ridge, as well as support the exposed flanks of this movement. The Fifth Virginia Infantry chased the overmatched Union skirmishers off the height and took over their gun placements. The Twenty-seventh Virginia seized an empty hillock immediately west of the contested one, and the Second Virginia advanced between and behind their brigade comrades. The Thirty-third Virginia stayed in reserve, while Winder directed the Fourth Virginia to advance east of the Turnpike to support the three regiments across the road. A member of the Twenty-seventh claimed that his company "filed up a hill into some rifle pits and fire[d] a volley and thus commences the battle of Winchester." The time had just passed 4:30 A.M.[6]

As he was securing the base of the ridge with his infantry, General Winder ordered up a section of Poague's battery (the Rockbridge Artillery). Stapleton Crutchfield no longer superintended the artillery deployment, for he was still away on his mission to find General Ewell. General Winder, trained in the artillery profession early in his military career, was competent in this duty and—unlike Crutchfield at Front Royal—was successful at bringing up two rifled pieces in a timely manner. But like Crutchfield, Winder would have to wait to suppress the Union guns northeast of them across the pike, for the battery section's mission was immediately threatened by activity down the ridge from Winder's secured base. As Captain Poague unlimbered his rifled guns, he watched Colonel Gordon complete the deployment of his twenty-one hundred infantry. Anchoring westward from the Valley Pike, the Twenty-seventh Indiana infantry aligned in double line, followed by the Twenty-ninth Pennsylvania, and Third Wisconsin. The alignment formed uphill, following the contours of Bowers Hill from the valley traversed by the turnpike. They naturally formed in packed lines to assure cohesion in the hours before sunrise.[7]

The final regiment of the brigade, the Second Massachusetts, had begun to negotiate up the slope of the hill to extend the Union line westward. Confederate artillerists immediately discerned the threat posed by the Second Massachusetts as it attempted to anchor the right flank of Gordon's line. Captain Poague ordered his gunners to turn the two cannons to the left and end the threat to their position. Confederate gunners opened upon the Bay states, the only Union infantry atop the crest of the hill. Stonewall Brigade infantry, particularly the Fifth Virginia, volleyed lead to match the artillery iron screaming at the Second Massachusetts. The Union regiment completed its mission, its three right-hand companies in exposed position on top of the hill but for a stone wall, behind which they serendipitously found shelter.[8]

Union artillery magnified the firepower to overwhelm the Confederate position. Cothran's New York battery of Parrott guns was closest to Gordon's brigade, although its namesake leader was no longer in command. Lt. James H. Peabody took charge of the guns. As soon as the Twenty-ninth Pennsylvania skirmishers fell back to Gordon's main line, Lieutenant Peabody immediately deployed his six rifled pieces, placing two sections on knolls of Bowers Hill, while another section unlimbered on high ground east of the pike. The Parrotts could destroy targets one mile away, so the presence of Confederate infantry and artillery just six hundred yards to the south was too inviting. Peabody unleashed the fury of all six of his guns upon the Stonewall Brigade and the artillery they supported. "We are immediately assailed with a shower of grape," noted a horrified Confederate foot soldier. "The shells whistle close over our heads and explode in our rear. The shower of grape and canister is terrible."[9]

With Union artillery rounds exploding behind the Southern infantry, the Rockbridge Artillery suffered the brunt of the barrage. Confederate gunners and horses littered the clover-covered hill. Peabody's battery, with help from a section of Hampton's battery, had kept the Confederates at bay. As the sun rose, these eight Parrotts, deployed in two-gun sections on hillocks, had achieved suppression of the rifled section of the Rockbridge Artillery.

Winder was directly responsible for troop deployment on the southern sector of the height. He had already deployed Carpenter's battery on a hill to the right of Poague's section and closer to the Valley Pike. Capt. Wilfred Cutshaw arrived with his four guns. Winder ordered them onto the hill between Carpenter's and Poague's cannons. These ten Southern cannons well neutralized the two sections of Union artillery directly opposing them, but the enfilading fire by Lieutenant Peabody's four western-deployed Parrotts was still wreaking havoc on the ragged Confederate battle line. A member of Carpenter's battery explained, "We had engaged the enemy but a short time in front, when we were surprised with a terrific cross-fire from the left upon our line. The Rockbridge artillery immediately wheeled upon them, but no sooner fired till a second surprise—for still closer and within 500 yards of our line, lay a regiment of Yankee sharpshooters, with Belgian guns, who immediately commenced their usual work, upon the cannoneers—'picking them off.' "[10]

The sharpshooters were not specialized troops; they were the three right-flank companies of the Second Massachusetts. Taking advantage of the cover they afforded, two companies of skirmishers hustled into place behind several limestone walls running up and down the hill in front of them. These troops came from the left wing of the Third Wisconsin, which occupied a wall seventy-five yards in front of the regiment, close to the Valley Pike. Behind these two companies of detached infantry, thirty-eight companies of Union infantry

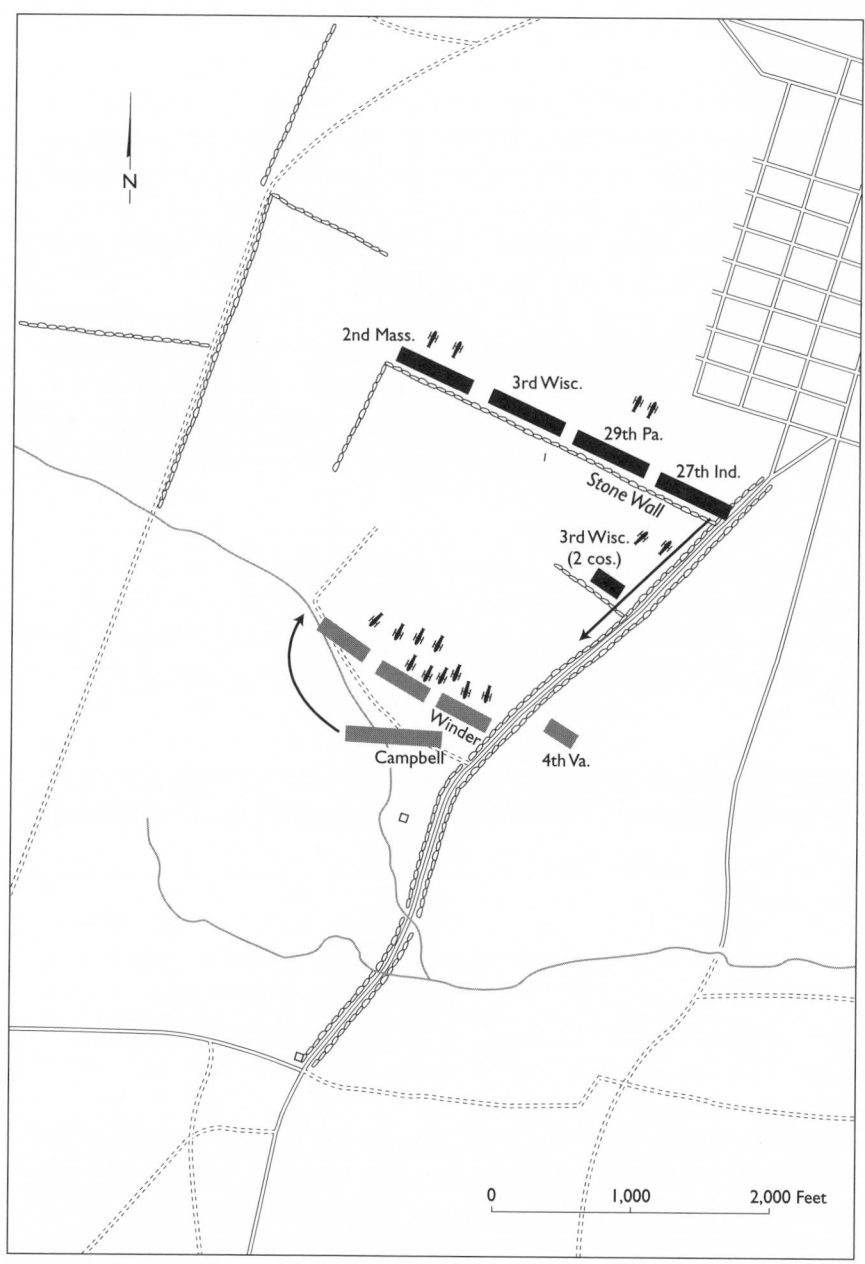

Battle of Winchester: Bowers Hill, 4:30–5:30 A.M., May 25, 1862

formed a battle line about two-thirds of a mile across. But it was the right-flank companies of the Second Massachusetts that inflicted the most damage on Winder's tactical deployment. They raked Winder's advanced position. Their volleys, in combination with frontal fire from a battery section directly in front of Poague's guns and blasts of enfilading fire from two sections to the northwest, rendered Poague's position untenable. Two artillery officers were mortally wounded, including Captain Cutshaw, while an additional twenty Confederate artillerists were struck by solid shot, shrapnel, shell, or bullets. The Stonewall Brigade also suffered a score of casualties before 5:30 A.M.

To this point, the most relieved body of Confederates engaged was the Fourth Virginia Infantry. Protecting the Confederate right flank by advancing east of the Valley Pike, the Virginians halted in a wheat field within eight hundred yards of the Union guns ensconced on Camp Hill ahead of them. Surprisingly, the cannon muzzles never oriented in their direction, despite the open view to their position. "I expected to draw the fire of this battery," reported Col. Charles Ronald, "but it did not open upon me, although in full view of it."[11]

Those Union guns belonged to Lieutenant Crosby's Battery F, Fourth U.S. Artillery. They did not orient toward the Fourth Virginia, for they had begun an artillery duel with Confederate batteries stationed on Bowles Hill near the junction of the Millwood and Front Royal Pikes, one mile southeast of their position. Lieutenant Crosby claimed these cannons "threw shell into us rapidly and with great precision."[12]

The initiation of the artillery barrage forewarned an infantry clash; therefore, an aide entered a dwelling where the Union brigade commander, Col. Dudley Donnelly, was sleeping. Donnelly's obtuse personality induced divergent views of him. A lieutenant in the Tenth Maine Infantry considered "Old Dud" (he was only twenty-four years old) a "hard fellow to manage," while his superior, Gen. Alpheus S. Williams, described him as "a great joker and full of humor." Both views were confirmed by the colonel's reaction when the staff man attempted to wake him at the stroke of dawn that Sunday. The response became camp fodder for weeks thereafter: "He rolled over, gave a grunt, growled at his awakener, and told him it was too early in the morning to turn out to fight rebels."[13]

As Donnelly got out of bed, Ewell's batteries harassed the three regiments of his brigade. The soldiers of the Fifth Connecticut had

just risen and were in the process of heating coffee and cooking breakfast when screaming iron intruded to interrupt their preparations. A
single shell was followed by a succession of rounds, one a solid shot
that hit a gun stack and strewed the rifles all around. Lt. Col. George
D. Chapman hustled his men into a hollow carpeted by a wheat field
off to the east of the road leading into Winchester. A Connecticut
infantrymen noted that "here we dropped out of sight and were entirely concealed by the hollow and standing grain which at that season of the year was pretty fully grown." The regiment had close to 620
men present for duty as they angled eastward from the road into the
hollow.[14]

Across the road from the Connecticut men stood the Forty-sixth
Pennsylvania, led by Col. Joseph F. Knipe. He protected his men from
the Confederate barrage by tucking them behind the crest of the hill
they had encamped on the night before. He closed them en masse to
deploy them when necessary, but the backside of the hill failed to
protect them. "Several men were killed and others wounded in the
Forty-sixth Pennsylvania by these shells," admitted Capt. William L.
Foulk, "and it is a matter of surprise that many more have not been
killed or wounded by them, as they fell and burst at every fire close
around it."[15]

The Twenty-eighth New York stood behind the Forty-sixth Pennsylvania. Many of their members sheltered themselves overnight in a
little church in the eastern part of Winchester. Having just arrived on
the ground, the bombardment horrified their rank and file, primarily
because a substantial fog shrouded their view. "We stood there ½ hours,
the shell falling thick and fast all around and among us," claimed a New
Yorker, although the time frame was likely half his estimate. Lt. Col.
Edwin F. Brown sent the ambulances to the rear and readied his men for
the infantry assault they all expected. Together, Donnelly's three regiments totaled seventeen hundred officers and men.[16]

General Ewell had not deployed his men as early as did Jackson on
May 25. The sun rose above the Blue Ridge several minutes before
5:00 A.M., but Dick Ewell could not use it to his advantage. A low-
level fog shrouded the position of Colonel Donnelly's brigade. Rail
and limestone fences that latticed throughout the valley of Abraham's Creek and Town Run also interfered with his view of the
Union deployment. Ewell never heard the crackle of small arms fire
one mile away from him when Jackson's soldiers opened the battle on

Bowers Hill at 4:30 A.M. But the cannon fire exchanged on that height could not escape Ewell's notice. "All doubts as to Jackson's intentions were dispelled soon after day break," remembered Ewell upon hearing the artillery, "& I at once pressed my attack with vigor."[17]

Although Ewell's infantry—the regiments of Trimble's brigade—rested instead of marched throughout the night as did Jackson's men, the stagnancy made them suffer. Nighttime temperatures dipped into the low forties, and since Jackson had stripped down the force to one wagon per regiment, blankets and overcoats were necessarily left behind. Ewell also had extinguished any plans to build campfires. The result was a universal complaint: "came very near freezing." Groups of fifteen to twenty soldiers braced together to ward off the cold, a participant claiming that without this adjustment, "we would have frozen to death." Col. William C. Oates complained that his regiment was ordered to stand in the road all night. "It was a precaution wholly unnecessary and a cruel punishment," he railed. "The men shivered and their teeth chattered with the cold."[18]

Ewell put the leading regiments of his infantry in motion; no longer would they complain about the cold even though the temperature likely remained in the forties during the first hour of light. His artillery attempted to soften the Union position, although the boggy landscape forced the artillerists to employ indirect fire. At 5:30 he bypassed the normal chain of command to deliver his assault directive. Rather than give his orders to General Trimble, Ewell rode up to the Twenty-first North Carolina infantry, the leading regiment of Trimble's brigade. He did not come alone, for a section of Courtney's battery rolled up with him. Lt. Joseph White Latimer, all of eighteen years old on May 25, commanded these two guns, and Ewell commanded him to fire on the Fourth U.S. Artillery from the roadbed. The baby-faced officer dutifully unlimbered his pieces and directed his gunners to open on the battery. On Camp Hill, Crosby immediately responded by sending spherical case and shell one-half mile back to Latimer's gunners.

During the cannonade, Ewell fed instructions to Col. William W. Kirkland, who two days later remembered the instruction, "[T]he Major-General directed me to move into the town with my regiment and drive the enemy out." Ewell took his message directly to the Tarheels assigned to the duty. "Now, old North Carolina, this is your chance," bellowed the general. "The Yankees are before you. Drive them out of the town!" Ewell obtained the reaction he anticipated. According to Colonel Kirkland, "The Twenty-first responded to this order with a cheer that convinced me that our regimental color would soon wave in the streets of Winchester."[19]

Kirkland's regiment consisted of only twelve companies. To alleviate the oddity, Companies A and B formed a battalion, separately designated as the "First Battalion of Sharpshooters." Since Maj. Saunders Fulton was temporarily away from the regiment with two of the companies, Kirkland called in the First Battalion to form with his eight available companies. Back to ten companies, Kirkland's strength returned to three hundred officers and men.[20]

Curiously, Ewell had decided to send a single regiment into unknown Union infantry and artillery defense essentially alone. The only support provided the Carolinians was to the west, off their left flank. This was provided by Col. Bradley Johnson's First (CSA) Maryland Infantry. Considering the depletion of the regiment by mutiny and hard service over the previous two days, plus detachments to guard prisoners and captured supplies at Front Royal, Johnson's regiment was no larger than a small battalion—perhaps two hundred officers and men, but likely fewer than this. No better evidence for the paltry size of Johnson's command exists than their duty for May 25. According to Colonel Johnson, Ewell ordered him "to deploy as skirmishers on the left of the road, and of the Twenty-first North Carolina, Colonel Kirkland, to watch his left and keep it from being turned, and look out for Jackson on the Valley road." Thus, Ewell looked to the Maryland regiment as little more than a link with Jackson's position, leaving Colonel Kirkland as the lone assaulting force against an opponent that clearly outnumbered them.[21]

Although the Marylanders skirmished off his left flank, Colonel Kirkland magnified General Ewell's mistake by not posting his own skirmishers to scour the region in front of the Twenty-first North Carolina. Under constant shelling by Crosby's cannoneers, Kirkland marched his men in line of battle toward Winchester, leading them on his beautiful bay mare. Passing the tollhouse on their right, the Confederates crossed over Abraham's Creek and started to march uphill on the opposite side of the creek valley. The road the Carolinians followed toward the city turned rather sharply from northwest to north near the top of the hill. Beyond this point, the terrain dropped and rose again to another hill. The valley between these hills remained shrouded in mist. Waiting in this curtained hollow, east of the road, was the Fifth Connecticut—unseen by Kirkland or his men.[22]

The left wing of the Twenty-first North Carolina—Companies C and M—pulled ahead of the other companies in the center and right wing. Upon reaching the top of the hill immediately north of Abraham's Creek, these two companies—many of their men packed four ranks deep in the narrow, double-stone-lined lane—found a stone wall about seventy-five yards off to their left. One hundred yards north of this wall, Colonel Knipe of the Forty-sixth Pennsylvania could sense the vulnerability of his position on open ground, somewhat downhill from that wall. Two of his companies, D and E, had positioned themselves closer to the wall, where they became the first targets of the North Carolinians' musket fire. Knipe immediately ordered his remaining companies to charge uphill upon the wall.[23]

The Pennsylvanians reached the wall before the left wing of the Tarheels, who saw the Union infantry suddenly rise up from it and were misled to believe that an entire brigade waited in ambush, concealed behind the fence the entire time. The Forty-sixth Pennsylvania loosed a volley from the wall. The small arms fire caught the Twenty-first North Carolina completely by surprise. The left-hand companies returned fire, as Kirkland quickly sought a position to cover his men. He pulled the left wing from the roadbed where they joined the rest of the Tarheels behind the low stone wall that lined the east side of the lane. From there Kirkland's men exchanged fire with the Pennsylvanians, while the colonel saw another regiment come in behind those Union troops to gain cover behind another wall on his side of the road. This was Lieutenant Colonel Brown's Twenty-eighth New York Infantry, which quickly showered bullets on Kirkland's now-exposed command. Making matters worse for the Tarheels was the sudden appearance of a force directly in front of them—Companies A and Company F of the Fifth Connecticut—brazenly challenging the Southerners from twenty yards.[24]

Colonel Kirkland had little choice but to disrupt the triple threat by aggression. He ordered a bayonet charge, and on his command, the Carolinians leapt the wall with a shout and rushed for the wall protecting the Forty-sixth Pennsylvania, temporarily ignoring the other Union soldiers on their flank. A volley by Knipe's Pennsylvanians rocked Kirkland's foot soldiers back. But unseen by Kirkland during

the charge were the remaining eight companies of the Fifth Connecticut, tucked away in the boggy hollow off to his right. Lieutenant
Colonel Chapman had ordered his four-hundred-man battalion up to
the support of his advanced two companies. They arose out of the fog
just as Kirkland's bayonet charge petered out directly in front of
them. The Connecticut major bellowed, "Now is your time, boys! Up
and give it to them."[25]

On this command, the eager Yankees fired into the unprotected
right flank of the Twenty-first North Carolina. The effect was devastating. "Up sprang every man, with his rifle leveled—" raved a Connecticut soldier, "along our line blazed a sheet of flame, and down like
ten-pins went the front ranks of the rebels." Lieutenant Colonel
Chapman reported that his regiment's volley "mowed down the enemy in scores." He ordered a second barrage. His men aimed at human targets closer than forty yards away; one defined it as "easy pistol
range." They could hardly miss. Minié balls tore through Carolina
flesh, snapping bones and shredding vital organs. Rebel yells turned
to shrieks, groans, and screams from the pain and terror of this point-
blank execution. Their agony stirred the Yankees. As each of two
Carolina flag bearers went down with their colors, the Union soldiers
cheered with blood lust. According to a participant, "[W]e hooted and
yelled at them in Yankee style."[26]

Scores of Southerners dropped out of the ranks, including Lt. Col.
Rufus K. Pepper, mortally wounded by a bullet that passed through
his hips as he waved his sword overhead to rally the right wing of the
regiment. (Pepper was the highest-ranking officer on either side to die
as a result of the three days of action.) Five company officers fell killed
or wounded—one with nine bullets through his clothes and body.
Somehow, Colonel Kirkland kept his cool as he attempted to deliver
his regiment from the maelstrom. He used the protection of the low-
walled lane again, this time by rallying his men into the roadbed.
Facing toward the Connecticut soldiers, Kirkland's infantrymen got
off a ragged volley, effective enough to knock back the right-wing
companies of Chapman's regiment. Colonel Kirkland summarized
the action: "They received us with a most withering fire, before which
my men fell like autumn leaves, but the Yankees fell back." But most
of the Union men remained. Realizing his advantage, Lieutenant
Colonel Chapman moved in for the kill. As he directed a third volley,

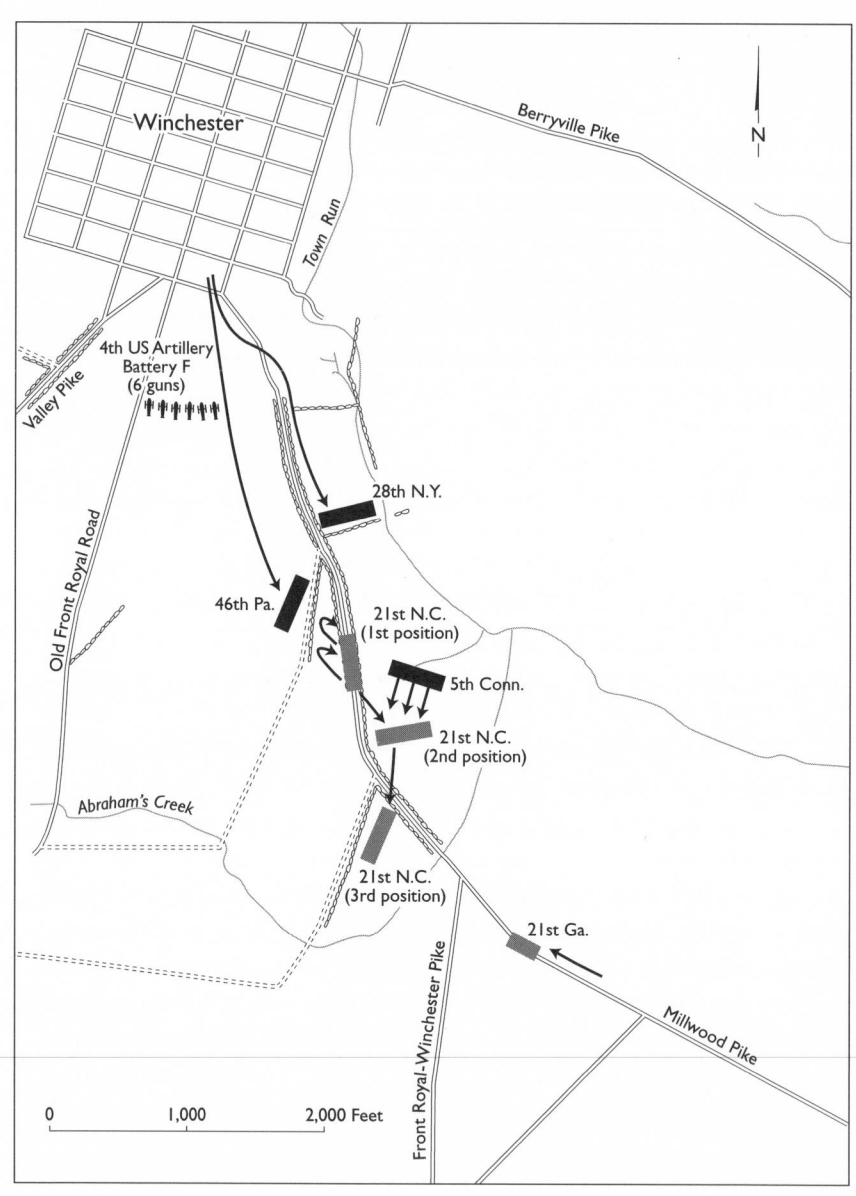

Battle of Winchester: General Ewell versus Colonel Donnelly

he ordered his two left-flank companies (I and B) to half-wheel to the right. From this position they delivered an appalling crossfire into Kirkland's ranks, sending his men into more agony and confusion.[27]

The Confederate regiment broke under the pressure and fled rearward. In under two minutes, the Twenty-first North Carolina suffered at least seventy-five casualties. Kirkland's total losses in twenty minutes of action were eighteen killed and seventy-eight wounded. One out of every three men fell in the desperate charge. Colonel Kirkland, hobbled by a bullet in his thigh, located a more substantial limestone wall just north of Abraham's Creek, three hundred yards south of but parallel to the wall protecting the Forty-sixth Pennsylvania. This east–west wall extended to the left of the road, lining a lane that led to a mill. The Twenty-eighth New York moved eastward and a little south toward an orchard near Town Run. The Fifth Connecticut dropped back to the stone wall previously held by the New Yorkers. Kirkland's Tarheels huddled behind their protection, eventually joined by Major Fulton's two companies, but the minor reinforcement was pointless. The Confederates were outnumbered five to one as they watched a three-quarter-mile-long, crescent-shaped Union formation surround them.[28]

The First (CSA) Maryland Infantry provided no succor to the Carolina regiment. Advancing to the left of the Tarheels, Johnson permitted a five-hundred-yard gap (four hundred yards west and one hundred yards south) to develop between them. Impaired by mist, fog, and battle smoke, Johnson and his men lost sight of Colonel Kirkland, but they could tell he was heavily engaged with a Union force. Johnson wheeled his men to the right after they advanced past the Twenty-first North Carolina. They scaled a fence line near some farm outbuildings and rested in an apple orchard. The civilized setting surrounding the Marylanders convinced some members that they had actually penetrated into the town of Winchester. More likely, they were just off the old Front Royal road, between the turnpikes that converged in Winchester, their backs to the Valley Pike. Colonel Johnson sent a courier back to General Ewell, to inform him that he would attack on the flank if another demonstration was made in front of the Union position.[29]

At 7:00 A.M. the battle was well into its third hour, with no progress in Ewell's sector. His careless deployment of the Twenty-first

North Carolina not only sacrificed nearly one hundred men; it also stalled any momentum he hoped to carry. The Tarheels had been unable to dent the Union defense or inflict any appreciable casualties. Soon after the destruction of the Confederate regiment, General Banks and General Williams rode out to inspect the progress of the troops. As much relieved as they were pleased by the performance of Donnelly's brigade, the two generals must have believed that these three regiments had merely slowed down the inevitable—an expected onslaught by overwhelming opposing numbers.[30]

Unknown to Banks was the reality facing General Ewell—he did not possess overwhelming numbers to assault the regiments of Donnelly's brigade, nor did he outgun Lieutenant Crosby's battery on Camp Hill. Trimble's brigade plus the First (CSA) Maryland did not exceed two thousand men; they likely had numbers closer to Donnelly's seventeen hundred infantrymen. Ewell's only formula for success was to outmaneuver the Federal defense. The only gain from the debacle of sending the North Carolina men "up the gut" was to expose the Union positions.

General Ewell had already committed another regiment up the center. He had General Trimble send the Twenty-first Georgia forward, ostensibly to relieve the pressure on Kirkland's right flank before they turned the Union east flank. The Georgians moved up to the Carolina line by 7:00 A.M. Colonel Donnelly had already countered Ewell's advances. He not only sent the New Yorkers to protect the flank but also pulled the Pennsylvanians back closer to the battery. He also pulled out a section of the battery, under Lt. Henry Cushing, to counter the Confederate reinforcements. Cushing trained his pieces on the Georgians to slow their advance.[31]

Col. John Thomas Mercer and his Twenty-first Georgia performed well, notwithstanding the focused attention they received from the Union brigade. After firing at the Pennsylvanians during their retrograde movement to the artillery, the Georgians got a surprise. "We received a volley from another Regiment behind a fence at right angles to the first," recalled Maj. James Nisbet. The volley came from the Twenty-eighth New York, anchored to a stone wall looping northward from the front of the eighteenth-century Hollingsworth house. Casualties mounted among the Georgians as Colonel Mercer turned his attention to the right. An orchard stood on high ground, north of Abraham's Creek and east of its junction with Town Run,

which flowed southward into it from Winchester. Mercer led his
men eastward as they negotiated along the southern bank of Abraham's Creek in an effort to sweep onto the orchard covered hill from
the south.

Lt. Col. Edwin Brown anticipated this attempt to gain his flank
and hustled his men to the same destination. "We at once started on,
amid a shower of bullets, crossing a creek and passing over a hill,"
claimed a New Yorker. "Beyond the hill was an orchard in which the
rebels tried to find shelter, but we gave them a taste of our lead before
they got to it." The taste was hot for the Southerners, who took seventeen casualties in the brief exchange with Brown's regiment. Mercer and his men quickly disappeared from view behind Bowles Hill.[32]

The entire battlefield began to disappear at 7:30 A.M., the end of
the third hour of battle. Temperatures in and south of Winchester
neared fifty degrees (it was fifty-four degrees in Georgetown at 7:00
A.M.), and the promise of a lifting mist at sunrise had reversed into a
starkly different reality. A heavy fog was settling on the terrain, wip-
ing out all visibility for the opposing soldiers. Thus far, the contest
found Banks achieving more success against Jackson and Ewell than
he had expected. The choice of good defensive ground and tenacious
fighting by Union soldiers in their first battle had stymied Confederate progress to the point where the Southerners had penetrated only
one mile closer than where they stood in the predawn hours of that
Sunday morning.

The other reason for Northern success was the absence of cohesion between Jackson and Ewell. The latter did not have the numbers
to punch his way into Winchester, and the settling fog delayed his
opportunity to do so by maneuver. Jackson had more than five thousand available men in reserve, but he had no intention of sending
them to Ewell, primarily because at 7:30 A.M., he did not yet know
where Ewell was. Jackson's immediate problem at this time was not
a lack of numbers, but he seemed puzzled where to place his troops.
By the time General Ewell's three deployed regiments had stalled in
their tracks southeast of Winchester, or were forced back from those
tracks, Jackson had deployed not three regiments but three brigades
southwest of Winchester—with the same fruitless results. Colonel
John A. Campbell's brigade and Colonel Fulkerson's brigade extended
to the left of the Stonewall Brigade, but with no success against the
four Union regiments extending onto Bowers Hill. Jackson's three

thousand deployed infantrymen could not make any headway against the twenty-one hundred Federals opposing them.

Union artillery on Bowers Hill, supported by the two companies of the Second Massachusetts perched behind a wall in front of them, wreaked continuous havoc on General Winder's deployment. He had placed his infantry primarily to support the three batteries on the southern edge of Bowers Hill. "A regiment behind a stone fence did much execution," admitted Winder about the Second Massachusetts infantrymen, who continued to pick off his artillerists and infantry-men supporting them. For three hours he endured the constant pressure applied by the Union detachment. Eighteen members of the Second Virginia fell dead or wounded, more casualties than were recorded by the rest of the regiments of the Stonewall Brigade combined.[33]

In addition to the few thousand infantrymen, close to two hundred artillerists manned the three Confederate batteries deployed along the southern ridgeline of Bowers Hill. By 7:30 A.M. Winder felt he had neutralized the six cannons six hundred yards in front of him, but the enfilading section and the wall-protected Massachusetts infantry to the left continued to threaten his position. He was unable to place the remaining four smoothbore cannons of the Rockbridge Artillery (Poague's battery) on a hill to the left of the two suppressed rifled pieces; therefore, these guns deployed closer to the harassed section.

At least half an hour earlier, General Winder had ordered up the Thirty-third Virginia to support Carpenter's battery, but the unit had yet to materialize on the hill. The order miscarried, and Winder was forced to reissue it. Col. John F. Neff hustled his tiny command—only 150 officers and men—up to the battery. Within half an hour, Carpenter's guns fell silent after firing forty rounds. They moved off leaving Neff's men on the hill awaiting a section of Cutshaw's battery to take Carpenter's place. While they waited in the interim, General Jackson made his initial appearance on the height, escorted by some staff officers—Col. John A. Campbell, the commander of the second brigade of Jackson's division, and another officer who assisted Stonewall in reconnoitering the height. A shower of lead and iron from the Union defense thudded all around them, wounding both officers near Jackson's side.

Undaunted, Jackson rode onto the hill covered by the Thirty-third Virginia. Jackson ordered Neff forward, admonishing him to keep an eye out for the unattended hillock directly in front of him. This was the highest point of Bowers Hill, and no Confederate battery dared to occupy it because Peabody's guns and Union infantry would destroy the first to try. Jackson appeared more concerned that the Union guns would be rolled forward to this point and render his entire line untenable. Jackson pointed out this possibility to Colonel Neff. "They must not do it!" Stonewall declared, ordering Neff to charge the height with bayonet if Yankees attempted to claim the ground. Neff tried to explain the difficulty of doing so with 150 officers and men, but Jackson would not hear excuses. "Take it," he repeated.[34]

No attempt by either side was made to occupy the hill between the lines. The loss of Colonel Campbell shortly before reaching Neff's position underscored a serious problem developing within the ranks of the second brigade, the infantry subsequent to the Stonewall Brigade that had come up to support Confederate batteries. They did not suffer the same number of casualties as did the Stonewall Brigade, but their casualties were more detrimental, for there was a disproportionate number of regimental officers incapacitated by wounds received on Bowers Hill. When Colonel Campbell went down near Jackson's side, he was immediately replaced by Col. John M. Patton, a capable officer, but one who would be out of the war in three months as his weight dwindled from the hardships of campaigning to 128 pounds. Lt. Col. R.H. Cunningham, who took over the Twenty-first Virginia when Colonel Patton ascended to brigade command, reported no casualties in his regiment. But he felt obligated to inform Patton, "It is my painful duty to report that some were not at their posts. Owing to the fact that a large number were broken down by the hard duty we had performed, it is impossible to separate those who were really broken down from those who were lost to all pride and patriotism as to desert their posts in the hour of danger."[35]

Part of Cunningham's problem was the dearth of line officers to support him. John B. Moseley, the major of the Twenty-first Virginia, was ordered to lead the Forty-eighth Virginia after its commanding officer left the field with a wound, leaving captains and lieutenants as the only commissioned officers within the unit. The major commanding the Forty-second Virginia was also struck early in the action and forced from the field. No line officers remained in the regiment, nor were there available officers to transfer from other regiments in the brigade. This left John E. Penn, the senior captain of the Forty-second Virginia, to take the helm of ten companies. Benjamin Watkins Leigh, commanding the First Virginia Battalion, was the only officer of the second brigade who began and finished the day at the helm of his unit, but he, too, was a captain.[36]

Under the best of circumstances, a commander of a three-regiment, one-battalion brigade could rely on eleven regimental officers for optimal function and discipline of that brigade (a colonel, lieutenant colonel, and major for each regiment; and the latter two for the battalion). By 7:30 A.M. Colonel Patton was down to a total of two regimental officers for his entire brigade. Desertion and disciplinary problems on May 25 were not reported in the Forty-second Virginia, Forty-eighth Virginia, and the First Virginia Battalion, but given the stretched duties of company officers, it is likely that dereliction of duty was as prevalent in these units as what Lieutenant Colonel Cunningham reported for his Twenty-first Virginia.

General Winder, for all intents and purposes, acted as a division commander on Bowers Hill. General Jackson delegated his authority to Winder, who performed as soundly as possible under the circumstances, not only deploying the Stonewall Brigade but also superintending the movements and actions of the artillery and regiments attached to Jackson's second and third brigades. If Winder was aware of the unraveling structure within the regiments on Bowers Hill, he paid little heed to it because of the immediacy of what confronted him. As the fog began to roll over Bowers Hill, he studied a repositioning of troops in Gordon's brigade. "The enemy soon commenced to move by his right flank," observed Winder, who quickly looked for troops to equalize this chess move.[37]

What Winder witnessed was a redeployment of the Second Massachusetts Infantry atop Bowers Hill. Lieutenant Colonel Andrews superintended this movement in response to observing General Winder continue to extend his line westward. He ordered Companies D and I to rush upon an unoccupied wall forty yards southwest of the right flank of the Union regiment. These hundred soldiers were there within minutes, increasing the threat upon the Confederates' left flank. One Massachusetts officer behind this wall was Lt. Robert Gould Shaw, who had returned to his regiment less than twelve hours earlier from his mission in Washington. Denied by Secretary Stanton the opportunity to raise a black regiment, Shaw was now fighting his first battle with troops of any color.[38]

General Winder reacted swiftly to the Massachusetts maneuvers. Matching strength with more strength, Winder brought up three regiments of Fulkerson's brigade and wheeled them in to extend his left to threaten the Union batteries and infantry flank. He got Poague's remaining four guns into position where the Parrotts had opened the battle, and directed these guns to divide their fire between Peabody's guns behind the Second Massachusetts and the advanced wall protecting those Bay State soldiers. Plastering the wall with the solid shot, Poague and Winder were relieved to see the Massachusetts skirmishers abandon the wall and return to the brigade line behind them. As the work of killing continued on Bowers Hill, some could hear the surreal sounds of Sunday off to the northeast in the city of Winchester —the rhythmic tolling of church bells.[39]

The abandonment of the skirmish wall resulted more from Confederate maneuver than from the solid shot hurled at the wall. Maj. Wilder Dwight, while at the stone wall, had detected two regiments moving westward at the bottom of the hill, a finding he relayed to Colonel Gordon. This was most likely the Tenth and Thirty-seventh Virginia Infantry regiments of Colonel Fulkerson's brigade, the third and final brigade of Jackson's division deployed by General Winder. In response, Gordon ordered the skirmishers to return to the regimental line. He also ordered Lieutenant Peabody to roll one of his pieces forward and to the right to cover this potential threat.[40]

As the battle of Winchester entered its fourth hour, the citizens of Winchester attempted to conduct their normal routines. But the thundering sounds of continuous battle alerted all in town that this was no normal Sunday. The anticipation of liberation after two months and two weeks of Union control was unbearable to the secessionists in town. Equally unbearable to the Unionists and African American refugees was the fear of Confederate victory and the repercussions that were sure to follow. Turning their ears to the acoustics of battle southeast and southwest of town, Winchester residents were startled to hear a sudden cessation to the cannonading that had awoken them before 5:00 A.M.

The fog came down upon the battlefield like a white curtain, closing act 1 of the battle. For the participants the play had no theme, no decision. More than two hundred casualties mounted within Jackson's army compared to less than half as many among Banks's troops —a predictable result for an attacking force against stubborn defenders. But the battle lines had barely budged since dawn and Banks's wagons were all rolling past Martinsburg. General Banks had to be satisfied with the Union defense to this point. They had withstood well. Together, Jackson and Ewell had deployed fewer than five thousand infantrymen and fired about as many cannons as Banks. Unless Jackson could throw overwhelming numbers against him, Banks hoped the battle to remain a standstill.

With the exception of ordering the Thirty-third Virginia to charge with the bayonet ninety minutes earlier, General Jackson had not been personally involved with the action on Bowers Hill. That all changed beginning at 7:30 A.M. on May 25, 1862. Jackson stepped forward to direct this performance, preparing to add a new cast of characters to begin act 2. Riding up to General Winder, Jackson asked him about the progress of the battle. Winder's response was succinct: the enemy was vulnerable on the right flank. "Very well," acknowledged Jackson to his subordinate, "I will send you Taylor's brigade."[41]

9

EXHILARATION AND DESPAIR

The Louisiana brigade was in an unusual position at 7:30 A.M. on May 25, compared to the previous three days in the Valley. It stood in reserve on the Valley Pike at Kernstown on Sunday morning while Jackson's entire division, as well as half of Ewell's division under General Trimble, battled Banks's men for three hours along the turnpike approaches to Winchester. Since May 22, Brig. Gen. Richard Taylor's Louisianans had marched in the van of the entire army. They initially led the approach to Front Royal; they were the first infantry to strike blue-clad troops at Middletown, but ever since Jackson took them on a wayward excursion to Cedar Creek Saturday afternoon, the Pelican State soldiers had been eating the dust of the Virginians, who marched in front of them.

Their vanguard position had produced mixed results. The Eighth Louisiana had performed well at Front Royal, as did Wheat's Battalion in the first two hours of the action on May 23. But Wheat's men broke from their duties to raid the First (USA) Maryland's camps, negating the tenacious pressure they had applied to Colonel Kenly's position for two hours before that. The Seventh Louisiana darkened the stain on the Louisianans' record of poor discipline on May 24 by breaking ranks and raiding the captured supply wagons near Middletown (a dereliction of duty that was cited in Colonel Crutchfield's report).

More puzzling was General Taylor's leadership, particularly at Front
Royal. Ordered away from the main body with three regiments, Taylor seemingly disappeared from view with these two thousand men
for the first two hours of the battle. This resulted in the deployment
and engagement of barely a third of his command during the constant
action of May 23–24, despite holding a position and orders that afforded him the opportunity to commit at least twice as many of his
men in battle during that time.[1]

Despite the question marks on the brigade's recent record, General Jackson called for them specifically to strike the Union flank on
Bowers Hill. Perhaps Jackson was impressed with Taylor and his men
during the approach to Cedar Creek sixteen hours earlier, but it cannot be ruled out that he chose them primarily because of their numbers. While none of the brigades of Jackson's division exceeded thirteen hundred men available for duty on May 25, Taylor's massive
brigade was clearly the largest of the army with twenty-five hundred
officers and men. When Lt. Henry K. Douglas led Jackson back to
General Taylor, the Louisianans were still working the stiffness out
of their bodies, but they were ready to take part in the engagement.[2]

General Taylor, the son of the twelfth President of the United
States, rode toward Winchester while his regiments marched in tow.
General Jackson greeted him near Milltown, then sent him beyond
the Confederate flank. Marching in column, Taylor's men negotiated
the ground along the northern bank of Abraham's Creek. As Taylor
moved westward around General Winder's deployed troops at the
southern lip of Bowers Hill, Winder intercepted Taylor and fed him
instructions to reach the flank. Taylor's men continued, taking advantage of a fog-laden creek bottom and nearby woods to conceal
their movement.

Notwithstanding nature's cover for the Louisianans, Union deployment had already foiled what would have been an easy flank
march. Colonel Gordon made sure that his flank was secured. He sent
orders back to the Twenty-seventh Indiana. Col. Silas Colgrove's 446
Hoosiers stood with their left flank anchored on the Valley Pike, but
somewhat behind the line formed by the Wisconsin and Massachusetts regiments (the Twenty-ninth Pennsylvania had reformed to the
right of the Indianans). Essentially unengaged throughout the morning action, Colgrove received his orders from Gordon's assistant adjutant general, and had his regiment on the move in immediate re-

sponse. In columns of fours they followed a ravine that led them toward the crest of the hill to their right. Within minutes after the Hoosiers marched out on their mission, Col. John K. Murphy of the Twenty-ninth Pennsylvania received similar orders from brigade headquarters and prepared his regiment to respond.[3]

As the Twenty-seventh Indiana crested the hill, they received brisk fire from the skirmishers of the Tenth Virginia Infantry, commanded by Capt. Isaac G. Coffman. The Virginians, concealed behind trees and rocky outcroppings along the western base of Bowers Hill, fired sporadically at the Hoosiers as soon as they entered their field of vision. One Company A corporal became the first casualty for the Indianans, shot through the forehead. "We were obliged to break ranks somewhat to avoid stepping upon him, as he writhed in the convulsions of death," recalled Corporal Edmund Brown, who was only seventeen years old at the time. Those not looking down at the soldier in death throes were preoccupied by an even more foreboding sight. Down the hill an expansive body of timber teemed with Confederate soldiers. A Hoosier in Company H observed that the rebels "were all marching to our right" and easily discerned they were "undertaking to outflank and surround us."[4]

Gordon's machinations to secure his flank were apparently not instigated by the westward movement of Taylor's Louisiana brigade but by Fulkerson's brigade, which was visible to Major Dwight just before fog enveloped the lowland. The Louisianans had reached the flank minutes after the Hoosiers crested the hill above them. Fulkerson's brigade, already split when the Twenty-third Virginia stayed near Winder's batteries while the two other regiments of the brigade filed to the west, split again with the arrival of the Louisianans. Colonel Fulkerson, personally leading his former regiment, the Thirty-seventh Virginia, while the Tenth Virginia had already secured a wooded hill, decided to send the Tenth Virginia to the left as the Thirty-seventh replaced them on the hill. Colonel Edward T. H. Warren escorted the Tenth Virginia to the left of Taylor's brigade, once it reached its position.[5]

The morning fog lay thickest in the Abraham's Creek valley between the ridge lines of Camp Hill and Bowles Hill, southeast of Winchester. This was the locale where Col. Dudley Donnelly and Gen. Richard S. Ewell had squared off for three hours—to a draw. The heavy fog cover caused a hiatus in the action. Donnelly, a native of

Niagara Falls, New York, was certainly accustomed to morning mist and fog, but being in a defensive position he could do nothing during the forced respite. His brigade was fully deployed.

General Williams rode up to Donnelly to be apprised of the situation with his former brigade. "I was rejoiced to find my old brigade doing so well," expressed Williams, but Donnelly misinformed him that nine rebel regiments threatened his position, when in fact there were only five. Williams studied the position and decided that Donnelly needed reinforcements. Behind him, in Winchester, more than eight hundred members of the Tenth Maine Infantry stood in reserve (they only had skirmishing duty in the overnight hours before the battle). The Maine troops had marched into Winchester less than twelve hours before. They had been officially organized in the Railroad Brigade of Maj. Gen. John A. Dix's Middle Department and thus were not attached to Williams's division. Surprisingly, Williams did not seek Banks's consent to order them forward. Instead, the general decided to pull troops from Gordon's brigade on Bowers Hill to reinforce Colonel Donnelly. At about 8:00 A.M. he left his old command and rode out to consult with Colonel Gordon. This further protracted the inactivity of the Tenth Maine Infantry, thus wasting 20 percent of the available strength at Banks's and Williams's disposal.[6]

General Ewell, being on the offensive, was better able to act during the fog cover. This he did, following the sound advice of his brigade commander, Gen. Isaac Trimble. Trimble was one of the oldest field generals of the Confederacy; he had celebrated his sixtieth birthday ten days before the Battle of Winchester. Under cover of the fog, he pulled back the harried Twenty-first North Carolina Infantry. The Twenty-first Georgia collected their companies on a high hill, flanking their main nemesis of the morning, the Twenty-eighth New York Infantry. As the fog began to lift close to 8:00 A.M., Ewell was prepared to flank westward toward Winchester. He still had two regiments in reserve, the Fifteenth Alabama and the Sixteenth Mississippi, to throw into the fray when needed. According to General Ewell, his brigadier decided the best time to deploy them: "the mist then admitting a better view, I adopted the suggestion of Brigadier-General Trimble and marched them to the right." The Sixteenth Mississippi moved out first, covered by Courtney's battery, which had repositioned north of the earlier battery line on Bowles Hill and now raked the Union batteries on Camp Hill with shell fire.[7]

Ewell followed Trimble's advice because it was clear and appropriate. Near the same time, however, Ewell received an order that left the major general and his staff scratching their heads. The source was Jackson's chief of artillery, Col. Stapleton Crutchfield, who finally completed the mission Jackson sent him on nearly five hours earlier. He had ridden from the mills south of Winchester up to Newtown, then crossed over on the Richmond Road to Nineveh expecting to find Ewell near there. With no signs of Ewell's force and hearing the sounds of battle to the north, Crutchfield headed down the Front Royal–Winchester Pike for twelve miles until he found Ewell upon the field shortly before 8:00 A.M. Crutchfield would claim in his report two months later that he rode twenty-nine miles on this mission. (Unless he was misdirected to the outskirts of Front Royal, he likely traversed twenty-three miles of Lower Valley roads.)

More puzzling than Crutchfield's route to find Ewell was the content of Jackson's message: to pull back to Double Tollgate, cross over to Newtown, then head up to Strasburg to check a suspected Union force there from threatening Jackson's rear. The threat did not exist, which rendered Jackson's 3:00 A.M. message a clear overreaction, but the fact that the message was not delivered for five hours, and subsequently handed over in the midst of a battle, made it absolutely mind-boggling. Although a member of his staff maintained the order was one hour old instead of five, General Ewell had the good sense to piece the time line together enough to ignore the message as an outdated one.[8]

Across the battlefield on Bowers Hill, Jackson sent Taylor's brigade to the flank intending to break the stalemate. Including the regiments from Fulkerson's brigade, the Confederate flank consisted of close to three thousand infantrymen, poised to crush the Union regiments, a force they outnumbered by a thousand men. More important for Jackson's designs, the Union regiments were expected to be facing southward, unsuspecting of what was about to hit them.

Colonel Gordon's troop realignment now hindered Jackson's plan. Not only was the Twenty-seventh Indiana on the Union flank and facing the Louisianans, but help was coming their way in the form of the Twenty-ninth Pennsylvania Infantry, led by sixty-five-year-old Col. John K. Murphy. They marched over the crest a few minutes after 8:00 A.M. and aligned to the left of the Indiana troops, facing obliquely to the southwest. Although these nine hundred troops presented a significant obstacle to the Confederates, they had little artillery support, save for one gun from Peabody's battery that had reoriented toward the area of suspected threat.

Apparently by orders of Colonel Gordon, no horses were allowed to carry officers in the Union regiments on Bowers Hill. This of course affected the familiarity and visibility of seeing the leaders elevated on horseback. It also must have been an additional burden for the venerable and irascible Colonel Murphy, one of the few Civil War field commanders born in the 1700s and a veteran of the War of 1812. The two flank-protecting regiments were too exposed on the side of the rocky hill. As Murphy's Pennsylvanians completed their alignment, Colonel Colgrove ordered his Twenty-seventh Indiana forward about twenty yards farther down the hill to a line of rail fencing. They fired as they advanced, volleying minié balls toward the waiting Southerners in the woods. Once they reached the fence, the officers directed the men to hurry but still take enough time to aim as they continued to shoot away. "We fired from three to five rounds each from that position," reported Corporal Brown of the action at the fence line, "and could clearly see that our shots were taking effect."[9]

The plunging rifle fire caught the Confederates at the tail end of their march to the flank. Fulkerson's Virginians were generally spared, for his two regiments had pulled back to a supporting position. Taylor's Louisianans bore the brunt of the bullets from the Hoosier rifles. General Taylor recalled artillery harassing his moving column with a fire that "became close and fatal." This was confirmed by a soldier in Fulkerson's brigade, who revealed that "cannon shots almost took our hats off" during the march. A member of the Eighth Louisiana, marching in front, noted it was the first time he witnessed his men wounded in battle; he also noted another "first": "I felt different from anything I had ever felt before." Despite the mounting casualties, Taylor flew into a profanity-laden rage after watching his men duck their heads to escape the maelstrom, but at the same time he acknowledged that "many men fell."[10]

Indeed they did. Scores of Louisianans were ripped up by small arms fire. Oddly, the Pelican State soldiers did not stop to return fire, at least with any precision; Colonel Colgrove's troops would suffer fewer than twenty battle losses for the day. The Indiana soldiers' advantageous position made it easy for them to surprise the rebels. One Northerner compared it to "the pot shooting of quails," alluding to how hunters could fire into a covey of the game birds. "Some dropped all in a heap," wrote another; "some turned half way round and fell side ways, some fell forward, some backward, some fell prone on the ground, while others caught themselves on their hands."[11]

The pot-shooting advantage of the Indiana troops was short lived. As soon as Taylor reached his designated position, he deployed his men from column into double line of battle. The shoulder-to-shoulder formation extended for more than one thousand yards flank to flank. The fog had lifted; the formation was in full view of the two regiments now facing them. Fulkerson's brigade bookended the formation, the Thirty-seventh Virginia on the right (south) and the Tenth Virginia wedging off the northern flank, closed in by a stone wall on their left. This stone wall ran uphill from a farm lane that traversed the countryside one mile west of Winchester, connecting the Cedar Creek Grade Road with the Northwest Turnpike.[12]

Close to the eastern end of this wall stood the right flank of Colonel Murphy's Twenty-ninth Pennsylvania Infantry, who marched past the Hoosiers before stopping at this position. Their formation ran southeast from this eastward running wall; the Twenty-seventh Indiana stood at the fence slightly southeast of the Pennsylvanians and perhaps 150 yards from Taylor's men. With these nine hundred blue-clad soldiers opposing him, Taylor ordered his men to charge.[13]

Perhaps as many as two thousand Louisianans launched from the woods (Taylor kept the Seventh Louisiana in reserve). The Sixth and Ninth Louisiana formed the right wing of the line; the Eighth Louisiana and a portion of Wheat's battalion brought up Taylor's left flank. The left immediately expected a tough contest for the crest of Bowers Hill. A regiment ahead of them, "behind a rock fence," opened on them. This was likely the Twenty-ninth Pennsylvania, which raked the regiment much like the Hoosiers had ten minutes earlier. "For a moment the enemy seemed to stagger," reported a Pennsylvania captain, "but only for a moment." General Taylor benefited from a Union miscue. Just as the Twenty-seventh Indiana was prepared to join the Pennsylvanians in an infantry clash, the lieutenant colonel of the Indiana regiment, Abishya L. Morrison, ordered the men to about-face and march to the rear![14]

Colonel Colgrove was on foot and positioned to the right of the regiment, linking with the Pennsylvanians by convincing Colonel Murphy to drop his men back twenty paces while Companies A and F

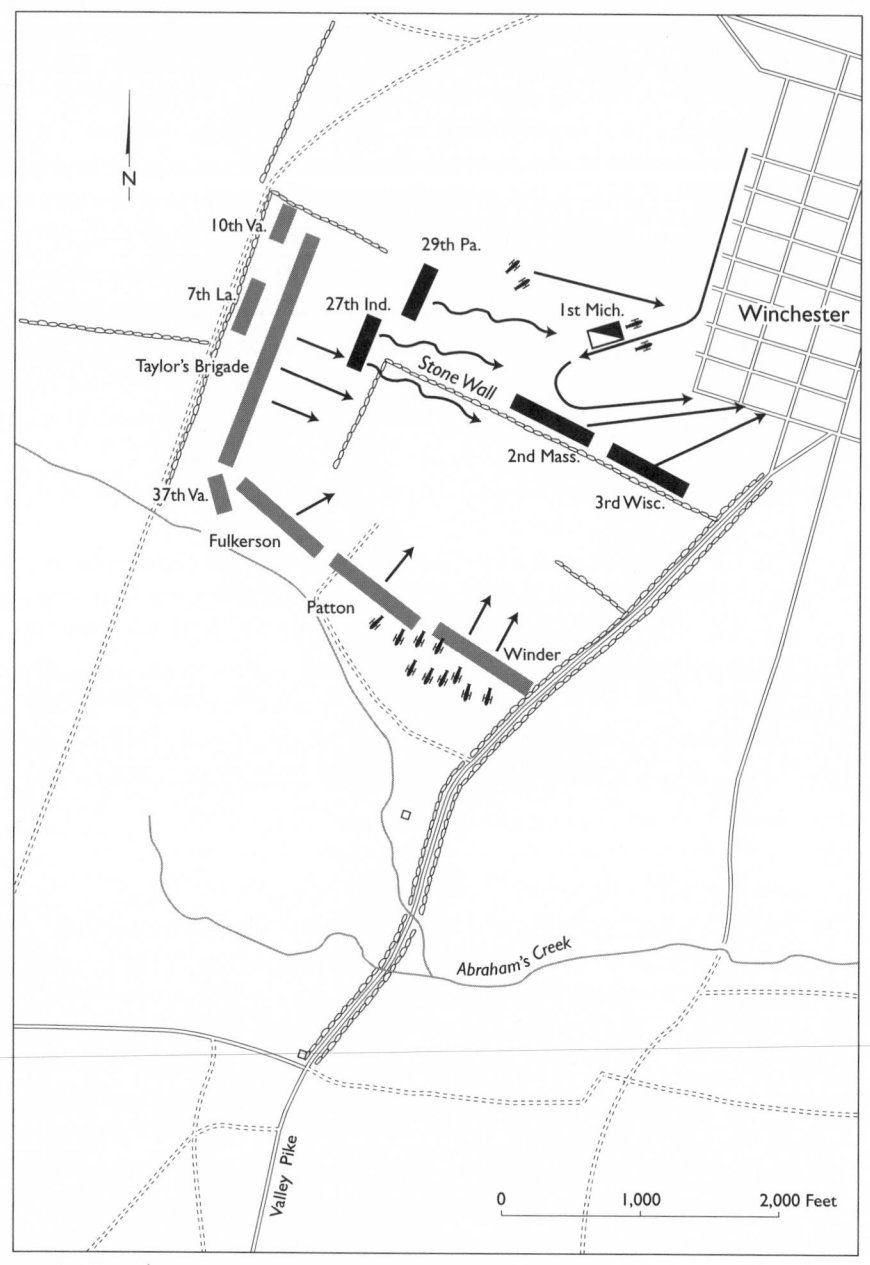

Battle of Winchester: Charge of Taylor's Brigade

of the Twenty-seventh Indiana joined Murphy's men in firing on the Louisianans. After temporarily checking the Eighth Louisiana with the combined volleys, Colgrove turned to his left to find that the remaining eight companies had abandoned them. Colgrove raced up the hillside and brought his command to a halt and quickly reversed them again to face the troops attacking them from the base of the hill.

As Colgrove attempted to correct his regiment's wayward movement, the Twenty-ninth Pennsylvania and the two Hoosier companies with them tried to stem the tide of two thousand Confederate soldiers coming toward them—a daunting task. After observing half the enemy resistance apparently flee the scene, General Taylor sent orders for all his regiments to move forward at the double-quick. A Louisianan told his diary that the faster movement was a relief; still, he recalled, "Many of our men fell in this charge, but we succeeded in routing the enemy without firing a gun."[15]

The Louisianans had no need to fire, for all nine hundred Union men disappeared from their front. Colonel Murphy refused to stay in his position with both flanks unprotected; so—with thousands of Confederates renting the air with the "rebel yell"—he ordered his regiment to retire. Up the rocky slope from Murphy, Colonel Colgrove not only succeeded in turning his regiment around, but he got them to commence firing again. This ended when Lieutenant Colonel Morrison found his colonel and told Colgrove that the order to give up the position came from Colonel Gordon, through the brigade commander's aide-de-camp, Lt. Henry B. Scott.

When Colonel Gordon learned about the reason for the retreat, he was incredulous. Insisting that he never sent such an order, Gordon later queried the direct source—Lieutenant Scott—about what order he delivered. Gordon's aide-de-camp also denied delivering the retreat order. The issue was never resolved. After receiving written reports from the Indiana and Pennsylvania regiments implicating his aide as the source of misinformation, Gordon added an addendum to the reports: "The statement that Lieutenant-Colonel Morrison received the order to retire from Lieutenant Scott is incorrect, as has been proved to the satisfaction of Lieutenant-Colonel Morrison."[16]

Assuming Colonel Gordon was factual regarding the order and Lieutenant Colonel Morrison's response, it did not meet the satisfaction of the rest of the Twenty-seventh Indiana. What order did Lieutenant Scott intend to deliver? According to a member of the Hoosier

regiment who spoke with Silas Colgrove, the colonel believed that
Gordon intended the regiment to change fronts to the other side of the
ridge to more effectively oppose the broad-flanked column approaching
them. But neither Scott nor Gordon made a confirming statement for
the public record. More problematic for Lieutenant Scott was his failure to deliver the order to the commander of the regiment, exacerbating
the confusion within the ranks of the Twenty-seventh Indiana.[17]

Lieutenant Colonel Morrison shockingly took it upon himself to
retire the regiment without telling his commanding officer. (He probably could not find him as Colgrove was dismounted and at the right
of the regiment rather than mounted thirty-five paces behind the
battle line as indicated by textbook tactical protocol.) So by the time
Colgrove thought he had rectified the situation, he saw the Twenty-
ninth Pennsylvania scale the hill toward his right, followed by the
vast column of Louisiana soldiers pacing toward him in well-formed
ranks. Colgrove felt he had no choice but to continue the withdrawal.
Like dominoes the Massachusetts and Wisconsin soldiers peeled
away from their lines and dropped down eastward toward Winchester. Notwithstanding the stubborn and obstinate defense they displayed for three and one-half hours, the subsequent fifteen minutes
stained an otherwise solid performance on Bowers Hill, one in which
to this point 180 casualties had been inflicted on Confederate soldiers
at the cost of fewer than 80 on Union infantry. General Hatch's analysis to his father shed light on the misleading characterization of
Banks's fight that would prevail: "Our troops did not do very well."[18]

Union high command quickly attempted to fill the void caused
by the mass infantry evacuation of Bowers Hill. General Williams
watched the leading retreating elements of Gordon's brigade descend
the hill as he rode out of Winchester to inspect the position at 8:15
A.M. Banks sent his adjutant, Capt. William D. Wilkins, up the hill to
rally retreating elements. Wilkins succeeded only with three companies of Indiana soldiers, directing them behind a stone wall just
below the crest of the hill. General Williams detached one of his staff
officers to rally a portion of the Third Wisconsin to occupy another
stone wall closer to town. Both Banks and Williams rode to and fro,
pleading with fleeing infantry to rally.

Failing to turn anyone around, Williams rode to the right at the
western edge of Winchester where he found a squadron of cavalry—
more specifically, four companies of the First Michigan Cavalry,

commanded by the major of the regiment, Charles H. Town. He had performed well during the retreat from Strasburg the day previous, and General Williams—appreciating the zeal Major Town exuded— ordered the spirited major to lead his two hundred men to the top of the hill and, if possible, charge the Louisianans who had begun to marching uphill. Town galloped to the crest with his command, the only organized body of Union troops on Bowers Hill. Closing within one hundred yards from them was Taylor's attacking line of four regiments and battalion. Seeing the sudden appearance of the cavalry fronting his left flank, Taylor ordered Lt. Col. Francis T. Nicholls, commanding the Eighth Louisiana, to withhold his flank companies in an effort to refuse the marching left flank.

Nicholls ordered the regiment to fire—the first volley fired by Taylor's men during the charge. General Williams was caught in the volley as he stayed with the Michigan cavalry to view the position of the Southerners. "The air seemed literally to be full of whizzing bullets," wrote Williams to his daughter. Although the general was fortunate to escape injury, the Louisiana volley emptied at least a dozen saddles, perhaps as many as twenty. Major Town decided that to charge the Confederate flank was suicide; he wisely ordered his men off the hill. General Williams spurred his horse and also fled the hill.[19]

The Louisiana brigade—sans the Seventh Regiment—surged forward, accompanied by the Tenth Virginia of Fulkerson's brigade. All of the military obstacles in their path to and over the crest of Bowers Hill were gone, except for one section of artillery. Barely five minutes elapsed between the misguided departure of the Twenty-seventh Indiana and that of the four companies of First Michigan Cavalry. General Jackson would later commend how Gordon's infantry "preserved their organization remarkably well" when they abandoned Bowers Hill. But the two westernmost sections of Battery M of the First New York Light Artillery required time to limber up. Ordered to fire two rounds of canister from each cannon, they complied, but one section was almost too late. Artillerist Leander Davis confessed to his wife, "I come near losing my piece by their charge. I gave canister shots. . . . They got within eight rods [about forty-five yards] when I gave my parting gift which killed about 30 or 40 of the rebs." Although he overestimated the destruction caused by his "parting gift," the New York artillerist did account for the first casualties suffered by the Louisianans while scaling the ridge.[20]

The artillerists limbered and rode down the hill toward Winchester. By 8:15 A.M., the Louisianans owned the hill, accomplished before they reached the crest and by firing only one volley. General Taylor rode in front holding his uplifted sword, occasionally turning in his saddle to inspect the integrity of his line. He did not need to do so, for his men marched in perfect order. As they neared the crest in double-quick step, Taylor bellowed the order to charge. Col. Henry B. Kelly of the Eighth Louisiana Infantry declared, "This was done in a style that elicited the admiration of all who witnessed it, including General Jackson."[21]

Colonel Kelly spoke well for the witnesses, for it was a magnificent sight, one that embedded into the minds of all who witnessed it. No soldiers enjoyed a better view of the charge than the Virginians in Jackson's division, particularly those on the southern rim of Bowers Hill. "This charge of Taylor's was the grandest I saw during the war," declared Sergeant John H. Worsham of the Twenty-first Virginia Infantry. "There was all the pomp and circumstance of war about it that was always lacking in our charges." A member of the Stonewall Brigade captured the stirring ten minutes in his diary entry for May 25: "We peep over the rifle pits and lo! The Louisiana Brigade is coming up on our left. Steadily and in unbroken column they advance through a storm of rifle balls and cannon shot. . . . Nothing can withstand the impetuous charge of Taylors [sic] Brigade."[22]

General Winder, the consummate professional, did what he could to support Taylor's awesome charge. When he saw Peabody's battery spew canister at close range, Winder tried to suppress the sections with the Rockbridge Artillery, but Poague's battery was too shot up; not enough horses existed to move the Confederate guns into an advantageous position. Relieved to see that his artillery support was unnecessary to protect the Louisianans, Winder sensed the importance of magnifying the charge and chasing down the Union infantry. He called forward all his available infantry to conduct a secondary assault from the south.[23]

No single person was more caught up in the moment than Stonewall Jackson. Often known to display anger, Jackson rarely indicated the other extreme—happiness, excitement, and exhilaration—to members of his staff. At 8:15 A.M. on Bowers Hill, Jedediah Hotchkiss sat on his horse at Jackson's side; he was treated to a rare show of emotion by his commanding general. The sight and sounds of Taylor's performance, all playing out in front of him, captured Jackson's spirit unlike any previous battle scene of the war. As he watched Taylor's men confront Union infantry, cavalry, and artillery, Hotchkiss turned to stare at Jackson raising both hands above him, as if he were seeking divine intervention. When the opposition peeled away from the Louisianans, Jackson pulled the gray cap from his head. "Now," announced Jackson, gesticulating and swinging his cap at his fellow Virginians, "Let's shout."[24]

Shout they did, and much more. Renting the air with the rebel yell, the division infantry caught their leader's spirit. "After the enemy, men!" Jackson yelled, piqued with excitement. "And all dashed forward in pursuit," raved Hotchkiss to his wife, capturing a moment with his pen that he would limn again with the same electricity thirty-three years later. From a different angle they swept the crest already attained by the Louisianans. The meager resistance offered by three companies of Indiana troops clinging to the wall near the crest melted away. The last military obstacle before Winchester was a remnant of Wisconsin troops. They held out until General Winder got a single gun from Cutshaw's battery deployed on the hill and facing Winchester. The two or three rounds thrown at Colonel Ruger's Badgers convinced them the time was up. They fired a final time before peeling away from the wall. One of the Yankee bullets shattered the elbow of Colonel Nicholls, damaging his arm so much as to require amputation. Maj. Arthur McArthur of the Sixth Louisiana was even more unfortunate. He was struck at the helm of his command by the same Wisconsin volley; a bullet entered his skull upward through his bearded chin, killing him instantly.[25]

The Union collapse on Bowers Hill portended a catastrophe for Banks's army—not only for Colonel Gordon's men trying to escape through Winchester but also for Colonel Donnelly's brigade, now threatened in front and on flank. General Banks sent an aide to Donnelly, ordering him to retreat immediately. By the time he received this order, Donnelly was facing a horrific barrage from Courtney's guns. In a moment of rhetorical flourish, General Trimble officially reported: "For half an hour the fire exchanged between these batteries was incessant and well directed on both sides, displaying a scene surpassing interest and grandeur on that sunny but far from peaceful Sabbath." Donnelly extricated his battery and infantry and hustled into town as Ewell's batteries took advantage of the clear field of vision to send shells screaming toward them. Trimble's brigade had just begun to work on the Union left flank, marching northward east of Winchester. Trimble later took a swipe at General Ewell when he reported that the movement started much later than he proposed it, due to nebulous causes discussed between superior and subordinate. "Had this movement been permitted half an hour sooner...," insisted Trimble, "the retreat of the enemy's reserves would have been completely cut off."[26]

Sunday mornings in Winchester would never again be as dramatic as what transpired beginning at 8:30 A.M. on May 25. The last troops to strike the streets of Winchester, Donnelly's men conducted an orderly retreat through the town. They hustled down Kent Street and Cameron Street, two parallel avenues on the eastern side of town that carried the Union men northward through the ten city blocks of Winchester to the macadamized Martinsburg Pike. Already on the pike and past Martinsburg was Banks's supply train, five hundred wagons afforded a four-hour head start from the battle.

The seventeen hundred infantrymen and artillerists from Donnelly's brigade skirted through with relative ease, for they escaped a flank strike by Jackson's men from the west and were chased through town by only a small portion of Ewell's command. The First (CSA) Maryland Infantry entered the town from the southeast but were several minutes behind Donnelly's brigade and were unable to disrupt the Union retreat. But the Marylanders received a greeting they would never forget. One year removed from the event, Colonel Johnson clearly was still affected by it all, as indicated by his enthusiastic description: "Down the street we went, cheering like mad, and open flew doors and windows, old men, women, and children rushed out, dressed and undressed in their Sunday clothes, and in their night clothes, hurrahing, crying, laughing, screaming.[27]

Donnelly's brigade's relatively quick and smooth-flowing trek through Winchester was not duplicated by the forces in Gordon's brigade filing through the western side of town. These troops were more heavily and closely pressed and were forced to filter through several east–west avenues before they could turn left on Market or Loudoun streets to gain access to the Martinsburg Pike. Their confusion about Winchester's layout hindered their attempt to escape.

The Union troops also were forced to withstand unexpected Confederate reinforcements in the form of Winchester's civilian population. These citizens were by and large strongly secession-minded women (only fifty households in the city were known to harbor pro-Union sympathies). Although the secessionists had endured ten weeks of Union occupation, the most recent six weeks of Union control was by one regiment of provost while the rest of Banks's army had toiled more than twenty miles south of Winchester. With Banks's remaining army in Winchester's environs for the last twelve hours, it was only natural that the citizenry would lend a hand in their liberation. Perched in the upper floors of their houses and public buildings, as well as on a few street corners, the civilians were armed and dangerous. They shot at Gordon's foot soldiers and artillerists scurrying down and across the roads seeking safety. When the citizens read of this charge by Union officers in their after-battle reports, they vehemently denied these rumors, insulted by the low characterization of their Victorian principles. "They tell the most infamous lies about the Winchester ladies," complained Cornelia Wilson to her brother upon reading the reports. "Swear that we all shot at them from our windows. . . . There was not a gun fired by a lady in town."[28]

The evidence suggests otherwise. Few Civil War–era controversies accumulated as many contemporary, first-hand accounts as did this one. No fewer than sixty-four soldiers registered their observations and complaints against the gun-toting women and civilian men of Winchester. The testimony is locked in posterity in a variety of contemporary accounts: letters, diaries, after-battle reports, and in a special investigation by the U.S. government entitled "Outrages performed by. . ." Clearly, many of the testimonies were embellished; others were complete fabrications. However, two soldiers were positively identified as killed by a citizen of Winchester, including Pvt. Andrew Johnson of the Third Wisconsin Infantry. Lt. Robert Gould Shaw of the Second Massachusetts Infantry revealed his animus to Winchester's citizens when he complained about the incident to his mother: "The inhabitants did their share from the windows—women as well as men. I hope that town will be destroyed when we go back there. We had time to burn part of it while the fight was going on."[29]

The fires burning during the retreat through the town were indeed set by Union soldiers, on direct order to burn the supplies that could not be carried away. They torched the buildings used by the Union Commissary, but the fire inadvertently spread to civilian homes. Before it was controlled and eventually extinguished, five homes were destroyed or damaged. The fire was in full flaming fury during the Union retreat. One of the citizens noted the surrealism, "The fire was burning furiously but no one seemed to notice it."[30]

A street fight ensued in Winchester as soldier fired at opposing soldier. Several casualties were inflicted in the town, but most of these were captures. Scores and scores of blue-clad soldiers were rounded up, either chased down in their confusion or forced to surrender when no other viable option remained. No discrimination between rank and file could be detected as ample representatives from both classes of the Union army were taken prisoners of war. The top prize for the Confederates was a colonel, the elderly John K. Murphy of the Twenty-ninth Pennsylvania. Forced to flee into Winchester on his sixty-five-year-old legs, Colonel Murphy had little chance to outrun foot soldiers forty to fifty years his junior.[31]

The next highest-ranking capture was Maj. Wilder Dwight, the Second Massachusetts second in command who had performed so admirably from Bartonsville on May 24 to Bowers Hill on May 25. True to form, he was heading out of town to safety when he stopped to carry a wounded comrade to a house. After he placed the injured man in bed, Dwight explained the circumstances of his capture: "I then turned to go out, but the butternut soldiery were all around the house, and I quietly sat down." He was escorted to the center of town to the Taylor Hotel, under the charge of Col. Bradley Johnson of the First (CSA) Maryland Infantry. Looking across the street to the courthouse, he saw the fenced-in courtyard teeming with fellow POWs.[32]

Both captor and captive bore witness to the effects of the Confederate victory on Winchester's civilian populace. Major Dwight saw Confederate flags displayed everywhere: "the town was full of soldiers and rejoicing." The soldiers were exhilarated by the ecstatic citizens. The near unanimous consensus was that it was the most exciting event of their lives. A rare voice of dissent came from an angry soldier in the Twenty-first Virginia Infantry, too consumed by hostilities and suspicions to enjoy the moment. "I think Winchester is a very 'fishy' place," he opined to his father the following day, expressing disappointment. "I saw too many men wearing citizen's clothes & feel a most intense desire to run against some of them & knock them in the gutter."[33]

No curmudgeon could crash this Sunday morning party, for it was a singular moment for patriots of the Confederacy. "I cannot describe the beaming countenances and the congratulations passed between citizens," raved a Winchester resident. A Louisiana soldier exclaimed, "The ladies seemed so well pleased that I really believe I lost several kisses by not stopping for them." General Jackson remained as excited as he did on Bowers Hill, due to the reaction he received in Winchester. "I do not remember having ever seen such rejoicing as was manifested by the people of Winchester," he tried to explain to his wife. ". . .The people seemed nearly frantic with joy; indeed, it would be almost impossible to describe their manifestations of rejoicing and gratitude. Our entrance into Winchester was one of the most stirring scenes of my life."[34]

Jackson passed through the frenzy, his arousal piqued by the sights and sounds of jubilation. He trotted to the northern sector of Winchester as Jedediah Hotchkiss rode ahead of him. The time passed 9:00 A.M. as Hotchkiss trotted down the Martinsburg Pike. "I soon discovered," Hotchkiss recalled, "that we were rapidly approaching the rear of the retreating army." Hotchkiss galloped back to Stonewall, informing him that no Confederate troops were in front of them. Keeping with the mission General Lee telegraphed to him nine days earlier, Jackson had accomplished the first section—"Whatever movement you make against Banks do it speedily"—with stunning success. Jackson used the next line of Lee's message as his new command order. Jackson turned to Hotchkiss and said, "Order the whole army to press on to the Potomac."[35]

Jackson's troops followed in his path and quick-stepped down the turnpike out of Winchester toward Martinsburg. The spirit was willing, but their bodies could no longer function. Too many consecutive days of marching and not eating or sleeping had caused the army to break down. As was the case at Front Royal, the Confederate infantry could not decide the issue. Watching his dilapidated infantry tire early in the pursuit north of town, Jackson realized he would need his cavalry to run down Union infantry. But neither of his two cavalry commands were with him.[36]

At Front Royal Lt. Col. Thomas Flournoy's Confederate horse soldiers—outnumbered fivefold—had annihilated fleeing infantry in dramatic fashion. The same body of troops, under the command of Brig. Gen. George Steuart, then succeeded at disrupting the Union train and supplying Jackson with valuable intelligence concerning Banks's retreat route on May 24. Since then, Jackson had relied on

Ashby's Seventh Virginia Cavalry and railed against its performance, believing it failed him on May 24 in the late-afternoon wagon plunder at Middletown and during the night-long pursuit from Newtown to Kernstown. Steuart's men succeeded; Ashby's men failed. The decision for Jackson at 9:00 A.M. on May 25 was not difficult to make.

Lt. Alexander S. "Sandie" Pendleton, Jackson's top aide and essentially his assistant adjutant general, galloped from Stonewall's side back to Winchester with verbal orders for General Steuart: "to move as rapidly as possible and join me on the Martinsburg turnpike, and carry on the pursuit of the enemy with vigor." Pendleton believed it was 10:00 A.M. when he left Jackson (it was at least half an hour earlier), and it took him perhaps half an hour to find Steuart's cavalry, which he accomplished two and one-half miles east of Winchester on the Berryville Pike. Pendleton's odyssey continued when Lieutenant Colonel Flournoy refused to accept the order unless it came from General Steuart who was not with the men at the time. This consumed several more minutes, but Pendleton likely thought the frustration was over when he delivered Jackson's order directly to Steuart. But Steuart continued to dismay the young aide by refusing to act on Jackson's directive without the consent of General Ewell, his immediate superior. Pendleton remonstrated that Jackson's order "was peremptory and immediate," but attempted to appease Steuart by promising to inform Ewell of the cavalry mission after they departed.

Pendleton rode southwestward two miles out to General Ewell and informed him that Steuart had taken the cavalry by Jackson's order, but that Ewell must write out his consent for Steuart's satisfaction. (Ewell expressed surprise that Steuart insisted on this protocol.) With General Ewell's written consent in hand, Lieutenant Pendleton rode back onto the Berryville Pike. Here, he was stunned to see that General Steuart and his cavalry had not ridden out to General Jackson. Immensely irritated, Pendleton showed Steuart the order and stayed to make sure that they finally departed down a byroad toward Stephenson's Depot, two miles north of Winchester. By the time Pendleton arrived at the destination, the time passed 11:00 A.M. More than ninety minutes had elapsed from the issuance of the order to its delivery and subsequent compliance, a costly waste of at least half an hour considering that the cavalry was no more than three miles away from Jackson and could have been at his side in half that time.[37]

Jackson had called a halt to his infantry shortly after sending

Lieutenant Pendleton away. They no longer pursued Banks's men, who were flying north at a pace of four miles per hour. Notwithstanding their orderly retreat from Bowers Hill, Gordon's brigade appeared panic-stricken as it fled down the pike toward Martinsburg. This was not surprising, given the melee they had escaped in Winchester. Now, five miles out of town and fearing a potential cavalry charge from behind, Banks found ground where he could make a stand, only to realize a significant portion of his army was inconsolable. Failing to rally a horde of Wisconsin men, Banks vented his frustration at them. "My God, men, don't you love your country?" postured the general. "Yes," came the reply from one who refused to stop, "and I am trying to get to it as fast as I can."[38]

General Banks was able to rally most of his army with the sound of approaching reinforcements. But the help turned out to be a mere two squadrons of First (USA) Maryland Cavalry. Although their approach instilled a little élan in the men, it was not sufficient for Banks to stay and make a stand. He proceeded to Martinsburg. His main column continued to advance on the Martinsburg Pike, but because of the disorganization in Winchester, Union troops fled on at least two other roads as well. Hundreds scurried on the Pughtown Road, heading toward the Potomac River via Unger's Store and Hancock (This included troops who were still cut off from the main body back on May 24.) Still others took a more northeasterly route through Charlestown and Harpers Ferry.[39]

Jackson's cavalry started its pursuit during the final hour of the morning of March 25. The delay was costly, but another unexpected impediment stifled their progress. Not only did Banks's men flee Winchester, but so did the refugees—mostly African Americans, and most of them escaped slaves. As Shields's infirmed men had tied up Steuart's cavalry on May 24, so did the fleeing blacks from Winchester on May 25. In addition to the blacks, additional scores of fleeing infantry were rounded up; in all Jackson's infantry and cavalry captured more than one thousand soldiers after the battle ended. An additional 750 infirm Union soldiers stayed behind in the huge hospital Banks had set up in town. All told, for the Battle of Winchester, Jackson's army had killed, wounded, and captured nearly 2,000 Union soldiers at the cost of only 350 Confederate casualties.

Notwithstanding the stunning success, Jackson had expected much more. The heart of Banks's army was escaping, with most of their wagons, and Jackson had little left to punch through this. His infantry was too fatigued to do anything, Steuart's cavalry was too small to inflict significant damage, and Ashby's cavalry was scattered and unaccounted for. "I had seen but 50 of Ashby's cavalry since prior to the pillaging scenes of the previous evening," Jackson seethed. He insisted, "There is good reason for believing that, had the cavalry played its part in this pursuit as well as the four companies had done under Colonel Flournoy two days before . . . but a small portion of Banks's army would have made its escape to the Potomac." Finally seeing Ashby in the early afternoon, Jackson queried him as to why he was absent at the close of the battle. Ashby responded he was working east of Winchester to flank Banks's left.[40]

Banks became the beneficiary of Confederate miscues at the most opportune time. He had yet to realize that more than one-quarter of his army was hors de combat, but he did know that five hundred supply wagons continued to roll in front of him. Four thousand Union soldiers, on three different avenues, headed toward the Potomac River. Among his other responsibilities was to notify the U.S. War Department. He had sent a courier northward at the close of the battle to inform his superiors that he was retreating, a message received in Washington—ostensibly by telegraph from Harpers Ferry—before 11:00 A.M. Banks had not personally communicated with Washington since midnight. The next opportunity was dependent on telegraph operations to communicate.

Banks rode into Martinsburg at 2:30 P.M. He was now twenty miles from Winchester. He found a telegraph operator there and wired Secretary Stanton a brief report of the Winchester battle and subsequent retreat. He assured the secretary, "Our trains are in advance, and will cross the river to safety." To make sure, Banks did what he proved to be his only real consistent achievement as a field commander: establish a rear guard to delay the enemy while the advance continued its retreat. As the wagons continued to roll, the army remained in Martinsburg until 5:00 P.M. They then proceeded to the Potomac, across from Williamsport, Maryland. There would be no assaults upon the train or army during the twelve-mile trek.[41]

At the U.S. War Department, President Lincoln and Secretary Stanton endured a second long and uneasy day at the telegraph office. The two juggled two functions: gaining information from General Rufus Saxton and General Geary, and coordinating the transfer of troops from Baltimore to Harpers Ferry, from Frémont's Mountain Department into the Valley, and from General McDowell's army at Falmouth directly to the Valley by the route of the Manassas Gap Railroad and indirectly by sending one brigade to Harpers Ferry. They also called on states close to the northern Valley to send out their militia. For Lincoln, this was his most active role as commander in chief. He had changed Frémont's direction from the planned campaign to eastern Tennessee, and more significantly, he rerouted all but one-fifth of McDowell's force, which remained at Falmouth with no plans to join McClellan on the Peninsula.[42]

Lincoln well knew that General McClellan had been expecting McDowell's army to reinforce him in front of Richmond. (That had been the plan as late as the midafternoon of the previous day.) Although Banks had wired a dispatch from Martinsburg in the afternoon of May 25, two hours later Lincoln still had not received it and was yet to be assured that Banks had really escaped. By ordering in excess of forty thousand troops to the Valley and Harpers Ferry, he had overreacted to Jackson's presence, perhaps believing Geary's wild estimates of Jackson's strength. He must have understood twenty-four hours after issuing the orders that altered grand strategy in Virginia that sending these troops out to Banks's aid was never going to help the general, for these men could not possibly trod into the Valley for several days. He also convinced himself, perhaps after discussing the matter with Secretary Stanton, that his response to Jackson's presence was not playing into the hands of war planners in Richmond. So, with a full day of hindsight, Lincoln decided to use his decision as a showdown with McClellan.[43]

At 5:00 P.M. on May 25, Lincoln wired McClellan with a summary of what they knew and did not know about Jackson's operation against Banks. He admitted to his top general that he did not know what strength the Confederates possessed in the northern Valley. He also believed General Geary's exaggerated intelligence that Confederate threats extended out of the Valley to Leesburg and the Manassas Gap Railroad from the north and south. He went on to assess that because of the enormity and character of the Southern offensive, it could not be a mere decoy for "the purpose of a very desperate defence of Richmond." Lincoln concluded his communiqué: "I think the time is near when you must either attack Richmond or give up the job and come to the defence of Washington."[44]

General McClellan was in the process of writing a letter to his wife when Lincoln's message was handed to him. He interrupted his letter to answer the president immediately. He informed Lincoln that two of his corps were between the Chickahominy and Richmond—six miles from the capital—with the rest of his army ready to cross with the completion of the bridges. He also corrected Lincoln's assessment about the reason for the Southern Valley offensive: "The object of the enemy's movement is probably to prevent reinforcements being sent to me." McClellan assured Lincoln that, independent of the president's attempt to prod him, "the time is very near when I shall attack Richmond."[45]

McClellan fumed at Lincoln's telegram and did his best to suppress his rage in his immediate response. But Lincoln's words and deeds irritated him to the core. McClellan was astounded at how the president overreacted to Jackson's assault on Banks, and how this overreaction had likely played into the plans of the Confederate War Department. He knew that the administration in Washington had not been happy with the pace of the campaign on the Peninsula, but he also knew that since the beginning of the war he had not failed in any campaign he personally superintended in the state of Virginia. Returning to his letter to his wife, McClellan could no longer control the animus he felt at the interference with the operation he presently had been conducting. "It is perfectly sickening to deal with such people & you may rest assured that I will lose as little time as possible in breaking off all connection with them," ranted McClellan. "I get more sick of them every day—for every day brings with it only additional proofs of their hypocrisy, knavery & folly."[46]

General Jackson had absolutely no idea how dramatically his offensive against Banks had altered the plans of the U.S. War Department. Three weeks earlier, he admitted that his lack of knowledge about operations outside his district prevented him from authoring grand strategy, leaving General Lee and the Confederate War Department in charge of war plans. Jackson only knew on the afternoon of May 25 that he had performed the mission Lee sent to him on May 16. Banks had been swept away speedily and driven to the Potomac. He had one portion of the mission to accomplish: "create the impression, as far as practicable, that you design threatening that line [of the Potomac River]." Unaware that that was already happening, Jackson planned on sending his army to the river, but that would have to wait;

his entire department was in no condition to move. The army needed rest, as did their commander. A soldier in his division saw him that day. "He was so fatigued," observed the Virginian "that, after the fight, he actually went to sleep on his charger."[47]

Jackson's fatigue had appeared to affect him in the early morning hours of that Sunday morning, when he intended on sending General Ewell back to Strasburg to counter a nonexistent threat, thus potentially removing his right-hand force for the Battle of Winchester. By the afternoon of May 25, the surge of adrenaline released from the excitement of battle and the frenzy of its aftermath had dissipated. Unlike his opponent, Jackson chose to wait before sending a campaign summary to his respective War Department. He had not communicated with Richmond since May 21, and he would not communicate with them on May 25. Instead, the weary victor entered his room in the Taylor Hotel and—while the citizens of the town he liberated continued to celebrate—he disappeared for the remainder of the day.

Epilogue

The military news emanating from the Shenandoah Valley stunned Washington on May 23 and continued to disorient the capital for the next two days. After fighting and retreating for fifty-five miles in thirty-six hours, Banks crossed his remaining army unmolested into Williamsport, Maryland, on the morning of May 26. By the middle of that day, the U.S. War Department not only was more at ease about his predicament but was also encouraged by the gathering force concentrating at Harpers Ferry to block any potential threat posed by Jackson from the Valley. They prepared for good news to generate from the Valley once Frémont's and McDowell's armies entered into the mountain corridor before the end of the week.

The ripples of Jackson's grand achievements did not permeate Richmond until late on Monday, May 26. The Valley victories infused hope into a beleaguered capital starving for victories. The news also appeared to have hobbled the grand Union offensive on Richmond. Expecting McDowell's presence from the north, the Confederate War Department was relieved to see no sign of his formidable army. By May 28 General Lee was so encouraged by McDowell's absence that he sent Jackson a short dispatch that encouraged a daring and aggressive continuation of his mission. "We rejoice at your brilliant success," wired Lee to Jackson. "If you can make demonstrations on Maryland and

Washington, it will add to its great results." This telegram and a similar one received from General Johnston shortly afterward strongly indicated giving Jackson permission to carry the campaign over the Potomac and onto Northern soil.[1]

General Lee was thrilled that Jackson not only had accomplished the parameters of his mission but had exceeded them. For Jackson did not just drive the Union army to the Potomac; he effectively forced Banks to cross that river. Sending the suggestion for an offensive across the Potomac demonstrated that the Confederate War Department had no idea of the internal obstacles Jackson had to overcome to complete his mission in the northern Shenandoah Valley. Perhaps some of the obstacles were ones Jackson himself did not fully comprehend. Discipline in his army had been so lax as to allow incredibly high rates of desertion in three weeks—more than fifty percent in his own division. His cavalry performed poorly on May 24–25, his artillery never suppressed the guns of the opposition, and his infantry never overpowered an outnumbered and inexperienced opponent in a stand-up fight. This is especially true for the action on Bowers Hill. All the grandeur associated with the May 25 charge of the Louisianans fails to conceal the fact that Taylor's brigade stormed a nearly abandoned height.

Other factors impeded Jackson. His staff committed critical errors affecting battlefield performance and intelligence gathering. General Ewell was unspectacular and unsteady, allowing his opponent to outnumber his offensives at Front Royal and Winchester. General Taylor's good day at Winchester at best neutralized his hours-long absence at the Battle of Front Royal. General Winder was the only brigade commander in either Jackson's or Ewell's divisions who consistently excelled in this three-day action. His stellar performance earned Jackson's respect and confidence to handle his entire division, including artillery, on Bowers Hill. Lt. Col. Thomas Flournoy's achievement with Virginia cavalry on May 23 was the only noteworthy performance by a regimental officer in Jackson's army, a feat that failed to prevent Jackson from replacing him the following morning with George Steuart, a general who was of little help to Jackson in the Winchester aftermath on May 25.

Jackson was also beset with personal flaws in his generalship. His tendency for snap and unorthodox decisions, laxity in early morning scouting, confusion at understanding time requirements to transfer vital messages, and lack of appreciation of how fatigue had plagued the efficiency of his command are not usually considered the hall-marks of successful field commanders, particularly when they all occur at the same time in a campaign. Added to this was a serious tactical shortcoming of Jackson's, displayed for the first time in the battles of May 23–25: piecemeal deployment. At Front Royal and Winchester, Jackson's infantry engaged its opponent one regiment at a time until four regiments of Taylor's brigade stormed Bowers Hill at the end of the contest. Although Jackson had seven infantry brigades at his disposal, never during this sustained offensive did he, or General Ewell for that matter, deploy even two of them at once to overwhelm the lone regiment of Union infantry at Front Royal and two brigades of Union infantry at Winchester.

Jackson's tendency to trickle his troops onto battlefields on May 23 and May 25 helps explain how these two seemingly lopsided contests became four- to five-hour affairs. Valley topography sometimes prevented division-sized assaults; however, the landscape south of Winchester and immediately north of Front Royal allowed for the deployment of three to four brigades of infantry in line of battle. Yet Jackson never took advantage of the favorable terrain or his numerical dominance at the point of attack. His tactic is not typical of deployments on Civil War battlefields during March through May 1862. At Shiloh, Williamsburg, and Seven Pines, large-scale deployments were characteristic of Confederate battlefield offensives, but these contests had more troops available than the seven brigades of infantry in Jackson's army. A more appropriate comparison can be made during the first day of the Battle of Pea Ridge (Arkansas) on March 7, 1862, where Maj. Gen. Earl Van Dorn attacked through Cross Timber Hollow with an entire division of his two-division Army of the West to overwhelm a Federal brigade near Elkhorn Tavern. Clearly, these four examples of Confederate tactical offensives indicate that Jackson's piecemeal assaults were not a product of the times.

Nor were they an aberration, for this flaw in Jackson's generalship would be exposed again against opponents he numerically overwhelmed at Port Republic and Brawner's Farm, contests both won by Jackson but each made more difficult by his inability to concentrate en masse on these battlefields. From May 1862 until his untimely death in May 1863, General Jackson never had fewer than two divisions of troops under his command in seven battles in which he directed them on a tactical offensive. In only three of those seven contests did Jackson assault his opponent with more than one brigade at a time.

Jackson overcame his own flaws and those of his subordinates to achieve a grand victory—in Lee's words, a "brilliant success." More remarkable of the victory was that it was achieved against an opponent who did not create many openings for him to exploit between May 23 and May 25. General Banks's decisions and attempts at intelligence gathering after receiving the first information about the defeat at Front Royal were timely and sound, despite insistence to the contrary by his most vocal critics and subordinates. His leadership during the retreat from Strasburg, and subsequently from Winchester, served as glue to hold his army together. His decision to fight on May 25 was reasonable to allow time to roll his supply train to safety. Given the fact that he had an aggressive opponent on his flank and rear on the night of May 23, with battle-tested opposing infantry that outnumbered his own green troops by nearly three to one, it is remarkable that Banks was able to cross the Potomac River on May 26 with more than 80 percent of his supply train and 75 percent of his Strasburg army.

But Banks did commit two costly errors that aided Jackson in his victorious Lower Valley sweep. The greatest error was his decision to send none of his cavalry to cover the mouth of the Luray Valley south of Front Royal in the days leading up to the battle there. Had cavalry been available to Colonel Kenly during the evening of May 22 or at least in the morning of May 23, they could have easily and safely patrolled southward along the Gooney Manor Road, from where they could have gazed upon Jackson's entire army as it tarried for nearly five hours along twelve miles of turnpike below them between Asbury Chapel and Compton's Creek that fateful Friday morning. There would then have been no surprise about Jackson's intentions, and Banks would have learned about the location and strength of the Confederate threat to his flank at least six hours earlier than he did.

Banks's second error was one of tactical deployment during the Winchester battle. The Tenth Maine Infantry was not officially attached to General Williams's division; therefore, it was Banks's responsibility as army commander to insert this regiment into his defense line, particularly when Williams sought reinforcements for Bowers Hill. One must consider the altered or at least delayed outcome of the May 25 battle had eight hundred more infantrymen extended the Union right flank, exactly to the point where Taylor's Louisiana brigade had marched to exploit the opening on the western slope of Bowers Hill. Banks's shortcoming is worsened considering the help available to him. In addition to his and General Williams's staff, Banks had two commissioned generals, Samuel Crawford and George S. Greene, to aid in defensive deployment. Both generals and, unfortunately for Banks, the largest regiment in his army went unused that Sunday morning.

Banks could hardly be considered a tactical genius, but he had the self-awareness to appreciate his own limitations and delegated (perhaps too much) to subordinates more talented to make decisions on the battlefield. Unlike the Confederates, several examples of quality leadership and infantry and artillery performances from May 23 to 25 could be cited on the Union side. Colonel Kenly found himself in an impossible situation on May 23 at Front Royal, but he drew out what should have been an easy Confederate victory into a five-hour marathon (eventually earning a brigadier's star for his performance). Col. George H. Gordon paralleled Kenly's achievement on Bowers Hill, also receiving a general's commission for his leadership. Col. Dudley Donnelly ably handled his small brigade at Winchester. On May 24 Banks's rear guard performed admirably at Newtown. The Second Massachusetts Infantry turned in a consistently outstanding performance, first in slowing Jackson to a crawl between Newtown and Winchester, and again on the crest of Bowers Hill on May 25. The First New York Light Artillery, Battery M, performed so well on Bowers Hill that it not only held three brigades of Confederate infantry at bay, but also outperformed three batteries of artillery deployed against it, even achieving suppression against a section of rifled guns.

Given the numerous deserving accolades for those in Banks's command and the myriad troubles in Jackson's army, the success of the latter can be attributed only to generalship qualities that superseded his interpersonal flaws. Jackson's dominance at maneuver, his refusal to allow obstacles to paralyze his momentum, and his insurmountable determination outshone his tactical shortcomings and split-decision miscues to conquer his adversary and overcome adversity. General Lee and Jefferson Davis were unaware of any of this, nor did they care. They only saw victory and success with Jackson—and to this point, only with Jackson.

It is clear Lee telegraphed instructions to Jackson to demonstrate on Washington buoyed by a combination of Jackson's success and the apparent side effect of that success: holding General McDowell in place at Falmouth. It is equally clear that Lee had no idea that when he sent that May 28 dispatch, the leading brigades of McDowell's army would penetrate the Valley two days after he wrote it, thus jeopardizing Jackson's existence north of the Union entry into the Valley. What is unclear of Lee's dispatch is its true genesis, for one cannot discount President Davis's role in not only permitting but masterminding the notion of Jackson carrying the campaign across the Potomac River.

As uneasy as Davis must have felt about the result of the certain battle that would transpire at the gates of Richmond between the armies of General Johnston and General McClellan, he must have been pleased about the result of Jackson's campaign against Banks, and how it could help give his army a fighting chance against the blue-clad force Lincoln sent to the Peninsula. He must have been equally proud of how the perceived outcomes of Jackson's Valley Campaign coaxed Lincoln to divert more forces into the Valley. This exceeded Confederate expectations when the campaign was first discussed in the middle of April.

President Davis was reminded of that mid-April discussion by reading a late-May letter from his wife. In her missive she congratulated her husband on the success of Jackson's campaign, alluding to her husband's hand involved with the planning of it. "Thank you for congratulations on success of Jackson," Davis responded to his wife. He must have contemplated about the idea that had Jackson conducted the offensive one month earlier, perhaps the capital would not be in jeopardy with the approach of June. He reflected back on the overnight conference of April 14–15, 1862, when he finished his thoughts on Jackson to his wife. "Had the movement been made when I first proposed it, the effect would have been more important," he reasoned. "In the night's long conference it was regarded impossible."[2]

Two days after writing this assessment, President Davis could breathe easier. General Johnston attacked General McClellan on May 31 to initiate the Battle of Fair Oaks. Wounded at the end of the battle day, Johnston was replaced by Gen. Robert E. Lee, who completed the Confederate victory the following day by pushing the Army of the Potomac from the gates of Richmond. Davis would eventually learn that on the same day, June 1, Stonewall Jackson slid his army between two opponents attacking from opposite ends of the Valley. Not only did he escape from two Union armies; he sucked those two commands of Frémont and McDowell into the Valley where they would both be defeated on subsequent days at the Battles of Cross Keys and Port Republic. Perhaps Johnston and Lee would have beaten McClellan even with McDowell secured on the Union flank—a force that would have exceeded one hundred forty thousand officers and men—but to have done so would have ranked it as the greatest victory of the war, considering the disparity of troops deployed.

Thus, the combination of tactical and strategic Confederate success in the Shenandoah Valley from May 23 to 25 has to be considered the heart of the Valley Campaign, for this three-day segment of the campaign imparted the greatest impact beyond the Valley. Although President Jefferson Davis deserves credit for masterminding the notion of using Jackson's offensive to accomplish broader strategy, he was not the man chiefly responsible for Jackson's Valley offensive sustaining benefits for the Confederacy east of the Blue Ridge.

That honor belongs to President Abraham Lincoln. A close and chronological read of all the dispatches sent to and from the War Department on May 24 suggests that his decision to send General McDowell's army to the Shenandoah Valley was at worst flippant, and at best a poorly conceived and exaggerated response to Jackson's presence in the northern Valley. Furthermore, Lincoln's denial that Jackson's campaign in the Valley was planned as a measure to protect Richmond argues against a sound grasp of Confederate strategy. Both in hindsight and foresight, it is difficult to see Lincoln's drastic move as anything but a military blunder performed by the president in his most active role as Commander in Chief.[3]

Ample evidence supports the conclusion that poorly phrased telegrams on May 24 misled the U.S. War Department to believe that Banks was about to be captured or annihilated. Lincoln's noontime assurance to General McDowell that despite the poor news from the Valley, all but two brigades of his army would march to Richmond. This argues against the notion suggested by modern scholarship that he designed an admirable plan to urge McClellan to attack at Richmond by officially holding McDowell's entire force from him. If Lincoln indeed had planned this move, the aforementioned dispatch would likely have been sent purposely to mislead McDowell into believing he was going to Richmond, only to have that order abruptly rescinded six hours later. Thus, this decision by Lincoln could hardly be regarded as reacting admirably to the situation if he planned to mislead two army commanders.[4]

The available evidence argues more strongly that Lincoln's decision to send McDowell away from McClellan and to the Shenandoah Valley was exactly as it appears—a poorly formulated response to Stonewall Jackson's threat against an army whose strength was halved by Lincoln three weeks earlier. How ironic it was that the division leading McDowell's westward trek was that of Brig. Gen. James Shields, the same division that departed from Banks's army on May 16 and induced the Confederate War Department to urge Jackson's offensive.

Whether it was designed or impetuous, Lincoln's response fed into Jefferson Davis's plan and turned the Valley Campaign of 1862 into something even more than a marvel at the operational level of warfare. Nevertheless, the marvel of determined maneuver within the mountain corridor of the Blue Ridge and Alleghenies cannot be overlooked. Despite sloppy tactics and personal miscues, Stonewall Jackson turned the heart of the campaign into a grand Confederate success. The result is more dramatic when one appreciates the state of his army on the evening of May 22, 1862. Dissatisfaction with Jackson's generalship would likely have spread from the rank to the file had Jackson not defeated Banks in three consecutive and near continuous days of battles. Success on the battlefield was vital for the integrity of Jackson's command. Victory they needed; victory they achieved.

Here the legend of Stonewall Jackson was born, based on the contemporary words of his soldiers. "Jackson is completely idolized by this army," claimed a Louisiana soldier to his wife after the Winchester battle. A Marylander took to calling him "my earthly God." General Ewell, who dismissed Jackson as an "enthusiastic fanatic" ten days before the Front Royal battle, admitted to a subordinate less than two weeks after the battle of Winchester that he was so very wrong in his assessment. "I take it all back," he confessed.[5]

Jackson's enemies also took it all back. Perhaps the greatest conversion on the matter of Jackson's abilities from a Northern perspective is evidenced in comments of John Hay, President Lincoln's secretary. In February Hay belittled Stonewall Jackson as "a queer, thick-skulled, blundering, honest dunce." In May Hay appears to have gained respect for him "when Stonewall Jackson was rushing invincible through the Shenandoah, driving the army corps of Banks under the guns of Harper's Ferry." From that point onward, Hay lauded Jackson as "our lively and enterprising contemporary," and believed Washington was never safe with an enemy at large who desired to raise the Confederate flag over the Capitol Building. Hay insisted, "It was certainly a bold and seducing idea to a man of Jackson's character, flushed with constant success, and fanatically sure of his cause."[6]

That was the reaction Jefferson Davis had sought since the middle of April.

ORDER OF BATTLE: MAY 23–25, 1862

CONFEDERATE: VALLEY DISTRICT, DEPARTMENT OF NORTHERN
VIRGINIA, MAJ. GEN. THOMAS J. JACKSON, COMMANDING

Jackson's Division: Maj. Gen. Thomas J. Jackson

First Brigade: Brig. Gen. Charles Winder
    Second Virginia Infantry: Col. James W. Allen
    Fourth Virginia Infantry: Col. Charles A. Ronald
    Fifth Virginia Infantry: Col. William S. H. Baylor
    Twenty-seventh Virginia Infantry: Col. Andrew J. Grigsby
    Thirty-third Virginia Infantry: Col. John F. Neff
    Alleghany Artillery: Capt. Joseph Carpenter
    Rockbridge Artillery: Capt. William T. Poague
Second Brigade: Col. John A. Campbell (wounded, May 25), Col.
John M. Patton
    First Virginia Battalion: Capt. Benjamin W. Leigh
    Twenty-first Virginia Infantry: Col. John M. Patton (Transferred
    to brigade command, May, 25), Lt. Col. Robert H. Cunningham
    Forty-second Virginia Infantry: Maj. Henry Lane (wounded, May
    25), Capt. John E. Penn
    Forty-eighth Virginia Infantry: Maj. John B. Moseley (transferred
    from Twenty-first Virginia, May 25)

Hampden Artillery: Capt. William H. Caskie
Jackson Artillery: Capt. Wilfred E. Cutshaw
Third Brigade: Brig. Gen. William B. Taliaferro (May 23), Col.
Samuel V. Fulkerson (May 24–25)
Tenth Virginia Infantry: Col. Edward T.H. Warren
Twenty-third Virginia Infantry: Col. Alexander G. Taliaferro
Thirty-seventh Virginia Infantry: Col. Samuel V. Fulkerson
(May 23), Maj. Titus V. Williams (May 24–25)
Danville Artillery: Capt. George W. Wooding
Division Cavalry: Brig. Gen. Turner Ashby
Seventh Virginia Cavalry: Brig. Gen. Turner Ashby
Horse Artillery: Capt. Roger P. Chew

Ewell's Division: Maj. Gen. Richard S. Ewell

Second Brigade: Col. William C. Scott
Forty-fourth Virginia Infantry: Maj. Norvell Cobb
Fifty-second Virginia Infantry: Col. Michael G. Harman
Fifty-eighth Virginia Infantry: Col. Samuel H. Letcher
Fourth Brigade: Brig. Gen. Arnold Elzey
Twelfth Georgia Infantry: Col. Zephaniah T. Conner
Thirteenth Virginia Infantry: Col. James A. Walker
Twenty-fifth Virginia Infantry: Col. George H. Smith
Thirty-first Virginia Infantry: Col. John S. Hoffman
Seventh Brigade: Brig. Gen. Isaac R. Trimble
Fifteenth Alabama Infantry: Col. William C. Oates
Sixteenth Mississippi Infantry: Col. Carnot Posey
Twenty-first Georgia Infantry: Col. John T. Mercer
Twenty-first North Carolina Infantry: Col. William W. Kirkland
(wounded, May 25), Maj. Saunders Fulton
Eighth Brigade: Brig. Gen. Richard Taylor
First Special Louisiana Battalion: Maj. Chatham R. Wheat
Sixth Louisiana Infantry: Col. Isaac G. Seymour
Seventh Louisiana Infantry: Col. Harry T. Hays
Eighth Louisiana Infantry: Col. Henry B. Kelly
Ninth Louisiana Infantry: Col. Leroy A. Stafford
Division Cavalry: Lt. Col. Thomas S. Flournoy (May 23), Brig. Gen.
George H. Steuart (May 24–25)
Second Virginia Cavalry (four Companies): Lt. Col. James W.
Watts

Sixth Virginia Cavalry: Col. Thomas S. Flournoy
Maryland Line: Brig. Gen. George H. Steuart
    First Maryland Infantry: Col. Bradley T. Johnson
    Baltimore Light Artillery: Capt. John B. Brockenbrough
Division Artillery: Col. Stapleton Crutchfield
    Henrico Artillery: Capt. Alfred R. Courtney
    Second Rockbridge Artillery: Capt. John M. Lusk
    Lynchburg Artillery: Capt. Charles I. Raine
    Eighth Star Artillery: Capt. Robert S. Rice

UNION: DEPARTMENT OF THE SHENANDOAH,
MAJ. GEN. NATHANIEL P. BANKS, COMMANDING

Front Royal: May 23, 1862

First Maryland Infantry: Col. John R. Kenly
Twenty-Ninth Pennsylvania Infantry (two companies): Lt. Col. Charles Parham
Fifth New York Cavalry (two companies): Maj. Philip G. Vought
Pennsylvania Light Artillery, Battery E: Lt. Charles A. Atwell
Pioneer Company: Capt. William H. H. Mapes

Middletown and Winchester: May 24–25, 1862

First Division: Brig. Gen. Alpheus S. Williams
First Brigade: Col. Dudley Donnelly
    Fifth Connecticut Infantry: Lt. Col. George D. Chapman
    Twenty-eighth New York Infantry: Lt. Col. Edwin F. Brown
    Forty-sixth Pennsylvania Infantry: Col. Joseph F. Knipe
Third Brigade: Col. George H. Gordon
    Second Massachusetts Infantry: Lt. Col. George L. Andrews
    Third Wisconsin Infantry: Col. Thomas H. Ruger
    Twenty-seventh Indiana Infantry: Col. Silas Colgrove
    Twenty-ninth Pennsylvania Infantry: Col. John K. Murphy (captured, May 25), Capt. Samuel M. Zulich
Artillery
    First New York Light Artillery, Battery M: Lt. James H. Peabody
    First Pennsylvania Light Artillery, Battery F: Capt. Robert B. Hampton

Fourth U.S. Artillery, Battery F: Lt. Franklin B. Crosby
Cavalry Brigade: Brig. Gen. John P. Hatch
First Maine Cavalry (five companies): Lt. Col. Calvin S. Douty
First Michigan Cavalry: Col. Thornton F. Broadhead
Fifth New York Cavalry: Col. Othneil De Forest
First Vermont Cavalry: Col. Charles H. Tompkins
First Maryland Cavalry (five companies): Lt. Col. Charles Wetschky
Unattached
Tenth Maine Infantry: Col. George L. Beal
Zouaves, Corps d'Afrique (one company): Capt. Charles H. T. Collis
Eighth New York Cavalry (five companies): Lt. Col. Charles R. Babbitt

Notes

PREFACE

1. Jedediah Hotchkiss to G. F. R. Henderson, May 1, 1895, Jedediah Hotchkiss Papers (hereafter cited as HP), 51:4–5, Manuscript Division, Library of Congress (LC).

2. Hotchkiss to Henderson, May 1, 1895, HP.

3. Ibid.; for Taylor's version of Jackson's night at his campfire, see in Taylor, *Destruction and Reconstruction*, 54.

4. Gordon, *Brook Farm to Cedar Mountain*, 196–97; Banks to George H. Gordon, May 24, 1862, George Henry Gordon Papers, Massachusetts Historical Society; U.S. War Department, *War of the Rebellion* (hereafter cited as *OR*—all citations referring to series 1; parts of each volume identified in parentheses), 12(1), 526; William D. Wilkins to George H. Gordon, May 23, 1862, RG 393, National Archives (hereafter cited as NA). The latter citation, a written order delivered to Gordon shortly after midnight of May 23, 1862, refutes Gordon's oft-cited claim that except for ambulance wagons, Banks made no preparation to retreat until the mid-morning of May 24, as does an excerpt from a letter of Banks's cavalry commander: "The baggage wagons were started during the night. The troops (infy) were directed to move in the morning" (Hatch to his father, May 27, 1862, John P. Hatch Papers, LC).

INTRODUCTION

1. Harsh, *Confederate Tide Rising*, 36. The most detailed description and analysis of this conference is in Newton, *Johnston and the Defense of*

Richmond, 95–111. For Lee's official position, see General Orders No. 14, March 13, 1862, in *OR* 5, 1099. For examples of subordinates' recognition of Lee's title of "Commanding General" of Confederate forces, see *OR* 12(3), 828, 834, 839, 862.

2. Sears, *To the Gates of Richmond*, 40–46. For troop numbers, see *OR* 11(3), 130, 484, 530–31.

3. Harsh, *Confederate Tide Rising*, 35, 42, 178; Daniel, *Shiloh*, 322.

4. Disagreement between twentieth-century scholars exists in relation to the plans Johnston discussed and supported. Douglas Southall Freeman suggests that Johnston used Smith's Northern invasion plan during his presentation as a ploy to accentuate his own option to strike a blow at McClellan near Richmond (*Lee's Lieutenants*, 149–50). An April 30 dispatch from Johnston to Lee suggests that Johnston advocated Smith's plan two weeks after the conference; therefore, it is likely he supported it at the meeting (Harsh, *Confederate Tide Rising*, 218n84). It cannot be ruled out that the Northern invasion portion of Smith's memorandum was a postwar addition to that document and was never discussed in the mid-April 1862 meeting (Newton, *Defense of Richmond*, 238n7).

5. Johnston, *Narrative of Military Operations*, 112–13; Smith, *Confederate War Papers*, 40–44; Davis, *Confederate Government*, 2:86–87.

6. Johnston to Jackson, March 19, 1862, Thomas J. Jackson Papers, Virginia Historical Society (hereafter cited as VHS).

7. For a description of the Kernstown battle, see Ecelbarger, *"We Are In for It!"* 84–203.

8. With years of reflection behind him, Johnston reiterated that he instructed Jackson to move "near the enemy as to prevent him from making any considerable detachments to reinforce McClellan, but not so near that he might be compelled to fight" (see Johnston, *Narrative of Military Operations*, 106).

9. On two occasions, Jackson admitted that his mere presence (without a battle) in front of the opposition could result in drawing troops into the Valley against him. See *OR* 12(1), 381, and Thomas J. Jackson, Testimony, August 5, 1862, Richard Garnett Court Martial Transcript, Museum of the Confederacy, Richmond, Va. He flatly denied attacking at Kernstown as a strategy to draw troops into the Valley. See *OR* 12(3), 840.

10. Lee to Johnston, March 20, 1862, Telegraph book, Lee's Headquarters Papers, series 2, VHS.

11. Davis to his wife, May 30, 1862, in Crist, Dix, and Williams, *Papers of Jefferson Davis*, 8: 203. The editors of Davis's papers claimed that he suggested Jackson's offensive in a May 12, 1862, meeting. This assertion has since been convincingly challenged and corrected to the April 14 session. See Harsh, *Confederate Tide Rising*, 188–89.

12. Ewell determined his strength on April 16. See *OR* 12(3), 850–51.

13. Jedediah Hotchkiss diary entries, April 17–24, 1862, in McDonald, *Make Me a Map*, 24–33.

14. *OR* 12(3), 844.

15. *OR* 12(3), 828–29; Hotchkiss diary entries, April 21–29, 1862, in McDonald, *Make Me a Map*, 30–34.

16. *OR* 12(3), 120, 879. The poor road condition is revealed in Hotchkiss diary, April 30–May 1, 1862, in McDonald, *Make Me a Map*, 35. A Union cavalry attack at Port Republic likely precipitated Jackson's decision to divert eastward through Brown's Gap. See Joseph M. Kern, diary and scrapbook, 8, University of North Carolina.

17. Jackson to Boteler, May 6, 1862, Boteler Papers, William R. Perkins Library, Duke University.

18. *OR* 12(3), 120, 134. Banks learned much about Confederate strength and deployment in the Valley in late April and early May from captured deserters See Nathaniel Banks's Intelligence Reports, RG 393, NA.

19. Harsh, *Confederate Tide Rising*, 179–80; *OR* 12(3), 118.

20. Lee, *Mr. Lincoln's City*, 114–15; Chase journal, May 1, 1862, in Niven, *Salmon P. Chase Papers*, 1:333–35.

21. Seward to Lincoln, April 30, 1862 (enclosing Scott to Seward, April 28, 1862), Lincoln Papers, LC.

22. Harsh, *Confederate Tide Rising*, 178; Lincoln to McClellan, May 1, 1862, in Basler, *Collected Works*, 5:203.

23. *OR* 12(3), 121–22.

24. *OR* 12(3), 126, 129.

CHAPTER 1

1. *OR* 11(3), 531; Harsh, *Confederate Tide Rising*, 39.

2. *OR* 11(3), 535–536.

3. *OR* 11(3), 500; *OR* 12(3), 892.

4. Hotchkiss diary entries, May 8–17, 1862, in McDonald, *Make Me a Map*, 39–46.

5. Lee to Jackson, May 11, 1862, Lee's Headquarters Papers, VHS; Pfanz, *Richard S. Ewell*, 180, 558n9; *OR* 12(3), 850–51, 879.

6. *OR* 12(3), 892–93.

7. *OR* 12(3), 898.

8. *OR* 12(1), 524.

9. Goss, *Union High Command*, 29–31; Hollandsworth, *Pretense of Glory*, 33–44.

10. Gould and Stedman, *Edmund Clarence Stedman*, 238; David H. Strother Diary, April 13, 1862, in Eby, *Virginia Yankee*, 28–29.

11. Hatch to his father, April 20, 1862, Hatch Papers, LC; Williams to his daughter, December 7, 1861, in Quaife, *From the Cannon's Mouth*, 40.

12. Letter of Edward G. Abbott, May 20, 1862, in Milano, "Letters from the Harvard Regiments," 44.

13. Strother Diary, May 6, 1862, in Eby, *Virginia Yankee*, 32.

14. J. S. Clark to his son, May 10, 1862, and to his wife, May 15, 1862, John S. Clark Papers, the Cayuga Museum, Auburn, N.Y.

15. A. S. Williams to his daughter, May 17, 1862, in Quaife, *From the Cannon's Mouth*, 74; Dwight, *Life and Letters*, 244–45.

16. Clark to his wife and family, June 21, 1862, Clark Papers; John Emerson Anderson memoir, p. 31, LC.

17. *OR* 12(1), 522–23.

18. Natural and man-made features, along with notations and descriptions, are best provided in the Jedediah Hotchkiss Sketchbook, Geography and Map Division, LC.

19. *OR* 12(1), 523–24.

20. Ibid.

21. Copeland to Banks, May 16, 1862, Nathaniel P. Banks Papers (hereafter cited as BP), LC; Shaw to Lt. Col. George Andrews, May 17, 1862, BP; Duncan, *Blue-eyed Child of Fortune*, 23–24, 202; Clark to "Friend Underwood," June 25, 1862, Clark Papers. Copeland's account, including the dispatches exchanged with Banks, is detailed in a pamphlet, *Statement of R. Morris Copeland . . . August 6, 1862*, 8–14.

22. *OR* 12(1), 524–25.

23. Various estimations of Confederate troop strength are determined in Allan, *Jackson's Valley Campaign*, 248, 256–57.

24. "Invisible" (William C. Crippen) to the *Cincinnati Daily Times*, in Hale, *Four Valiant Years*, 133–34; Map of Shenandoah Valley from Winchester to New Market, Hotchkiss Collection of Civil War Maps, LC. Jackson's location has been determined from the remark of a member of Jackson's staff, who told Jedediah Hotchkiss that headquarters were "at the church beyond White House Bridge" (McDonald, *Make Me a Map*, 47).

25. Jackson's chief commissary officer delineated the makeup of Jackson's army in an 1880 history. (See Allan, *Jackson's Valley Campaign*, 255–57.

26. Charles Winder diary, May 22, 1862, Maryland Historical Society, Baltimore (hereafter cited as MHS).

27. *OR* 12(3), 892–93.

28. *OR* 12(3), 898. Johnston's dispatch, written at 2:00 p.m., is reproduced in Freeman, *Lee's Lieutenants*, 1:371n28. Jackson expected at least a two-day delay in receiving nontelegraphed transmissions, advising Ewell on May 18 to comply with his request "unless you receive orders from a superior officer and of a date subsequent to the 16th" (*OR* 12[3], 897). Although most campaign historians and Jackson biographers surmise that Lee's approval reached Jackson the same day he asked for it, the May 21 dispatch copied into Lee's Headquarters Papers proves otherwise.

29. A long-held tradition that Jackson intended to enter the Luray Valley much earlier and shifted Ewell's men back and forth from May 17 to May 21 as a ruse has been effectively refuted by modern scholarship. See Tanner, *Stonewall in the Valley*, Appendix A, 449–59.

30. Hotchkiss diary, April 19, 1862, in McDonald, *Make Me a Map*, 26–27.

31. Tanner, *Stonewall in the Valley*, 165–66. As late as May 16, the Confederate War Department had not received Jackson's application for Crutchfield's appointment, nor did the officials know what artillery units Jackson possessed for Crutchfield to command. See Lee to Jackson, May 16, 1862, Lee's Headquarters Papers, VHS.

32. James J. Kirkpatrick diary, May 22, 1862, in Ott, *War Diary of James Kirkpatrick*, 43; Temperature reading, Georgetown, D.C., May 22, 1862, National Weather Records, National Weather Center, Asheville, N.C. (hereafter cited as NWR). Both quotes from Hale, *Four Valiant Years*, 144.

33. Members of Shields's division learned about the fate of the men when they returned to the Luray Valley in June. See Franklin Sawyer to the editor, June 17, 1862, *Norwalk (Ohio) Reflector*, July 1, 1862; Rev. Denison, *Sabres and Spurs*, 94–95.

34. Hotchkiss quote in Henderson, *Stonewall Jackson*, 1:416–17; Boswell to Jackson, March 31, 1863, HP; Hotchkiss diary, May 22, 1862, in McDonald, *Make Me a Map*, 47–48.

35. Harman to his brother, May 15 and 18, 1862, HP.

36. Boswell to Jackson, March 31, 1863, HP; Boswell to "My Dear Captain," May 14, 1862, George Hay Steuart Papers, LC.

37. Tanner, *Stonewall in the Valley*, 166; Robertson, *Stonewall Jackson*, 360.

38. Jackson's concerns about Ashby's command are detailed in a May 5 letter (ten days after Ashby's resignation and its subsequent withdrawal) to General Lee, who endorsed it by admitting, "I did not know before that Colonel Ashby's command embraced more than cavalry, which I have been endeavoring to get organized and instructed." (*OR* 12[3], 880).

39. *OR* 12(3), 879. Although the strength report was sent on May 3, it may have represented a troop count from April 30 or May 1.

40. Ibid.; *OR* 12(1), 738–39, 742. Desertions, rather than straggling, appear to be the chief cause for the rapid disappearance of so many soldiers. Winder's subsequent Valley reports reveal that his brigade strength continued to dwindle for the next eighteen days; therefore, no evidence exists to place the men lost between May 3 and May 23 back in the ranks.

41. Howard, *Recollections of a Maryland Staff Officer*, 105; Winder diary, May 22, 1862, MHS.

42. Lawson Botts to J. F. O'Brien, May 22, 1862, Botts Papers, Virginia Military Institute (VMI).

43. Fulkerson to his sister, May 16, 1862, Fulkerson Papers, VMI; *OR* 12(1), 776; *OR* 12(3), 879; E.H.T. Warren to his wife, May 23, 1862, Warren Papers, University of Virginia.

44. Fulkerson to his sister, May 16, 1862, Fulkerson Papers, VMI; *OR* 12(1), 776; *OR* 12(3), 879; Hall diary, May 22, 1862, in Dayton, *Diary of James Hall*, 57.

45. Harman to his brother, May 15, 17, 18, 20, and 22, 1862, HP; *OR* 12(1), 721–22.

46. This estimate amends the traditionally accepted strength of 15,000–16,000. See Allan, *Jackson's Valley Campaign*, 257.

47. Johnson, "Memoir of the First Maryland," 52–53.

48. Ruffner, *Maryland's Blue and Gray*, 98–104.

49. Ibid.; Johnson, *Maryland and West Virginia*, 69; Washington Hands memoir, VHS, 47. Disagreement exists between members of the regiment as to the number of malcontents who were led under guard. Colonel Johnson claimed one dozen in 1882 (Johnson, "Memoir of the First Maryland," 53), but in 1899 he amended the number to "half the regiment." Randolph McKim believed Johnson's ire was directed at one disgruntled company (*Soldier's Recollections*, 96). One participant whitewashed the whole ugly episode when he fondly recalled, "We were mustered out on the 17th day of May in

accordance with the law, but to the credit of the men be it stated that every man took his old place in the ranks." (Gill, *Private Soldier in the Confederate Army*, 52).

50. *OR* 51(1), 561.

51. Hotchkiss Sketchbook, LC; Walter Buck to Turner Ashby, n.d., published in *Frederick* (Md.) *Examiner*, June 18, 1862.

52. Lightsey, *Veteran's Story*, 12–13; W.P. Harper diary, May 23, 1862, Louisiana Historical Association: Civil War Papers, Tulane University; quote from Jones, "Down the Valley after 'Stonewall's Quartermaster,'" 189. Jones, a nephew of one of Ewell's staff officers, accompanied the staff during this phase of the Valley Campaign. General Charles Winder claimed that the Stonewall Brigade, three miles north of Luray, left at 5:00 a.m. (see Winder diary, May 23, 1862, MHS). Based on this, Ewell's division likely initiated the march closer to 4:45 a.m.

53. *Lexington Gazette*, May 22, 1862.

CHAPTER 2

1. Miers, *Lincoln Day by Day*, 3:114; Temperature readings, Georgetown, May 21–23, 1862, NWR.

2. Bowman, *Civil War Almanac*, 94–99.

3. *OR* 12(1), 10, 804–13.

4. Lincoln and Stanton arrived at Falmouth at 8:30 a.m. See Stanton to P.H. Watson, May 23, 1862, Telegrams received by the Secretary of War, M473, Reel #101:589 (hereafter cited as TSW), NA. "Western" in 1862 applied to soldiers hailing from today's Midwest states.

5. Campbell Brown, "Ewell's Division at Front Royal," monograph in Brown-Ewell Papers , Tennessee State Library and Archives (hereafter cited as BEP); Lightsey, *Veteran's Story*, 13; Hotchkiss Sketchbook, H1, 26, LC. Today, Spangler's Crossroads is the hamlet of Limeton. The time is based on a marching pace of two and one-half miles per hour.

6. Member of the "Wise Troop" to a friend, May 24, 1862, published in *Lynchburg* (Va.) *Daily Republican*, June 3, 1862; Buck to Ashby, in *Frederick Examiner*, June 18, 1862. The *Examiner*, as well as other Northern newspapers, published this dispatch after it and three others were found in a burned-out railroad car in Winchester early in June. That Jackson carried the dispatches was confirmed by Ewell's chief of staff in 1868 (see Campbell Brown memoir, BEP).

7. Buck to Ashby, in *Frederick Examiner*, June 18, 1862. Jackson's dispatch quoted in Johnson, *Maryland and West Virginia*, 69. Jackson's order helps to time his reception of Lieutenant Buck's dispatch. Had he known that a Union Maryland regiment occupied the town prior to arriving at the outskirts of Front Royal, logic dictates that he would have realigned his assaulting force *before* they marched from Bentonville that morning. Others have speculated that Jackson learned of the Union Marylanders from captured pickets (see Tanner, *Stonewall in the Valley*, 535). This is possible, but considering that the Union pickets were infantrymen, it is unlikely that they would have been scouting five or more miles south of town. A more plausible

alternative is that sympathetic citizens alerted Jackson during his march. Buck's dispatch was still necessary to confirm any unsubstantiated citizen report.

8. Randolph McKim's diary places the First (CSA) Maryland twelve miles from the front (McKim, *Soldier's Recollections*, 96). A captain in the First (CSA) Maryland stated that the regiment was eleven miles from the front (William H. Murray to a friend, n.d., Murray Papers, MHS). Another Marylander confirmed the rearward position when he remembered, "His [Jackson's] whole army filed past us cheering and in the best possible spirits" (John E.H. Post to his mother, June 17, 1862, MS 1860, Post Papers, MHS).

9. Johnson, *Maryland and West Virginia*, 69–70; Johnson, "Memoir of the First Maryland," 55.

10. Ibid.; Booth, *Personal Reminiscences*, 31–32.

11. Washington Hands memoir, 49, VHS; Post to his mother, June 17, 1862, Post Papers, MHS; Murray to a friend, n.d., Murray Papers, MHS; Johnson, "Memoir of the First Maryland," 53.

12. Hotchkiss quote in Henderson, *Stonewall Jackson*, 316; Boswell to Jackson, March 31, 1863, HP.

13. Robert Barton memoir, in Colt, *Defend the Valley*, 141; Franklin Riley journal, May 23, 1862, in Dobbins, *Grandfather's Journal*, 79; McClendon, *Recollections of War Times*, 53; *OR* 51(2), 561; *OR* 12(3), 898.

14. Hotchkiss Sketchbook, 23, 25–27, LC; "A Mosby Ranger Recalls Battle," *National Tribune*, July 11, 1935 (exerpts from a *Washington Post* article originally published on May 24, 1935); Thornton V. Leach was the former Mosby Ranger who recalled the Colonel King story. He was merely fifteen years old at the time and was likely not a witness to the conversation. His version matches well with Front Royal lore and dovetails nicely with subsequent events of the day. See Hale, *Four Valiant Years*, 145–47.

15. Brown, "Ewell's Division at Front Royal," BEP.

16. *OR* 12(1), 702, 733; member of the "Wise Troop" to a friend, May 24, 1862, in *Lynchburg Daily Republican*, June 3, 1862; William L. Wilson diary, May 23, 1862, in Wilson, *Borderland Confederate*, 15. Ashby would not strike Buckton Station, twelve miles from McCoy's Ford, until 4:00 p.m.; therefore, it is unlikely he left Spangler's Crossroads well before noon to accomplish this mission. This is confirmed by Jackson's chief of staff, who states that Ashby and Flournoy were detached "in the forenoon" (Dabney, *Life and Campaigns*, 366). It is noteworthy that Jackson's rather late deployment of his cavalry becomes an oft-repeated trait over the next two days.

17. McKim diary, May 23, 1862, in McKim, *Soldier's Recollections*, 96; Lightsey, *Veteran's Story*, 13; Brown, "Ewell's Division at Front Royal," BEP. Today the mountain road (Route 671) is called "Rocky Lane." A postwar Asbury Chapel rests on the original foundation. The roads have realigned so much that the church is on the west side of the modern highway instead of the east side as it was in 1862. Dickey's Hill is now known as Dickey Ridge, the initiation point of Skyline Drive.

18. Hotchkiss Sketchbook, 32; Johnson, "Memoir of the First Maryland," 54; Allan, *Jackson's Valley Campaign*, 114; member of the "Wise Troop" to a friend, May 24, 1862, in *Lynchburg Daily Republican*, June 3, 1862.

19. Boswell to Jackson, March 31, 1863, HP.

20. Ibid. Boswell states in the report that "about 1 p.m., I rejoined you about three miles above Front Royal and remained with you." Because of the Shenandoah Valley's inverted nomenclature, "above" means "south of" because the land descends as one moves northward or "down" the Valley toward the Potomac River. This pinpoints Boswell finding Jackson on the Gooney Manor Road near the T intersection with the Asbury Chapel byroad.

21. Charles Parham to Banks, May 23, 1862, RG 94, NA.

22. Shaw to his sister, June 6, 1862, in Duncan, *Blue-eyed Child of Fortune*, 207; Johnson, *Maryland and West Virginia*, 71; Murray to a friend, n.d., Murray Papers, MHS. Shortly after the war, General Ewell was struck by the irony that Front Royal was garrisoned by what "proved to be the Md. Regt of the Northern Army & chance directed that the only Southern Regt from the same state should be instrumental in its discomfiture" ("Ewell's account of the 1862 Valley Campaign—undated manuscript fragment," folder 18, BEP). Ewell's belief that the clash between the two Maryland units was mere coincidence is evidence that General Jackson did not discuss with him his reasons for shifting regiments within Ewell's division prior to the attack.

23. *OR* 12(1): 800; Oates, *War between the Union and the Confederacy*, 96.

24. Johnson, "Memoir of the First Maryland," 54; Brown, "Ewell's Division at Front Royal," BEP; Douglas, *I Rode with Stonewall*, 59–60; Boyd, *Camp and Prison*, 125–27. The fact that the First (CSA) Maryland was already in the van was proof positive that Boyd's piece of intelligence was neither new nor particularly valuable. Jed Hotchkiss was adamant about this point to one of Jackson's biographers thirty-three years later when he wrote, "Jackson's information about Front Royal was largely derived from members of Ashby's cavalry. . . . Don't make too much of the Belle Boyd story" (Hotchkiss to Henderson, May 1, 1895, HP).

25. Parham to Banks, May 23, 1862, NA. Parham's dispatch, alluded to in his published report, has been listed as "not found" when the after-action report was published in volume 12 of the *OR* series (see 561n); however, it exists in the folder with the original report in the National Archives.

26. Lucy Buck diary, May 23, 1862, in Buck, *Sad Earth, Sweet Heaven*, 78; Ashby, *Valley Campaigns*, 114–15.

27. Hale, *Four Valiant Years*, 150; "The Fight at Front Royal: Statement of Captain George Smith," *Philadelphia Inquirer*, May 27, 1862; George Thompson to the editors of the *Baltimore American*, May 29, 1862, in Moore, *Rebellion Record*, 5:140; Charles Parham to the editor, n.d., published in *Cincinnati Daily Gazette*, May 31, 1862; Parham to Banks, May 23, 1862, NA; *OR* 12(1), 560–61.

28. Johnson, "Memoir of the First Maryland," 54; member of the "Wise Troop" to a friend, May 24, 1862, in *Lynchburg Daily Republican*, June 3, 1862. Another version has the exchange occur between Colonel Johnson and General Ewell (see Johnson, *Maryland and West Virginia*, 71).

29. William H. Murray to a friend, n.d., Murray Papers, MHS; James Thomas diary, May 23, 1862 (TS in Fredericksburg-Spotsylvania National Military Park; hereafter cited as FSNMP).

30. Bergeron, *Louisiana Confederate Military Units*, 149–50; Smith and Younghusband, *American Civil War Zouaves*, 59; Dufour, *Gentle Tiger*, 5–6, 140–41, 151; McClendon, *Recollections of War Times*, 37.

31. Dufour, *Gentle Tiger*, 6–9.

32. Brown memoir, BEP; member of the "Wise Troop" to a friend, May 24, 1862, in *Lynchburg Daily Republican*, June 3, 1862.

33. Ruffner, *Maryland's Blue and Gray*, 347; Camper and Kirkley, *First Maryland Infantry*, 32–33; Post to his mother, June 17, 1862, Post Papers, MHS.

34. Member of the "Wise Troop" to a friend, May 24, 1862, in *Lynchburg Daily Republican*, June 3, 1862; Post to his mother, June 17, 1862, Post Papers, MHS; Ashby, *Valley Campaigns*, 115–16.

35. Lucy Buck diary, May 23, 1862, in Buck, *Sad Earth, Sweet Heaven*, 79. Tom Ashby does not identify Walter Buck by name, but his description of the cavalier—"I met a Confederate soldier on horseback,—a man I knew well. . . . He was a gallant fellow and was killed in battle in 1863"—leaves little doubt. Walter Buck was killed at the battle of Upperville in June 1863.

36. *OR* 12(1), 556; Kenly to Lorenzo Thomas, January 27, 1864, U.S. Army Generals' Reports of Civil War Service, Papers of the Adjutant General's Office, M1098, 1:431, NA.

37. Parham to the editor, in *Cincinnati Daily Gazette*, May 31, 1862; *OR* 12(1), 560–61.

38. *OR* 12(1): 556, 558–59, 565. Kenly's strength is routinely listed as 1,063. The revised estimate removes the cavalry that had yet to arrive, does not include the 160 men between and north of the river branches who did not get engaged, and assumes a loss of 100 men from the three picketing companies. For a participant's map showing Atwell's guns east of the turnpike, see Camper and Kirkley, *First Maryland Infantry*, 47. The cannon fire beginning half an hour after the pickets were driven in is supported by a member of the Fifteenth Alabama (see Joseph M. Ellison to his wife, May 26, 1862, Richmond National Battlefield Park, bound volume no. 66).

39. Member of the "Wise Troop" to a friend, May 24, 1862, in *Lynchburg Daily Republican*, June 3, 1862; Lucy Buck diary, May 23, 1862, in Buck, *Sad Earth, Sweet Heaven*, 79.

40. Washington Hands memoir, MHS, 49–50; Johnson, *Maryland and West Virginia*, 71–72; Booth, *Personal Reminiscences*, 32; Murray to his friend, n.d., Murray Papers, MHS.

41. Johnson, "Memoir of the First Maryland," 54; member of the "Wise Troop" to a friend, May 24, 1862, in *Lynchburg Daily Republican*, June 3, 1862.

42. *OR* 12(1), 556.

43. Douglas, *I Rode with Stonewall*, 63; Brown memoir, BEP.

44. *OR* 12(1), 725. According to local tradition, the height where Southern guns first deployed is today the Prospect Hill Cemetery. The smoothbore battery that Crutchfield rejected likely fired from this hill. The rifled cannons deployed on the height currently dominated by the Randolph Macon Academy, a hill that cuts the distance to Richardson's Hill in half. A twentieth-century account claims that Prospect Hill was used first, then the guns were

rolled to the hill on which the academy now sits (see "A Mosby Ranger Recalls Battle," *National Tribune*, July 11, 1935). Crutchfield never mentions two positions in his report.

45. Jones, "Down the Valley after 'Stonewall's Quartermaster,'" 189.

46. Ashby, *Valley Campaigns*, 116–17.

47. *OR* 12(1), 800; Charles Eckardt diary, May 23, 1862, Warren County Historical Society, Front Royal, Va.

48. James Kirkpatrick diary, May 23, 1862 (TS at FSNMP); J.J. Wilson to his father, May 27, 1862, Wilson Papers, Reel 6368, Department of Archives and History, Mississippi State University; McClendon, *Recollections of War Times*, 54. Kirkpatrick places the time of the Sixteenth Mississippi deployment at "3 o'clock." This account matches McClendon's memoir. The Alabaman specifically mentions that Courtney's battery passed by while they were in line of battle.

49. Parham to the editor, in *Cincinnati Daily Gazette*, May 31, 1862; *OR* 12(1), 561, 564; Charley Greenleaf to his parents, May 26, 1862, published in *Hartford Daily Times*, May 30, 1862.

50. Sue Richardson diary, May 23, 1862, in Hale, *Four Valiant Years*, 149–151; Johnson, "Memoir of the First Maryland," 55; Johnson, *Maryland and West Virginia*, 72; Charles Atwell, "The Battle of Front Royal," *Pittsburgh Gazette*, May 29, 1862; *OR* 12(1), 556, 564–65. Johnson's two accounts conflict on the east side deployment. In the former monograph, he places two companies on the flank; in the latter, he claims only Company F.

51. Ibid.; Booth, *Personal Reminiscences*, 33.

52. *OR* 12(1), 725, 760, 777, 788; It is noteworthy that all those who sent their cannons forward specified that the orders came from General Jackson, not Stapleton Crutchfield.

53. Dabney, *Life and Campaigns*, 367.

54. Johnson, "Memoir of the First Maryland," 56.

55. Boswell to Jackson, March 31, 1863, HP; Boswell likely performed his reconnaissance to a hill west of the "Rose Hill" estate, but he reported that "before the guns could be brought up, the enemy retired."

56. *OR* 12(1), 778, 800. Richard Taylor appears to be most responsible for not supporting the assault of Richardson's Hill. Taylor did not specify the action in his report to General Ewell, explaining that "the details of the engagement having occurred under the eye of the major-general commanding, it is not necessary to mention them any further." Since Taylor directed his report to General Ewell, the phrase "major-general commanding" likely refers to Ewell, his division commander, rather than General Jackson. Ewell muddied the water when he wrote in his report that "the attack and decided results at Front Royal, though this division alone participated, were the fruits of Major-General Jackson's personal superintendence and planning." Interestingly, General Jackson acknowledges neither Ewell nor Taylor as directing the infantry assault at Front Royal in his report, nor does he claim that he took charge of the deployment.

57. *OR* 12(1), 702; George P. Ring diary, May 23, 1862, Tulane University Library; Eckardt diary, May 23, 1862, Warren County Historical Society;

S. Z. Ammen, "Maryland Troops in the Confederate Army," vol. 1 (1879), Clemens Papers, U.S. Army Military History Instiutute (hereafter cited as USAMHI); George Wren diary, May 23, 1862, Robert W. Woodruff Library, Emory University (hereafter cited as RWL).

58. *OR* 12(1), 556; Kenly to Lorenzo Thomas, January 27, 1864, U.S. Army Generals' Reports, 1:433, NA.

CHAPTER 3

1. John S. Clark to "Dear Friend Underwood," June 25, 1862, Clark Papers.

2. Hotchkiss Sketchbook, 7, LC.

3. Ibid.; Brown, *Twenty-seventh Indiana*, 127; Bryant, *History of the Third Wisconsin*, 53; Charles Parham to Banks, May 22, 1862, BP; Hewett, *Supplement to the Official Records of the Union and Confederate Armies* (hereafter cited as *SOR*), 75:271. The strength of the Union force is estimated by the author. No morning report exists for the two companies at Buckton, but three other companies of the Third Wisconsin reported numbers "for duty" in the seventies for this period (see Third Wisconsin Regimental Books, RG 94, NA).

4. Hotchkiss Sketchbook, 7, LC; Avirett, *Ashby and His Compeers*, 187; Hale, *Four Valiant Years*, 151.

5. Although three Union sources time the attack at 2:00 p.m., the most convincing evidence that the attack occurred at 4:00 p.m. comes from the dispatch written by the Union commander within an hour of the fight (Hubbard to Banks, May 23, 1862, BP; see also Hinkley diary, May 23, 1862, Hinkley Papers, Wisconsin State Historical Society). The distance between Spangler's Crossroads and Buckton station is nearly ten miles. It would have been difficult for Ashby to turn off the crossroads shortly before noon, ride ten miles, carefully reconnoiter the Buckton region, and launch the attack all within two hours. The fact that General Banks will learn of the Buckton attack *after* he is informed that Kenly has been attacked at Front Royal is stronger evidence for a 4:00 p.m. encounter.

6. Brown, *Twenty-seventh Indiana*, 127–29; Avirett, *Ashby and His Compeers*, 187–88. A conflicting source claims that Sheetz's horse was retained by Daniel E. Steele of the Seventh Virginia Cavalry. Steele placed the dead man "across the riderless horse and took it to the rear." Steele relayed the story to historian E.T. Stuart, who wrote it at the bottom of his copy of Charles T. O'Ferrall's *Forty Years of Active Service*, 33. The sources agree if Sheetz was laid across a different animal than his own horse.

7. Raab, *With the 3rd Wisconsin Badgers*, 66–67.

8. Ibid.; Bryant, *History of the Third Wisconsin*, 54; William Lyne Wilson diary, May 23, 1862, in Wilson, *Borderland Confederate*, 15.

9. Raab, *With the 3rd Wisconsin Badgers*, 66; McKim Holliday Wells diary, May 23, 1862 (TS at FSNMP; Wayland, *Virginia Valley Records*, 287. The primary source for Wayland's anecdote has not been found, but it likely comes from Captain Winfield's version of the battle relayed to his daughter,

Paulina, who compiled the captain's letters for Wayland's anthology in 1928. The flag Winfield captured would likely not have been a regimental flag since a detached company would not have any regimental standards in their possession.

10. Raab, *With the 3rd Wisconsin Badgers*, 66; Bryant, *History of the Third Wisconsin*, 54; Walker, *Biographical Sketches*, 193–94; Third Wisconsin soldier to unknown addressee, May 30, 1862, published in *Columbus Gazette*, June 13, 1862.

11. Thomas, *General Turner Ashby*, 98.

12. Avirett, *Ashby and His Compeers*, 188.

13. Bryant, *History of the Third Wisconsin*, 54–55.

14. Avirett, *Ashby and His Compeers*, 188–190; Wilson diary, May 23, 1862, in Wilson, *Borderland Confederate*, 15.

15. Bryant, *History of the Third Wisconsin*, 56; Thomas Ruger to Banks, May 23, 1862, BP.

16. *OR* 12(1), 556–57, 560–61.

17. Kenly to editor, n.d., John R. Kenly Papers, MS 1696, MHS.

18. *OR* 12(1), 564–65.

19. Wilson diary, May 24, 1862, in Wilson, *Borderland Confederate*, 16; Goldsborough, *Maryland Line*, 51; Post to his mother, June 17, 1862, Post Papers, MHS; Ammen, "Maryland Troops in the Confederate Army," 1:27 (TS in Clemens Papers, USAMHI). One of the many traits associated with Stonewall Jackson was his legendary penchant for lemons. Front Royal is a known documented source of this fruit.

20. Johnson, "Memoir of the First Maryland," 55; Gill, *Private Soldier in the Confederate Army*, 53.

21. *OR* 12(1), 557, 561–62, 565; "From General Banks's Division," *New York Daily Tribune*, May 29, 1862.

22. Dabney, *Life and Campaigns*, 365–66. This is the second time Jackson reportedly said these words. It is possible that both accounts describe the same exclamation. If so, then Dabney was mistaken as to when Jackson ordered up the artillery. Since Captain Poague, five and one-half miles south of Front Royal, acknowledged receiving Jackson's order for his rifled pieces at 4:00 p.m., then Jackson likely lamented about the artillery no later than 3:15 p.m., an hour before Kenly retreated from Richardson's Hill.

23. *OR* 12(1), 725, 788; Kirkpatrick diary, May 22–23, 1862, 43–44, FSNMP; Riley journal, May 23, 1862, in Dobbins, *Grandfather's Journal*, 79.

24. Taylor, *Destruction and Reconstruction*, 56. Although Taylor's egocentric memoir has several passages of proven fiction in it, there is no counterevidence to dispute his claim that he suggested the subsequent movement to General Jackson.

25. Kelly to Richard Ewell, January 9, 1863, Henry Kelly Compiled Service Record (CSR), M331, NA.

The commander of the Fifteenth Alabama claimed that two men from the Eighth Louisiana drowned in the river (Oates, *War Between the Union and Confederacy*, 97). The secondhand account is not supported by Taylor's casualty list, which shows no losses for the regiment (*OR* 12[1], 800). Taylor refuted his own report seventeen years later with a colorful (but likely fictitious) account that claimed, "Several men fell to disappear in the dark water beneath." (Taylor, *Destruction and Reconstruction*, 53).

26. Mrs. Richards diary exerpted in Hale, *Four Valiant Years*, 151.

27. *OR* 12(1), 725; Myers, *Comanches*, 51.

28. Beyer and OKeydel, *Deeds of Valor*, 30–31.

29. Kelly to Ewell, January 9, 1863, Henry Kelly CSR, NA; Robert A. Rowe to the editor, June 22, 1862, published in *Opelousas* (La.) *Courier*, September 6, 1862.

30. *OR* 12(1), 557; "Statement of Daniel Riwell, Private, Co. G 29th Penn. Vol.," BP.

31. Kelly to Ewell, January 9, 1863, Henry Kelly CSR, NA; Wren diary, May 23, 1862, RWL.

32. *OR* 12(1), 733–34; Ellison to his wife, May 26, 1862, Richmond National Battlefield Park; *SOR*, 69 (pt. 2): 781, 785–86; Kelly to Ewell, January 9, 1863, Henry Kelly CSR, NA.

33. Taylor, *Destruction and Reconstruction*, 54. Campbell Brown wrote that Davis participated in the charge "by way of a frolic. The poor fellow was intoxicated for the first time since entering the service" (Brown, "Ewell's Division at Front Royal," BEP).

34. Donohoe, "Fight at Front Royal," 133; Jonathan T. Mann to his wife, May 27, 1862, JonathanT. Mann letters, FSNMP; *OR* 12(1), 734. The number is estimated for seven companies, although only four would be heavily involved in the subsequent action. Mann believed that his regiment "only had about three hundred men in it then the balance of them on picket, some dodgeing some sick some with crippled horses." It seems more likely that four companies could bring only half that number based on the conditions he described. It must be noted that Mann, a participant, was from Company I, a unit not supposedly engaged. Officers heading two other companies also insist that their men were involved. Capt. D.T. Richards of Company D claims, "This company was in the fight at Front Royal where the regiment charged the First Maryland Yankee Infantry and captured the whole regiment." Capt. John E. Throckmorton also credits his Company F as one of the units "that charged in the pursuit of the enemy when routed in which [the] captain's horse was shot under him and three lieutenants wounded (*SOR*, vol. 69, pt. 2, 781, 785–86). Flournoy's report credits Companies D and I for their participation but does not mention Company F.

35. Kenly to Lorenzo Thomas, January 27, 1864, U.S. Army Generals' Report, 1:433.

36. Greenleaf to his parents, May 26, 1862, in *Hartford Daily Times*, May 30, 1862; Gordon, *Brook Farm to Cedar Mountain*, 190; Banks to Colonel Parham, May 23, 1862, BP; *OR* 12(1), 601.

37. *OR* 12(1), 557, 562.

38. Ibid. Although no known primary account mentions the Fairview house, local tradition places the final fight there (Hale, *Four Valiant Years*, 149), and much primary evidence supports this conclusion. On a map of the engagement, Jed Hotchkiss circled the road in front of the McKay house and wrote next to it, "May 23, 1862" (Hotchkiss Maps, H5, LC). Jonathan Mann of the Sixth Virginia Cavalry confirmed the plateau position when he wrote his

wife, "They [the Union forces] ran up the turnpike about four or five miles and made a stand on a hill [and] planted their cannon in the road" (Mann to his wife, May 27, 1862, FSNMP).

39. *OR* 12(1), 557, 562, 564, 733.

40. *OR* 12(1), 734; Hale, *Four Valiant Years*, 149; James H. Brown CSR, NA.

41. Donohoe, "Fight at Front Royal," 134; Henry Grueninger Pension Record, RG 94, NA; Kenly's revealing description of being shot—the only such known account of it—appears in his letter to Lorenzo Thomas, January 27, 1864, U.S. Army Generals' Report, 1:433; *OR* 12(1), 565.

42. "Arrival of Colonel Kenly," *Baltimore American and Commercial Advertiser*, June 6, 1862; Frederick Tarr Pension Record, RG 94, NA.

43. Donohoe, "Fight at Front Royal," 134.

44. *OR* 12(1), 562, 565–66.

45. Charles H. T. Collis to Banks, May 24, 1862, BP; Thompson to the editors, May 29, 1862, published in *Baltimore American and Commercial Advertiser*, June 2, 1862.

46. *OR* 12(1), 562–63; "The Disaster at Front Royal: Additional and Thrilling Details by an Eye-Witness," *Cincinnati Daily Gazette*, May 31, 1862.

47. "The Battle of Front Royal: Statement of Captain George Smith," *Baltimore American and Commercial Advertiser*, May 27, 1862; "Statement of Sergeant Henry Haugh," *Baltimore American and Commercial Advertiser*, June 6, 1862.

48. "Statement of David Powell," BP; "Statement of Captain George Smith," *Baltimore American and Commercial Advertiser*, May 27, 1862; Kenly to editor, n.d., Kenly Papers, MHS; *OR* 12(1), 553–54.

49. Jonathan Mann to Sarah, May 27, 1862, FSNMP; *OR* 12(1), 800; Nisbet, *Firing Line*, 79.

50. Dabney, *Life and Campaigns*, 368; Myers, *Comanches*, 51; Hotchkiss to his wife, May 26, 1862, HP. In 1895 Hotckiss remembered, "[T]he complete routing of Kenly's command . . . took place just about dark" (Hotchkiss to Henderson, May 1, 1895, HP). Sunset on May 23 took place at 7:07 p.m., according to Freeman, *Lee's Lieutenants*, 1:391n31 (refers to May 24).

51. Booth, *Personal Reminiscences*, 33; McClendon, *Recollections of War Times*, 55; Cockrell and Ballard, *Mississippi Rebel*, 74.

52. Ashby, *Valley Campaigns*, 118–19; Lucy Buck diary, May 23, 1862, in Buck, *Sad Earth, Sweet Heaven*, 80; Eckardt diary, May 23, 1862; Warren County Historical Society.

53. James Kirkpatrick diary, May 23, 1862, FSNMP; Cockrell and Ballard, *Mississippi Rebel*, 74; Buck, *With the Old Confeds*, 30.

54. Boyd, *Camp and Prison*, 133; Mrs. Richards diary, May 23 and 24, 1862, in Hale, *Four Valiant Years*, 151.

55. *OR* 12(1), 703. Eleven months after the battle, Jackson reported, "In order to watch both directions, and at the same time advance upon [Banks] if he remained at Strasburg, I determined, with the main body of the army, to strike the turnpike near Middletown" via the Chapel Road from Cedarville (ibid.). His subsequent actions early the following morning belied this decision.

56. Hotchkiss to Henderson, May 1, 1895, HP; Hotchkiss to Hunter McGuire, March 4, 1897, Hotchkiss-McCullough Papers, University of Virginia. Robert McKay's home stood across the road and west of Jacob's. Hotchkiss does not specify which McKay house (he mistakenly calls it "McCoy") Jackson stayed at, but his description makes Jacob McKay's the most likely location since it was nearest to the intersection. Although Front Royal lore places Jackson overnight at the Richards home near the River Station depot, Hotchkiss insists otherwise in two letters that vividly describe him sharing the blanket in "McCoy's front yard." There was a McCoy homestead near Nineveh, but Hotchkiss clarifies the location in his letter to Henderson ("where the road to Middletown left the Front Royal and Winchester Turnpike"), making it clear that it must have been the McKay rather than McCoy house.

CHAPTER 4

1. Miers, *Lincoln Day by Day*, 114; Lincoln to McClellan, May 24, 1862, in Basler, *Collected Works*, 5:231–32.

2. Strother journal, May 23, 1862, in Eby, *Virginia Yankee*, 38.

3. Ibid.

4. Saville to Banks, May 23, 1862, BP.

5. Strother journal, May 23, 1862, in Eby, *Virginia Yankee*, 39.

6. Gordon, *Brook Farm to Cedar Mountain*, 191–92.

7. Banks to George Gordon, May 23, 1862, Gordon Papers; Collis, *1st Brigade, 1st Division, 3rd Corps*, 13.

8. OR 12(3), 215; OR 51(1), 629.

9. OR 51(1), 629–30.

10. Gordon, *Brook Farm to Cedar Mountain*, 192–93.

11. OR 12(1), 525; OR 51(1), 628.

12. Wilkins to Gordon, May 23, 1862, NA; Hatch to his father, May 27, 1862, Hatch Papers, LC.

13. OR 12(1), 579, 585, 605, 623; Gettysburg Battlefield Commission, *Pennsylvania at Gettysburg*, 1:219.

14. Banks to Ruger, May 24, 1862, BP.

15. OR 12(1), 525–26, 564–65; Strother journal, May 23–24, 1862, in Eby, *Virginia Yankee*, 39.

16. Strother journal, May 23(4), 1862, in Eby, *Virginia Yankee*, 39; OR 12(1), 526.

17. Boyce diary, May 24, 1862, Boyce Papers, LC.

18. OR 12(1), 526; Banks to George H. Gordon, May 24, 1862, Gordon Papers. In his after-action report, Banks claimed that he decided to move his army away from Strasburg at 3:00 a.m. The paper trail of dispatches that flowed to and from headquarters belies the assertion.

19. Collis to Banks, n.d. (May 24, 1862), BP.

20. Strother, "Personal Recollections of the War," *Harper's New Monthly Magazine* 34 (March 1867): 442. Strother does not identify Greenleaf, but his account dovetails well with Greenleaf's letter to his parents.

21. OR 12(1), 526–27.

22. Murphy to Banks, May 24, 1862, BP.

23. Strother diary, May 24, 1862, in Eby, *Virginia Yankee*, 39.

24. *OR* 12(3), 225; William D. Wilkins to GeorgeH. Gordon, May 24, 1862, Gordon Papers.

25. Capt. S.B. Holabird, Banks's assistant quartermaster, performed his wartime duties so skillfully as to earn a brevet promotion to brigadier general in the United States Army afterward. Twenty years after the Valley Campaign, Holabird authored a monograph on transportation regulations, asserting that a twelve-thousand-man force required 150 wagons for ten days' provisions, and 300 wagons for twenty days of rations (Holabird, "Army Wagon Transportation," 100.

26. Report of hospitalized force at Strasburg, May 24, 1862, NA.

27. Boyce diary, May 24, 1862, Boyce Papers, LC.

28. Strength of Maine regiment in Allan, *Jackson's Valley Campaign*, 255.

29. Banks to his wife, May 24, 1862, BP.

CHAPTER 5

1. Chase journal, May 24, 1862, Salmon P. Chase Papers, LC.

2. Clark to "Dear Friend Underwood," June 25, 1862, Clark Papers; *OR* 12(1), 526.

3. *OR* 12(1), 703. Apparently, Jackson ruled out a fourth option for Banks: he could have headed westward through the Alleghenies to link with Frémont.

4. No report from the cavalry has been found to confirm the time that it began its mission. The prevailing traditional belief is that the mission began in Front Royal, but this would time their departure at 6:00 a.m. Since subsequent events will place their arrival at Newtown near 10:00 a.m., the Front Royal departure becomes an unreasonable assumption because the four-hour lapse of time to get there (three miles per hour) could almost be accomplished by foot soldiers. An 8:15–8:30 a.m. departure from Nineveh, resulting in a six-mile ride in one and one-half hours, is more reasonable. Although still a slow pace for horse soldiers, this scenario also encompasses time spent in preparation before their departure and after their arrival.

5. Warner, *Generals in Gray*, 290–91.

6. Hotchkiss diary, May 24, 1862, in McDonald, *Make Me a Map*, 48; Hotchkiss Sketchbook, LC. The time is approximated based on the documented hour of prior and subsequent events. Double Tollgate is never mentioned as the stoppage point for the van, but several Confederate letters and diaries mention mileage location that isolates the head of the army here. See member of the "Wise Troop" to his friend, May 24, 1862, in *Lynchburg Daily Republican*, June 3, 1862; the writer—obviously taking advantage of a long respite—heads his letter as "Nine miles North of Front Royal and Nine Miles from Winchester."

7. ASW to his daughter, May 27, 1862, in Quaife, *From the Cannon's Mouth*, 78; Francis G. Schoff to his "friends at home," May 30, 1862, Schoff-Sturtevant Papers, William Clements Library, University of Michigan. Times

of departure vary depending on the source, claiming as early as 9:00 a.m. (*OR* 12[1], 601), or as late as 11:00 a.m. (*OR* 12[1], 620). Given the size of the army moving and the order of march, it appears the artillery marched off shortly after 9:00 a.m. in the van, while Gordon's brigade moved last at approximately 10:00 a.m. In Winchester, diarist Laura Lee watched wagons roll past her home on the north side of town at "about ten Oclock this morning" (Laura Lee diary, May 24, 1862, Handley Library, Winchester, Va.; hereafter cited as HL); this reasonably places the same leading wagons at the southern outskirts of Winchester half an hour earlier. General Williams claimed a twenty-two-mile wagon train (Williams to his daughter, May 27, 1862, in Quaife, *From the Cannon's Mouth*, 78), but it is unlikely that the wagons covered more than fifteen miles in front of Banks's army.

8. Hotchkiss diary, May 24, 1862, in McDonald, *Make Me a Map*, 48; Hotchkiss to his wife, May 26, 1862, HP. Jackson's decision not to scout on the Chapel Road earlier in the morning is almost too startling to believe. Hotchkiss insisted that they were aware that Union pickets were on the road early in the morning (Hotchkiss to Henderson, May 1, 1895, HP), but that force—the Twenty-ninth Pennsylvania, First Michigan Cavalry, and Wooding's section of Battery M, First New York Light Artillery—had begun to return to Middletown by 6:00 a.m., and perhaps earlier than that. Jackson could well have sent a small cavalry party on that road between 5:00 and 7:00 a.m., although no supporting documentation confirms this. It would explain why he marched past the crossroad at 7:00 a.m., and why Steuart was sent up a different road to look for Banks's army. If a scouting party was sent, it obviously failed to complete its mission, leaving Jackson without any intelligence into the waning morning hours. Jackson's suggestion in his April 10, 1863, report of this 1862 action that the Confederates "the following morning . . . advanced from Cedarville toward Middletown" is accurate, but very misleading, for the advance would not begin until the final hour of the morning.

9. In her May 24 diary entry, Laura Lee wrote, "Mr. Barton was at Spring Dale about 10 Oclock and a party of Stuart's [*sic*] cavalry dashed by from a cross road from Front Royal in pursuit of some Yankee wagons which had just passed" (Laura Lee diary, May 24, 1862, HL). Springdale (Bartonsville) is two miles north of Newtown. Although this claim of a 10:00 a.m. attack is secondhand, subsequent events confirm Steuart's attack time to match with the Lee diary entry.

10. *New York World* correspondent to the editor, May 25, 1862, republished in *Pittsburgh Daily Post*, May 30, 1862; Jonathan T. Mann to Sarah, May 27, 1862, FSNMP; *OR* 12(1), 734. Jackson's report claims that Steuart was sent to Newtown "to observe the movements of the enemy at that point." Thomas Flournoy reported that their mission was "to harass the enemy and intercept the trains" (*OR* 12[1], 703, 734). It appears that Flournoy's statement was affected by retrospection, since it is unlikely that the mission could have been to harass an enemy whose position was unknown at the outset of the mission.

11. The *New York World* correspondent believed the man's name was "David Dickerson" (*Pittsburgh Daily Post*, May 30, 1862), but no such soldier existed in the rolls. Derrickson's service and pension records confirm his

identity as the soldier who was shot. Although Banks's men were upset that Steuart's men "murdered him in cold blood" (Boyce diary, May 24, 1862, Boyce Papers, LC), it is equally as likely that an errant shot felled Derrickson.

12. Boyce diary, May 24, 1862, Boyce Papers, LC; *New York World* correspondent to the editor, May 25, 1862, in *Pittsburgh Daily Post*, May 30, 1862.

13. *OR* 12(1), 577, 579.

14. *OR* 12(1), 579, 703, 734; *OR* 51(2), 563.

15. *OR* 12(1), 605, 613; Boyce diary, May 24, 1862, LC; C.Wise to the editor, May 27, 1862, published in *Reading* (Pa.) *Daily Times*, June 2, 1862.

16. Strother diary, May 24, 1862, in Eby, *Virginia Yankee*, 39–40.

17. *OR* 12(1), 547; Anderson memoir, 36, LC.

18. Ibid.; *New York World* correspondent to the editor, May 25, 1862, in *Pittsburgh Daily Post*, May 30, 1862; *OR* 12(1), 568, 572; Strother diary, May 24, 1862, "Personal Recollections of the War," *Harper's New Monthly Magazine* 34 (March 1867): 443.

19. Hotchkiss diary, May 24, 1862, in McDonald, *Make Me a Map*, 48; Hotchkiss to his wife, May 26, 1862, HP; Hotchkiss to Henderson, May 1, 1895, HP.

20. *OR* 51(2), 563.

21. *OR* 51(2), 563; *OR* 12(3), 899–900; *OR* 12(1), 703.

22. Hotchkiss diary, May 24, 1862, in McDonald, *Make Me a Map*, 48; Hotchkiss to his wife, May 26, 1862, HP.

23. Charles Gardner memoir, USAMHI; *OR* 12(1), 576, 587.

24. Harper diary, May 24, 1862, Tulane University; Roger P. Chew to Avirett, January 18, 1867, in Avirett, *Ashby and His Compeers*, 269–70; *OR* 12(1), 760. Jackson's official report leaves the impression that Ashby had been sent on the Chapel Road in the morning, "supported by skirmishers from Taylor's brigade with Chew's battery and two Parrott guns from the Rockbridge artillery." (*OR* 12[1], 703). Historians have picked up on this statement to claim Ashby was first on the road to Middletown and left fairly early in the morning (Freeman, *Lee's Lieutenants*, 1:385). The contemporary evidence clarifies this to show that Ashby did not lead the march to Middletown but was sent to support Hotchkiss, who times the movement "after the position of the enemy had been ascertained by an advance of the cavalry on the Newtown Road"—that is, was well after 11:00 a.m. (Jed Hotchkiss MS journal, HP; Hotchkiss to his wife, May 26, 1862, HP). A member of the Seventh Virginia Cavalry confirms that the regiment "late in the morning was ordered to Middletown" (Wilson diary, May 24, 1862, in Wilson, *Borderland Confederate*, 16–17).

25. Temperature readings, Georgetown, 2:00 p.m., May 24, 1862, NWR; *OR* 12(1), 754; Hotchkiss diary, May 24, 1862, in McDonald, *Make Me a Map*, 48.

26. Gardner memoir, USAMHI.

27. Hotchkiss to his wife, May 26, 1862, HP; Hotchkiss to Henderson, May 1, 1895, HP. Since a member of the Seventh Louisiana Infantry claims his company was sent as skirmishers (Harper diary, May 24, 1862, Tulane University), the Eighth Louisiana Infantry companies (and Wheat's battalion) joined them on the skirmish line.

28. Gardner memoir, USAMHI; *OR* 12(1): 576, 588–89, 760–61.

29. George Neese diary, May 24, 1862,in Neese, *Three Years*, 56; Dabney, *Life and Campaigns*, 371; Gardner memoir, USAMHI.

30. Dixon Miles to Edwin Stanton, May 24, 1862, TSW, NA; Stanton to Miles, May 24, 1862, TSW, NA. No explanation exists for the delay in receiving these dispatches.

31. Geary to Stanton, May 24, 1862, TSW, NA; *OR* 12(3), 224.

32. *OR* 12(3), 222.

33. Hotchkiss Sketchbook, LC; Chew to Avirett, January 18, 1867, in Avirett, *Ashby and His Compeers*, 269–70.

34. *OR* 12(1), 576.

35. Hotchkiss to his wife, May 26, 1862, HP; Hotchkiss to Henderson, May 1, 1895, HP; Neese diary, May 24, 1862, in Neese, *Three Years*, 56–57.

36. *OR* 12(1), 574, 576.

37. Neese diary, in Neese, *Three Years*, 57; *OR* 12(1), 725; Hotchkiss Sketchbook, LC. The cavalry trains routinely moved separately from the infantry wagons. Their presence near Middletown at 3:00 p.m. is a logical point as Banks's massive train had passed the town four hours earlier.

38. Gardner memoir, USAMHI; G. M. Brown to his wife, May 26, 1862, published in *Bangor Daily Whig*, June 2, 1862.

39. *OR* 12(1), 574; Hatch to his father, May 27, 1862, Hatch Papers, LC.

40. *OR* 12(1), 576.

41. Neese diary, in Neese, *Three Years*, 57; Brown to his wife, May 26, 1862, in *Bangor Daily Whig*, June 2, 1862.

42. Gardner memoir, USAMHI.

43. Benedict, *Vermont in the Civil War*, 2:561–62.

44. Charles Blinn diary, May 23, 1862, University of Vermont.

45. Dabney, *Life and Campaigns*, 372; Hotchkiss to his wife, May 26, 1862, HP; Hotchkiss to Henderson, May 1, 1895, HP; Douglas marginalia in his copy of Henderson, *Stonewall Jackson*, 407 (custody of Henry K. Douglas Collection, Antietam National Battlefield Park).

46. Benedict, *Vermont in the Civil War*, 2:562; Brown to his wife, May 26, 1862, in *Bangor Daily Whig*, June 2, 1862; *OR* 12(1), 576, 726.

47. Douglas, *I Rode with Stonewall*, 62; Avirett, *Ashby and His Compeers*, 194.

48. *OR* 51(2), 562–63.

49. *OR* 12(1), 704.

CHAPTER 6

1. Chase to Horace Greeley, May 21, 1862, in Niven, *Chase Papers*, 3:202–203.

2. Chase, "Narrative of Operations," June 26, 1862, in Niven, *Chase Papers*, 4:345; *OR* 12(1), 643; *OR* 12(3), 225–26; Miles to Stanton, May 24, 1862, TSW, NA.

3. *OR* 11(1), 30.

4. *OR* 12(3), 219–20; F. A. Parker to Edwin M. Stanton, May 24, 1862, TSW, NA.

5. *OR* 12(1), 568, 572; Abert to Collis, March 17, 1891, in Collis, *1st Brigade, 1st Division, 3rd Corps*, 12.

6. Ibid.; Handerson, *Yankee in Gray*, 42.

7. Ibid.; *OR* 12(1), 568, 572, 600; Collis to Banks, May 26, 1862, BP; Abert to Collis, March 17, 1891, in Collis, *1st Brigade, 1st Division, 3rd Corps*, 12;.*OR* 12(1), 600.

8. Taylor, *Destruction and Reconstruction*, 55.

9. *OR* 12(3), 899.

10. *OR* 12(1), 567, 614; Gordon, *History of the Second Mass.*, 94–95.

11. Simpson Hamrick to his father, May 11, 1862, Hamrick Papers, Indiana Historical Society, Indianapolis; Shields to Banks, May 8, 1862, BP.

12. Wintz, *Memoirs of Two Rebel Sisters*, 48.

13. *OR* 12(1), 603; Lewis King, "Scraps from My Army Life," 28, Indiana State Library (hereafter cited as ISL); Brown, *Twenty-seventh Indiana*, 132–33; H.C. Cushing to Ned, June 15, 1862, Cushing Papers, University of Tennessee (hereafter cited as CP); Hotchkiss Sketchbook, LC.

14. King, "Scraps from My Army Life," 29, ISL; Chew to Avirett, January 18, 1867,in Avirett, *Ashby and His Compeers*, 270; Brown, *Twenty-seventh Indiana*, 133–34; Cushing to Ned, June 15, 1862, CP.

15. *OR* 12(1), 761; Barton memoir, in Colt, *Defend the Valley*, 143; Poague, *Gunner with Stonewall*, 23; Cushing to Ned, June 15, 1862, CP; Brown, *Twenty-seventh Indiana*, 132, 134–35.

16. Gordon, *History of the Second Mass.*, 95.

17. Neese, *Three Years*, 58; Dwight, *Life and Letters*, 253.

18. *OR* 12(1), 586; Benedict, *Vermont in the Civil War*, 2:555–56.

19. *OR* 12(1), 586; Benedict, *Vermont in the Civil War*, 2:564.

20. Benedict, *Vermont in the Civil War*, 2:563.

21. *OR* 12(1), 595, 615; Cushing to Ned, June 15, 1862, CP; Brown, *Twenty-seventh Indiana*, 188.

22. Cushing to Ned, June 15, 1862, CP; *OR* 12(1), 612; L. D. C. Gaskill to his father, May 29, 1862, published in (Albion, N.Y.) *Orleans American*, June 8, 1862; S.M. Quincy to Mary Jane Quincy, June 1, 1862, Quincy-Wendell-Upham-Holmes Family Papers (hereafter cited as Quincy et al. Papers), LC.

23. Neese, *Three Years*, 58; Williams diary, May 24, 1862, VHS; Dwight, *Life and Letters*, 253; S.M. Quincy to M.J. Quincy, June 1, 1862, Quincy et al. Papers, LC.

24. *OR* 12(1), 726, 761; Avirett, *Ashby and His Compeers*, 195; Hotchkiss Sketchbook, LC.

25. Brown, "Ewell's Division at Front Royal;" Brown memoir, BEP; *OR* 51(2), 562–63; *OR* 12(3), 899. No evidence exists that Ewell marched then halted in the late afternoon of May 24. This would have been the clear result of his receiving the two dispatches half an hour apart (*OR* 51[2], 562–63; *OR* 12[3], 899). Isaac Trimble claimed that the instructions written from Middletown at 4:00 p.m. to head to Winchester (*OR* 51[2], 562–63) were not received at this time because the courier lost his way (Allan, *Jackson's Valley Campaign*, 274n73).

26. Anderson memoir, 36–38, LC.

27. Ibid.; *OR* 12(1), 569, 572, 581–82, 586; Hotchkiss Sketchbook, 40, LC.

28. *OR* 12(1), 899; Handerson, *Yankee in Gray*, 42; Boswell to Jackson, March 31, 1863, HP. Jackson's dispatch to Ewell was headed "On the Road to Newtown." Timed at 5:45 p.m., the dispatch was likely dictated to Dabney close to Cedar Creek. Hotchkiss confirms this in a letter written two days later: "But we could not cross [Cedar Creek] to pursue them, so we could only drive them from their baggage at a distance, and then start at about 6 P.M. with our whole force." (Hotchkiss to his wife, May 26, 1862, HP).

29. Ewell, "Ewell's Account of 1862 Valley Campaign," BEP; Brown, "Ewell's Division at Front Royal," BEP.

30. *OR* 12(1), 735; Hotchkiss to his wife, May 26, 1862, HP.

31. *OR* 12(1), 704.

32. Hotchkiss to Henderson, May 1, 1895, HP; Hotchkiss to his wife, May 26, 1862, HP.

33. Thomas Hodgkins to his mother, May 27, 1862, Civil War Times Illustrated Collection, USAMHI; *OR* 12(1), 601.

34. *OR* 12(1), 761; Neese, *Three Years*, 58; Avirett, *Ashby and His Compeers*, 195–96.

35. S. M. Quincy to M.J. Quincy, June 1, 1862, Quincy et al. Papers, LC; *OR* 12(1), 574.

36. *OR* 12(3), 900.

37. Since he began his march (without orders) from Double Tollgate toward Winchester by 6:15 p.m., Ewell likely received Jackson's 7:00 p.m. message after 9:00 p.m. By this time he would have been within four miles of Winchester. He wisely chose to ignore it.

CHAPTER 7

1. *OR* 12(3), 222, 226; John S. Clark and AndrewG. Curtin to Stanton, May 24, 1862, TSW, NA.

2. Lincoln to Halleck, May 24, 1862, in Basler, *Collected Works*, 5:231.

3. Handerson, *Yankee in Gray*, 42.

4. *OR* 12(1), 549, 615, 621, 704.

5. Ibid.; S. M. Quincy to M.J. Quincy, June 1, 1862, Quincy et al. Papers, LC; King, "Scraps from My Army Life," ISL.

6. *OR* 12(1), 527.

7. *OR* 12(3), 224.

8. *OR* 12(1), 579, 609; Hotchkiss Sketchbook, LC; Gould, *First-Tenth-Twenty-ninth Maine*, 114–17. Colonel Beal and the Tenth Maine historian misidentified the cavalry as comprising Maryland instead of Michigan companies.

9. Boswell to Jackson, March 31, 1863, HP; Ewell, "Ewell's Account of 1862 Valley Campaign," BEP.

10. Ibid.; *OR* 12(1), 579, 609; Hotchkiss Sketchbook, LC; Gould, *First-Tenth-Twenty-ninth Maine*, 115.

11. Watkin Kearns diary, May 24, 1862, FSNMP.

12. *OR* 12(1), 706, 726, 735, 761; Neese, *Three Years*, 59–60; Williams diary, May 24, 1862, Williams Family Papers, VHS. Ashby's cavalry strength is determined from Jackson's report: "I had seen but some 50 of Ashby's cavalry since prior to the pillaging scenes [at Middletown]." (ibid.).

13. Hotchkiss to Henderson, May 1, 1895, HP.

14. Scott, *Fallen Leaves*, 131.

15. Dwight, *Life and Letters*, 253–54; Gordon, *History of the Seond Mass.*, 109; Quint, *Second Massachusetts Infantry*, 85; S.M. Quincy to Mary Jane Quincy, June 1, 1862, Quincy et al. Papers, LC; Hotchkiss diary, in McDonald, *Make Me a Map*, 64; Robert G. Shaw to his mother, May 31, 1862, in Shaw, *Memorial and Letters*, 157; Morse, *Letters*, 59.

16. Dwight, *Life and Letters*, 254; Quint, *Second Massachusetts Infantry*, 85; *OR* 12(1), 615, 621; Glazer, *Federal Cavalry*, 70.

17. Dabney, *Life and Campaigns*, 375; Douglas, *I Rode with Stonewall*, 63–64; *OR* 12(1), 754, 761; William H. Humphreys to his mother, June 14, 1862, WilliamH. Humphreys letters (TS at FSNMP).

18. Dwight, *Life and Letters*, 254; Gordon, *History of the Second Mass.*, 109; JuliusD. Rhodes, "The Shenandoah Valley," *National Tribune*, November 17, 1887; Quint, *The Potomac and the Rapidan*, 153.

19. Brown, *Twenty-Seventh Indiana*, 140.

20. Rhodes, "The Shenandoah Valley," *National Tribune*, November 17, 1887; Glazer, *Federal Cavalry*, 71; Massachusetts quotes in "The 2nd Massachusetts Infantry at the Battle of Winchester, 23–25 May, 1862: The Battle," http:////www.geocities.com/Pentagon/2126/winch.html (accessed 7/5/2007).

21. Dwight, *Life and Letters*, 254; Gordon, *History of the Second Mass.*, 109.

22. Dabney, *Life and Campaigns*, 375; Douglas, *I Rode with Stonewall*, 63–64; *OR* 12(1), 754, 761; William H. Humphreys to his mother, June 14, 1862, Humphreys letters, FSNMP; unknown member of 27th Virginia Infantry to his mother, May 26, 1862, Mary Kelly Smith Papers, North Carolina State Archives; Kearns diary, May 24, 1862, FSNMP.

23. Dwight, *Life and Letters*, 255; Gordon, *History of the Second Mass.*, 109–10; S.M. Quincy to his wife, June 1, 1862, Quincy et al. Papers, LC.

24. Ashby's presence with his cavalry at Bartonsville is not conclusively proven by primary accounts but is inferred by his acknowledged presence on each side of the contested hamlet before and after the skirmish. See Chew to Avirett, January 18, 1867, in Avirett, *Ashby and His Compeers*, 271, and Douglas, *I Rode with Stonewall*, 63–64. If both accounts are accurate, it is still possible that Ashby stayed in Newtown while his cavalry engaged the Union rear guard, then rode down the Valley Pike to join them as they approached Winchester.

25. *OR* 12(1), 735, 743, 751, 761; unknown member of the Twenty-seventh Virginia Infantry to his mother, May 26, 1862, Smith Papers, N.C. State Archives; Kearns diary, May 24, 1862, FSNMP; Barton memoir, in Colt, *Defend the Valley*, 144.

26. *OR* 12(1), 735, 743, 748; Winchester-Frederick County Historical Society, "Captain Kurtz's Account," 46–47 (hereafter cited as "Capt. Kurtz's Account").

27. Ibid.; Dwight, *Life and Letters*, 255; S.M. Quincy to Mary Jane Quincy, June 1, 1862, Quincy et al. Papers, LC. The Union soldiers referred to

the residence as a brick house. A Confederate captain identified it as Mahaney's residence ("Capt. Kurtz's Account," 47).

28. *OR* 12(1), 618; Morse, *Letters*, 60; Scott, *Fallen Leaves*, 131.

29. Gordon, *History of the Second Mass.*, 115; Dwight, *Life and Letters*, 256.

30. *OR* 12(1), 574, 576–77.

31. *OR* 12(1), 528, 549. Banks would fall victim to overestimation one week later and believe that thirty thousand men opposed him, but his May 25 dispatch to Edwin Stanton shows how accurate his earlier estimate was—a pure guess in regard to infantry, given that regiments from only three of the eight Confederate brigades engaged his army on May 24.

32. Hatch to his father, May 27, 1862, Hatch Papers, LC.

33. *OR* 12(1), 528, 549.

34. *OR* 12(1), 578; "Capt. Kurtz's Account," 47.

35. Elzey's brigade was the last one sent to Jackson from the Front Royal–Winchester Pike. According to a member of the Thirty-first Virginia in the brigade, "We marched on that night and encamped within 6 miles of Winchester" (Dayton, *Diary of James Hall*, 59).

36. *OR* 12(1), 623, 704.

37. A Richard Taylor anecdote details a discussion Jackson had with Harman at this time on the Valley Pike, where his wagons supposedly had rolled (Taylor, *Destruction and Reconstruction*, 55–57), but Harman wrote his brother from the other side of the Valley (letter, May 24, 1862, HP). William Allan places the wagons between Nineveh and Middletown on the night of May 24 (Allan diary, William Allan Papers, Southern Historical Collection, University of North Carolina. Harman confirms this the next day (Harman to his brother, May 25, 1862, HP).

38. Douglas, *I Rode with Stonewall*, 64.

39. Ibid.; John Apperson diary, May 24, 1862, Virginia State Library; General Winder reported, "The entire strength of the brigade on going into action was 1,529, rank and file" (*OR* 12[1], 138). Since Winder's report covered May 23–25, his strength estimate may have been for the morning of May 23, and not May 25. The action reports of his regiments for the Battle of Winchester add more evidence to this. For May 25, the following strength reports—totals for officers and men—are given (*OR* 12[1], 744, 746, 752, 756): Second Virginia, 392; Fourth Virginia, 200; Twenty-seventh Virginia, 136; and Thirty-third Virginia, 150; total for four regiments, 878. The Fifth Virginia report did not provide numbers engaged for May 25. Based on the May 3 strength reports (*OR* 12[3], 879), they were the largest of all the Stonewall Brigade regiments at 902 officers and men, but given the 48–80 percent reduction in numbers reported in their sister regiments three weeks later, it is unlikely that the Fifth Virginia suffered a mere 28 percent reduction over that time to muster the 651 officers and men necessary for Winder's strength report to apply to May 25. They likely carried no more than 400–500 officers and men into action that morning, 45–55 percent of what they reported on May 3, 1862.

40. Barton memoir, in Colt, *Defend the Valley*, 145.

41. Brown, "Ewell's Division at Front Royal," BEP.

42. *OR* 12(1), 572.

43. Douglas, *I Rode with Stonewall*, 63. The dispatch no longer exists, but is summarized by Ewell's adjutant, who read the order. See Brown, "Ewell's Division at Front Royal," BEP.

44. *OR* 12(1), 726.

45. Myers, *Comanches*, 52.

CHAPTER 8

1. *OR* 12(1), 549, 594–96, 602–603, 617.

2. *OR* 12(1), 552.

3. *OR* 12(1), 596, 601–605, 623. Geography and roads depicted in "Sketch of the second battle of Winchester, June 13th, 14th, and 15th 1863," Hotchkiss Maps, LC.

4. Winder diary, May 25, 1862, MHS; *OR* 12(1), 736, 738.

5. Howard, *Recollections of a Maryland Staff Officer*, 108–109.

6. Apperson diary, May 25, 1862, Virginia State Library; *OR* 12(3), 736, 744, 746, 748; Kearns diary, May 25, 1862, FSNMP.

7. Williams to his daughter, May 27, 1862, in Quaife, *From the Cannon's Mouth*, 79; *OR* 12(1), 595–96, 616–25.

8. Ibid.

9. *OR* 12(1), 602; Kearns diary, May 25, 1862, FSNMP.

10. Apperson diary, May 25, 1862, Virginia State Library.

11. *OR* 12(1), 746.

12. *OR* 12(1), 604.

13. Gould journal entry, July 14, 1862, *Civil War Journals of John Mead Gould*, 157; Williams to his daughter, August 17, 1862, in Quaife, *From the Cannon's Mouth*, 100.

14. Numerical strength derived from postbattle numbers (537 men) provided by George D. Chapman, plus adding back the 84 casualties reported for the unit. *OR* 12(1), 553, 608; Marvin, *Fifth Connecticut Volunteers*, 101.

15. *OR* 12(1), 613; W. L. Foulk to the editor, May 26, 1862, published in *Pittsburgh Evening Chronicle*, May 28, 1862.

16. *OR* 12(1), 596, 610–11; L. D.C. Gaskill to his parents, May 27, 1862, published in *Orleans American*, June 8, 1862; Charles Pickard to his aunt and friends, May 28, 1862, Charles Pickard letters, MHS.

17. Ewell, "Ewell's Account of 1862 Valley Campaign," BEP; Ewell, "Ewell's Report on First Winchester," original draft, BEP.

18. Kirkpatrick diary, May 24, 1862, FSNMP; Riley diary, May 24, 1862, in Dobbins, *Grandfather's Journal*, 80; Oates, *War between the Union and Confederacy*, 21. Winchester's overnight low temperature estimated from Georgetown readings of 49 degrees at 9:00 p.m., May 24, and 54.5 degrees at 7:00 a.m., May 25 (NWR). The estimate assumes lower temperatures in the Valley than in the District of Columbia, and a further dip in the ten hours that elapsed between the nighttime and morning readings.

19. Kirkland report, *SOR*, 2:669; 21st North Carolina letter, *Raleigh Register*, June 25, 1862; Eli S. Coble reminiscence, North Carolina Office of Archives and History, Raleigh (hereafter cited as NCOAH); *OR* 12(1), 604.

20. R. W. Wharton, "First Battalion (Sharpshooters)," in Clark, *Regiments and Battalions from North Carolina*, 4:15, 227–28. There are two known contemporary references to the numerical strength of the Twenty-first North Carolina. The first comes from a letter written three weeks after the battle by a member of the unit, who tells his parents the regiment engaged "about 300 men" (Augustus A. Clewell to his parents, June 13, 1862, Clewell letters); the second is Colonel Kirkland's report (*SOR*, 2:670), which confirms: "my men numbered 300."

21. Johnson, "Memoir of the First Maryland," 97–98.

22. Hotchkiss Sketchbook, LC; Coble reminiscence, NCOAH; William C. Oates memoir, Alabama Department of Archives and History, Montgomery; Kirkland report, *SOR*, 2:669; Marvin, *Fifth Regiment Connecticut Volunteers*, 101.

23. Coble reminiscence, NCOAH; Foulk to the editor, May 26, 1862, in *Pittsburgh Evening Chronicle*, May 28, 1862; Wise to the editor, May 27, 1862, in *Reading Daily Times*, June 2, 1862; *OR* 12(1), 613.

24. Ibid.; Wharton, "First Battalion," in Clark, *Regiments and Battalions from North Carolina*, 228; Kirkland report, *SOR*, 2:669; 21st North Carolina letter, *Raleigh Register*, June 25, 1862; *OR* 12(1), 608, 610.

25. *OR* 12(1), 608, 613; Gardner Stockman to the editor, May 29, 1862, published in (Waterbury, Conn.) *American*, June 13, 1862.

26. Ibid.; C. H. W. to the editor, May 27, 1862, published in *Windham County* (Conn.) *Transcript*, June 12, 1862; "D." to the editor, June 2, 1862, published in *Litchfield* (Conn.) *Enquirer*, June 12, 1862; Melzer Dutton to his mother, May 27, 1862, Dutton letters, HL.

27. Ibid.; Marvin, *Fifth Connecticut Volunteers*, 102; Coble reminiscence, NCOAH; Wharton, "First Battalion," in Clark, *Regiments and Battalions from North Carolina*, 228; Kirkland report, *SOR*, 2:669–70; 21st North Carolina letter, *Raleigh Register*, June 25, 1862; "Winchester" and "The 21st N.C. Regiment," *Raleigh Standard*, July 2, 1862.

28. *OR* 12(1), 608, 610; Kirkland report, *SOR*, 2:669–70; 21st North Carolina letter, *Raleigh Register*, June 25, 1862; Coble reminiscence, NCOAH; Wharton, "First Battalion," in Clark, *Regiments and Battalions from North Carolina*, 228–29.

29. Johnson, "Memoir of the First Maryland," 98; Ammen, "Maryland Troops in the Confederate Army," 28, USAMHI; Booth, *Personal Reminiscences*, 34; Goldsborough, *Maryland Line*, 55; Johnson, *Maryland and West Virginia*, 74.

30. Williams to his daughter, May 27, 1862, in Quaife, *From the Cannon's Mouth*, 78.

31. *OR* 12(1), 604, 606, 608, 610.

32. Kirkland report, *SOR*, 2:670; Nisbet, *Firing Line*, 86–87; Boyce diary, May 25, 1862, Boyce Papers, LC; R.M.C. Mansfield to his parents, May 27, 1862, published in (Albion, N.Y.) *Orleans Republican*, June 4, 1862; L.D.C. Gaskill to his parents, May 29, 1862, published in *Orleans Republican*, June 8, 1862; *OR* 12(1), 606, 610, 613, 780, 794.

33. *OR* 12(1), 736–37, 744.

34. *OR* 12(1), 736, 755, 758; Dabney, *Life and Campaigns*, 377–78.

35. *OR* 12(1), 764–65; Krick, *Lee's Colonels*, 275.

36. *OR* 12(1), 765, 767, 769.

37. *OR* 12(1), 736.

38. *OR* 12(1), 622; Dwight, *Life and Letters*, 257–58; Shaw to his father, May 26, 1862, in Shaw, *Memorial and Letters*, 154.

39. *OR* 12(1), 736, 761–62, 772; Dwight, *Life and Letters*, 258; Barton memoir, in Colt, *Defend the Valley*, 148.

40. Dwight, *Life and Letters*, 258.

41. Howard, *Recollections of a Maryland Staff Officer*, 110.

CHAPTER 9

1. *OR* 12(1), 704, 726. Although a careful reading of Crutchfield's report fails to specifically implicate Louisiana infantry in the wagon plunder, Jackson complained that "so many of Ashby's command, both cavalry and infantry, forgetful of their high trust . . . deserted their colors, and abandoned themselves to pillage." This excerpt implicates Louisiana infantry that attacked with Ashby's command at Middletown on May 24.

2. Handerson, *Yankee in Gray*, 42; Douglas, *I Rode with Stonewall*, 65.

3. Brown, *Twenty-seventh Indiana*, 144–45 (revealing sketch of Gordon's line on 147); *OR* 12(1), 619, 624.

4. *OR* 12(1), 775; Brown, *Twenty-seventh Indiana*, 145; King, "Scraps from my Army Life," 31, ISL.

5. *OR* 12(1), 772, 775, 777.

6. Williams to his daughter, May 27, 1862, in Quaife, *From the Cannon's Mouth*, 80; *OR* 12(3), 210–11, 237.

7. *OR* 12(1), 604, 779, 794.

8. *OR* 12(1), 726; Brown, "Ewell's Division at Front Royal," and Ewell, "Ewell's Account of 1862 Valley Campaign," BEP.

9. John Kidd Murphy Commission Branch File, M1064, NA; Gray and Ropes, *War Letters*, 42; Brown, *Twenty-seventh Indiana*, 146; King, "Scraps from my Army Life," 31, ISL.

10. Taylor, *Destruction and Reconstruction*, 58; Huffman, *Ups and Downs*, 47; Wren diary, May 25, 1862, RWL.

11. Brown, *Twenty-seventh Indiana*, 146; King, "Scraps from my Army Life," 31, ISL. Taylor reported a loss for May 25 of 15 killed and 90 wounded (see *OR* 12[1], 801). Perhaps as many as 80 of the 105 total losses occurred at the hands of the Twenty-seventh Indiana.

12. Sketch of this "cross lane parallel to V. Turnpike" in Hotchkiss Sketchbook, LC.

13. Brown, *Twenty-seventh Indiana*, 147–48; *OR* 12(1), 619.

14. *OR* 12(1), 619–20, 624, 800–801; Wren diary, May 25, 1862, RWL.

15. Ibid.; Brown, *Twenty-seventh Indiana*, 148–49; King, "Scraps from my Army Life," 31, ISL.

16. *OR* 12(1), 620, 624.

17. Brown, *Twenty-seventh Indiana*, 149.

18. *OR* 12(1), 617, 620, 622, 624–25; Hatch to his father, May 27, 1862, Hatch Papers, LC.

19. In his memoir written more than fifteen years after the battle, General Taylor claimed the cavalry charged his men (Taylor, *Destruction and Reconstruction*, 58), but Union and Confederate accounts—all written within days of the action—confirm that Town did not charge his men against the northern sector of Taylor's line. See *OR* 12(1), 580; Williams to his daughter, May 27, 1862, in Quaife, *From the Cannon's Mouth*, 81; and Wren diary, May 25, 1862, RWL.

20. *OR* 12(1), 602, 801; Leander E. Davis to his wife, June 9, 1862, Davis letters (TS at FSNMP.

21. Worsham, *One of Jackson's Foot Cavalry*, 46; Kelly to Ewell, January 11, 1863, Henry Kelly CSR, NA.

22. Worsham, *One of Jackson's Foot Cavalry*, 46; Kearns diary, May 25, 1862, FSNMP.

23. *OR* 12(1), 736–37.

24. Hotchkiss to his wife, May 26, 1862, HP.

25. Ibid.; *OR* 12(1), 600, 625, 737, 801; McDonald, *Woman's Civil War*, 53–54.

26. *OR* 12(1), 794.

27. Laura Lee diary, May 27, 1862, and Mary Charlton Greenhow Lee diary, May 27, 1862 (TS in HL); Johnson, "Memoir of the First Maryland," 99.

28. Cornelia L. Wilson to her brother, July 22, 1862, Ben Ritter Collection, Winchester, Va.

29. Shaw to his mother, June 6, 1862, in Duncan, *Blue-Eyed Child of Fortune*, 204.

30. Laura Lee diary, May 27, 1862 (TS in HL).

31. *OR* 12(1), 624.

32. Dwight, *Life and Letters*, 259–60.

33. Ibid.; Richard Waldrop to his father, May 26, 1862, Waldrop Papers, University of North Carolina.

34. Wren diary, May 25, 1862, RWL; John Peyton Clark diary, May 26, 1862, HL; Jackson to his wife, May 26, 1862, in Jackson, *Life and Letters*, 265.

35. Hotchkiss to his wife, May 26, 1862, HP; Hotchkiss to Henderson, May 1, 1895, HP.

36. *OR* 12(1), 706.

37. *OR* 12(1), 706, 709–10. Jackson reported that Steuart arrived "[a]bout an hour after the halt of the main body." Since it is unreasonable to assume, given the time necessary to find Steuart and the delays in getting the order issued, that Steuart reached Jackson one hour after Pendleton left Jackson, it is reasonable to conclude that Jackson halted his infantry half an hour after he sent his aide off to find Steuart.

38. Bryant, *History of the Third Wisconsin*, 69.

39. *OR* 12(1), 550–51.

40. *OR* 12(1), 706–707.

41. Banks to Stanton, May 25, 1862, Lincoln Papers, LC.

42. Lincoln to McClellan, May 25, 1862, in Basler, *Collected Works*, 5:236–37.

43. Lincoln did not receive Banks's dispatch until 10:00 p.m. (Banks to Stanton, May 25, 1862, Lincoln Papers, LC).

44. Lincoln to McClellan, May 25, 1862, in Basler, *Collected Works,* 5:235–36.

45. McClellan to Lincoln, May 25, 1862, in Sears, *Civil War Papers,* 276.

46. McClellan to his wife, May 25, 1862, in Sears, *Civil War Papers,* 275.

47. *OR* 12(3), 892–93; officer of the Irish Battalion to his uncle, May 26, 1862, published in (Richmond) *Daily Whig,* June 2, 1862.

EPILOGUE

1. Lee to Jackson, May 28, 1862, Lee's Headquarters Papers, VHS.

2. Davis to his wife, May 30, 1862, in Crist, Dix, and Williams, *Papers of Jefferson Davis,* 8:203.

3. For a completely antithetical opinion, see Gary W. Gallagher, "You Must Either Attack Richmond or Give Up the Job and Come to the Defence of Washington," *The Shenandoah Valley Campaign of 1862* (Chapel Hill: University of North Carolina Press, 2003), 3.

4. Ibid.; *OR* 12(3), 219.

5. These examples are among several detailed in Robert K. Krick's fine essay "The Metamorphosis in General Jackson's Public Image" (see Gallagher, *Shenandoah Valley Campaign of 1862,* 24–42).

6. Michael Burlingame, ed., *Lincoln's Journalist: John Hay's Anonymous Writings for the Press, 1860–1864* (Carbondale: Southern Illinois University Press, 1998), 212, 289, 293, 305.

Bibliography

MANUSCRIPT SOURCES

Alabama Department of Archives and History, Montgomery
    William C. Oates memoir
Antietam National Battlefield Park, Sharpsburg, Md.
    Henry K. Douglas Collection
The Cayuga Museum, Auburn, N.Y.
    John S. Clark Papers
Duke University, William R. Perkins Library, Durham, N.C.
    Boteler Papers
Emory University, Robert W. Woodruff Library, Atlanta (RWL)
    George Wren diary
Fredericksburg-Spotsylvania National Military Park, Fredericksburg, Va. (FSNMP)
    Leander E. Davis letters
    William H. Humphreys letters
    Watkin Kearns diary
    James Kirkpatrick diary
    Jonathan T. Mann letters
    James Thomas diary
    McKim Holliday Wells diary
Handley Library, Winchester, Va. (HL)
    John Peyton Clark diary
    Dutton letters
    Laura Lee diary

Mary Charlton Greenhow Lee diary
Cornelia L. Wilson letter
Indiana State Library, Indianapolis (ISL)
    Hamrick Papers
    Lewis King, "Scraps from My Army Life"
Library of Congress, Washington, D.C. (LC)

Geography and Map Division

Jedediah Hotchkiss Collection of Civil War Maps
Jedediah Hotchkiss Sketchbook

Manuscript Division

John Emerson Anderson memoir
Nathaniel P. Banks Papers
Boyce Papers
Samuel P. Chase Papers
John P. Hatch Papers
Jedediah Hotchkiss Papers
Abraham Lincoln Papers
Quincy-Wendell-Upham-Holmes Family Papers (Quincy et al. Papers)
George Hay Stuart Papers
Maryland Historical Society, Baltimore (MHS)
    Washington Hands memoir
    John R. Kenly Papers
    William H. Murray Papers
    Charles Pickard letters
    John E. H. Post Papers
    Charles Winder diary
Massachusetts Historical Society, Boston
    George Henry Gordon Papers
Mississippi State University, Department of Archives and History
    Wilson Papers
Museum of the Confederacy, Richmond, Va.
    Richard Garnett Court Martial Transcript
National Archives, Washington, D.C. (NA)
    Nathaniel Banks's Intelligence Reports, Record Group 393, entry 223
    James H. Brown Compiled Service Record, M331
    Henry Grueninger Pension Record, RG 94
    Henry Kelly Compiled Service Record, M331
    John Kidd Murphy Commission Branch File, M1064
    Charles Parham letter to Nathaniel Banks, May 23, 1862, RG 94
    Report of hospitalized force at Strasburg, May 24, 1862, RG 393
    Frederick Tarr Pension Record, RG 94
    Telegrams received by the Secretary of War, M473
    Third Wisconsin Regimental Books, RG 94
    U.S. Army Generals' Reports of Civil War Service, Papers of the Adjutant
        General's Office, M1098

National Weather Records Center, Asheville, N.C. (NWR)
    Georgetown, D.C., Weather Journal, 1858–1866
North Carolina Office of Archives and History, Raleigh (NCOAH)
    Augustus A. Clewell letters
    Eli S. Coble reminiscence
    Mary Kelly Smith Papers
Richmond National Battlefield Park
    Joseph M. Ellison letter
Tennessee State Library and Archives, Nashville
    Brown-Ewell Papers (BEP)
Tulane University, Louisiana Historical Association Collection, New Or-
    leans
    W. P. Harper diary
    George P. Ring diary
University of Michigan, William Clements Library, Ann Arbor
    Schoff-Sturtevant Papers
University of North Carolina, Southern Historical Collection, Chapel Hill
    William Allan Papers
    Joseph M. Kern, diary and scrapbook
    Waldrop Papers
University of Tennessee, Knoxville
    Cushing Papers
University of Vermont, Burlington
    Charles Blinn diary
University of Virginia, Charlottesville
    Hotchkiss-McCullough Papers
    E. H. T. Warren Papers
U.S. Army Military History Instiutute, Carlisle Barracks, Pa. (USAMHI)
    Ammen, S. Z. "Maryland Troops in the Confederate Army," vol. 1 (1879),
        Clemens Papers
    Charles Gardner memoir
    Thomas Hodgkins letters
Virginia Historical Society, Richmond (VHS)
    Thomas J. Jackson Papers
    Telegraph book, Robert E. Lee's Headquarters Papers
    Williams Family Papers
Virginia Military Institute, Lexington (VMI)
    Botts Papers
    Fulkerson Papers
Virginia State Library, Richmond
    John Apperson diary
Warren County Historical Society, Front Royal, Va.
    Charles Eckardt diary
Wisconsin State Historical Society, Madison
    Hinkley Papers

NEWSPAPERS

(Waterbury, Conn.) *American*
Baltimore American and Commercial Advertiser
Bangor Daily Whig
Cincinnati Daily Gazette
Cincinnati Daily Times
Columbus Gazette
(Richmond) *Daily Whig*
Frederick (Md.) *Examiner*
Hartford Daily Times
Lexington Gazette
Litchfield (Conn.) *Enquirer*
Lynchburg (Va.) *Daily Republican*
National Tribune
New York Daily Tribune
New York World
Norwalk (Ohio) *Reflector*
Opelousas (La.) *Courier*
(Albion, N.Y.) *Orleans American*
(Albion, N.Y.) *Orleans Republican*
Philadelphia Inquirer
Pittsburgh Daily Post
Pittsburgh Evening Chronicle
Pittsburgh Gazette
Raleigh Register
Raleigh Standard
Reading (Pa.) *Daily Times*
Windham County (Conn.) *Transcript*

BOOKS AND ARTICLES

Allan, William. *Stonewall Jackson's Valley Campaign from November 4, 1861, to June 17, 1862.* 1880. Reprint, New York: W.S. Konecky Associates, Inc., 1995.

Ashby, Thomas A. *The Valley Campaigns: Being the Reminiscences of a Non-Combatant While between the Lines in the Shenandoah Valley during the War between the States.* New York: Neale Publishing Company, 1914.

Avirett, James B. *The Memoirs of General Turner Ashby and His Compeers.* Baltimore: Selby and Dulany, 1867. Reprint, Baltimore: Williams and Wilkins Co., 1914.

Basler, Roy P. ed. *The Collected Works of Abraham Lincoln.* 8 vols. New Brunswick, N.J.: Rutgers University Press, 1953.

Benedict, George C. *Vermont in the Civil War: A History of the Part Taken by the Vermont Soldiers and Sailors in the War for the Union, 1861–5.* 2 vols. Burlington, Vt.: Free Press Association, 1886–88.

Bergeron, Arthur W., Jr. *Guide to Louisiana Confederate Military Units, 1861–1865.* Baton Rouge: Louisiana State University Press, 1989.

Beyer, W. F., and O. F. Keydel, eds. *Deeds of Valor: How America's Civil War Heroes Won the Congressional Medal of Honor*. 1903. Reprint, Stamford, Conn.: Longmeadow Press, 1994.

Booth, George W. *Personal Reminiscences of a Maryland Soldier in the War between the States, 1861–1865*. (1898. Reprint, Gaithersburg, Md.: Butternut Press, Inc., 1986.

Bowman, John S., ed. *The Civil War Almanac*. New York: Bison Books, 1983.

Boyd, Belle. *Belle Boyd in Camp and Prison*. New York: Blelock and Company, 1865.

Brown, Edmund R. *The Twenty-seventh Indiana Volunteer Infantry in the War of the Rebellion: 1861-1865, First Division 12th and 20th Corps*. Monticello, Ind.: n.p., 1899.

Bryant, Edward E. *History of the Third Regiment of Wisconsin Veteran Volunteer Infantry, 1861–1865*. Madison, Wisc.: Veteran Association, 1891.

Buck, Samuel D. *With the Old Confeds: Actual Experiences of a Captain in the Line*. Baltimore: H.E. Houck and Co., 1925.

Buck, William D., ed. *Sad Earth, Sweet Heaven: The Diary of Lucy Rebecca Buck*. Birmingham, Ala.: Cornerstone, 1973.

Burlingame, Michael, ed. *Lincoln's Journalist: John Hay's Anonymous Writings for the Press, 1860–1864*. Carbondale: Southern Illinois University Press, 1998.

Camper, Charles, and J. W. Kirkley. *Historical Record of the First Regiment Maryland Infantry*. Washington, D.C.: Gibson Brothers, 1871.

Clark, Walter, ed. *Histories of the Several Regiments and Battalions from North Carolina in the Great War, 1861–'65: Written by Members of the Respective Commands*. 5 vols. Goldsboro, N.C.: Nash Brothers, 1901.

Cockrell, Thomas D., and Michael B. Ballard, eds. *A Mississippi Rebel in the Army of Northern Virginia: The Civil War Memoirs of Private David Holt*. 1925. Reprint, Baton Rouge: Louisiana State University Press, 1995.

Collis, Charles H. T. *1st Brigade, 1st Division, 3rd Corps*. New York: n.p., 1891.

Colt, Margaretta Barton. *Defend the Valley: A Shenandoah Family in the Civil War*. New York: Orion Books, 1994.

Copeland, R. Morris. *Statement of R. Morris Copeland, Assistant Adjutant General and Major of Volunteers: Discharged from Service August 6, 1862*. Boston: Prentiss and Deland, 1864.

Crist, Linda L., Mary S. Dix, and Kenneth L. Williams, eds. *The Papers of Jefferson Davis*. 8 vols. Baton Rouge: Louisiana State University Press, 1995.

Dabney, Robert Lewis. *Life and Campaigns of Lieutenant-General Thomas J. Jackson (Stonewall Jackson)*. New York: Blelock, 1866.

Daniel, Larry J. *Shiloh: The Battle That Changed the Civil War*. New York: Simon and Schuster, 1997.

Davis, Jefferson. *The Rise and Fall of the Confederate Government*. 2 vols. New York: D. Appleton, 1881.

Dayton, Ruth Woods, ed. *The Diary of a Confederate Soldier: James E. Hall*. Phillipi, W.Va.: n.p., 1961.

Denison, Rev. Frederic. *Sabres and Spurs: The First Regiment Rhode Island Cavalry in the Civil War, 1861–1865*. Central Falls, R.I.: Regimental Veteran Association, 1876.

Dobbins, Austin C. *Grandfather's Journal*. Dayton, Ohio: Morningside House, Inc., 1988.

Donohoe, John C. "Fight at Front Royal." *Southern Historical Society Papers* 24 (1896): 133.

Douglas, Henry K. *I Rode with Stonewall*. Atlanta: Mockingbird Books, 1976.

Dufour, Charles L. *Gentle Tiger: The Gallant Life of Roberdeau Wheat*. 1957. Reprint, Baton Rouge: Louisiana State University Press, 1985.

Duncan, Russell, ed. *Blue-eyed Child of Fortune: The Civil War Letters of Colonel Robert Gould Shaw*. Athens: University of Georgia Press, 1992.

Dwight, Wilder. *Life and Letters of Wilder Dwight, Lieut.-Col. Second Mass. Inf. Vols*. Boston: Ticknor and Fields, 1866.

Eby, Cecil D., ed. *A Virginia Yankee in the Civil War: The Diaries of David Hunter Strother*. 1961. Reprint, Chapel Hill: University of North Carolina Press, 1998.

Ecelbarger, Gary L. *"We Are In for It!": The First Battle of Kernstown, March 23, 1862*. Shippensburg, Pa.: White Mane Publishing Company, Inc., 1997.

Freeman, Douglas S. *Lee's Lieutenants: A Study in Command*. 3 vols. New York: Charles Scribner's Sons, 1942–44.

Gallagher, Gary W., ed. *The Shenandoah Valley Campaign of 1862*. Chapel Hill: University of North Carolina Press, 2003.

Gettysburg Battlefield Commission. *Pennsylvania at Gettysburg: Ceremonies at the Dedication of the Monuments Erected by the Commonwealth of Pennsylvania*. 2 vols. Harrisburg, Pa.: William Stanley Ray State Printers, 1904.

Gettysburg Battlefield Commission. *Pennsylvania at Gettysburg: Ceremonies at the Dedication of the Monuments Erected by the Commonwealth of Pennsylvania*. 2 vols. Harrisburg, Pa.: William Stanley Ray State Printers, 1904.

Gill, John. *Reminiscences of Four Years as a Private Soldier in the Confederate Army, 1861–1865*. Baltimore: Sun Printing Office, 1904.

Glazer, Willard W. *Three Years in the Federal Cavalry*. New York: R.H. Ferguson Co., 1874.

Goldsborough, William W. *The Maryland Line in the Confederate Army, 1861–1865*. Baltimore: Press of Guggenheimer, Weil and Co., 1900.

Gordon, George H. *From Brook Farm to Cedar Mountain: In the War of the Great Rebellion, 1861–62*. Boston: JamesR. Osgood, 1883.

——. *History of the Second Mass. Regiment of Infantry: Third Paper*. Boston: Alfred Mudge and Son, 1875.

Goss, Thomas J. *The War within the Union High Command: Politics and Generalship during the Civil War*. Lawrence: University Press of Kansas, 2003.

Gould, George M., and Laura Stedman. *Life and Letters of Edmund Clarence Stedman*. New York: Moffat Yard and Company, 1910.

Gould, John M. *History of the First-Tenth-Twenty-ninth Maine Regiment.* Portland: Stephen Berry, 1871.

Gray, John C., and John C. Ropes. *War Letters, 1862–1865, of John Chipman Gray and John Codman Ropes.* Boston: Houghton Mifflin, 1927.

Hale, Laura Virginia. *Four Valiant Years in the Lower Shenandoah Valley: 1861–1865.* Front Royal, Va.: Hathaway Publishing, 1968.

Handerson, Henry E. *Yankee in Gray.* Cleveland: Western Reserve University, 1962.

Harsh, Joseph L. *Confederate Tide Rising: Robert E. Lee and the Making of Southern Strategy, 1861–1862.* Kent, Ohio: Kent State University Press, 1998.

Henderson, G. F. R. *Stonewall Jackson and the American Civil War.* 2 vols. 1898. Reprint, New York: Konecky and Konecky, n.d.

Hewett, James B., ed. *Supplement to the Official Records of the Union and Confederate Armies.* 95 vols. Wilmington, N.C.: Broadfoot Publishing Co., 1995–96.

Holabird, S. B. "Army Wagon Transportation." *Journal of the Military Service Institution of the United States* 3 (1882): 100.

Hollandsworth, James G., Jr. *Pretense of Glory: The Life of General Nathaniel P. Banks.* Baton Rouge: Louisiana State University Press, 1998.

Howard, McHenry. *Recollections of a Maryland Staff Officer under Johnston, Jackson, and Lee.* Baltimore: Williams and Winkins, 1914.

Huffman, James. *Ups and Downs of a Confederate Soldier.* New York: William E. Rudge's Sons, 1940.

Jackson, Mary Anna. *Life and Letters of General Thomas J. Jackson (Stonewall Jackson) by His Wife.* New York: Harper and Brothers, 1892.

Johnson, Bradley T. *Maryland and West Virginia.* Vol. 2 of *Confederate Military History,* ed. Clement A. Evans. 13 vols. Atlanta: Confederate Publishing Co. Reprint, Dayton, Ohio: Morningside Bookshop, 1975.

——. "Memoir of the First Maryland Regiment." *Southern Historical Society Papers* 9 (1881): 344–53, 481–88; and 10 (1882): 46–56, 97–109, 145–53, 214–23.

Johnston, Joseph E. *Narrative of Military Operations, Directed during the Late War between the States.* Edited by Frank E. Vandiver. Bloomington: Indiana University Press, 1959.

Jones, J. William. "Down the Valley After 'Stonewall's Quarter-master.'" *Southern Historical Society Papers* 9 (1881): 185–89.

Krick, Robert K. *Lee's Colonels.* Dayton, Ohio: Press of Morningside Bookshop, 1979.

Lee, Richard M. *Mr. Lincoln's City: An Illustrated Guide to the Civil War Sites in Washington.* McLean, Va.: EPM Publications, Inc., 1981.

Lightsey, Ada C. *The Veteran's Story.* Meridian, Miss.: Meridian News, 1899.

Marvin, Edwin E. *The Fifth Regiment Connecticut Volunteers.* Hartford, Conn.: Wiley, Waterman and Eaton, 1880.

McClendon, William. *Recollections of War Times by an Old Veteran While under Stonewall Jackson and Lieutenant General James Longstreet.* Montgomery, Ala.: Paragon Press, 1909.

McDonald, Archie P., ed. *Make Me a Map of the Valley: The Civil War Journal of Stonewall Jackson's Topographer.* 1973. Reprint, Dallas: Southern Methodist University Press, 1989.

McDonald, Cornelia Peake. *A Woman's Civil War: A Diary, with Reminiscences of the War, from March 1862.* Edited by Minrose C. Gwin. Madison: University of Wisconsin Press, 1992.

McKim, Randolph. *A Soldier's Recollections: Leaves from the Diary of a Young Confederate.* New York: Longman's, Green and Co., 1921.

Miers, Earl Schenck, ed. *Lincoln Day by Day: A Chronology, 1809–1865.* 3 vols. Washington, D.C.: Lincoln Sesquicentennial Commission, 1960.

Milano, Anthony J. "Letters from the Harvard Regiments." *Civil War: Magazine of the Civil War Society* 13 (June 1988): 15–73.

Moore, Frank, ed. *Rebellion Record.* 12 vols. New York: D.Van Nostrand, Publishers, 1866.

Morse, Charles F. *Letters Written during the Civil War, 1861–1865.* Boston: n.p., 1898.

Myers, Franklin M. *The Comanches: A History of White's Battalion, Virginia Cavalry, Laurel Brig. Hampton Div., A.N.V., C.S.A.* Baltimore: Kelly, Pier, 1871.

Neese, George M. *Three Years in the Confederate Horse Artillery.* New York: Neale Publishing Co., 1911.

Newton, Steven H. *Joseph E. Johnston and the Defense of Richmond.* Lawrence: University Press of Kansas, 1998.

Nisbet, James Cooper. *Four Years on the Firing Line.* Chattanooga: Imperial Press, n.d.

Niven, John, ed. *The Salmon P. Chase Papers.* 4 vols. Kent, Ohio: Kent State University Press, 1993–97.

O'Ferrall, Charles T. *Forty Years of Active Service.* New York: Neale Publishing Co., 1904.

Oates, William C. *The War between the Union and Confederacy and Its Lost Opportunities.* New York: Neale Publishing Co., 1905.

Ott, Eugene Matthew, Jr., ed. *The Civil War Diary of James J. Kirkpatrick, Sixteenth Mississippi Infantry, C.S.A.* Master's thesis, Texas A&M University, 1984.

Pfanz, Donald C. *Richard S. Ewell: A Soldier's Life.* Chapel Hill: University of North Carolina Press, 1998.

Poague, William Thomas. *Gunner with Stonewall: Reminiscences of William Thomas Poague.* Jackson, Tenn.: McCowat-Mercer Press, 1957.

Quaife, Milo M., ed. *From the Cannon's Mouth: The Civil War Letters of General Alpheus S. Williams.* 1959. Reprint, Lincoln: University of Nebraska Press, 1995.

Quint, Alonzo Hall. *The Potomac and the Rapidan.* Boston: Crosby and Nichols, 1864.

——. *The Record of the Second Massachusetts Infantry, 1861–65.* Boston: Joseph P. Walker, 1867.

Raab, Steven S., ed. *With the 3rd Wisconsin Badgers: The Living Experience of the Civil War through the Journals of Van R. Willard.* Mechanicsburg, Pa.: Stackpole Books, 1999.

Robertson, James I. *Stonewall Jackson: The Man, the Soldier, the Legend.* New York: Macmillan Publishing, 1997.

Ruffner, Kevin C. *Maryland's Blue and Gray: A Border State's Union and Confederate Junior Officer Corps.* Baton Rouge: Louisiana State University Press, 1997.

Scott, Robert Garth, ed. *Fallen Leaves: The Civil War Letters of Major Henry Livermore Abbott.* Kent, Ohio: Kent State University Press, 1991.

"The 2nd Massachusetts Infantry at the Battle of Winchester, 23–25 May, 1862: The Battle." http:////www.geocities.com/Pentagon/2126/winch .html (accessed 5/25/2007).

Sears, Stephen W., ed. *The Civil War Papers of GeorgeB. McClellan: Selected Correspondence, 1860–1865.* New York: Ticknor and Fields, 1989.

——. *To the Gates of Richmond: The Peninsula Campaign.* New York: Ticknor and Fields, 1992.

Shaw, Robert Gould. *Memorial and Letters.* Cambridge: Harvard University Press, 1864.

Smith, Gustavus Woodson. *Confederate War Papers, Fairfax Court House, New Orleans, Seven Pines, Richmond, and North Carolina.* 2nd ed. New York: Atlantic Publishing Co., 1884.

Smith, Robin, and Bill Younghusband. *American Civil War Zouaves.* London: Reed Consumer Books, 1996.

Tanner, Robert G. *Stonewall in the Valley: Thomas J. "Stonewall" Jackson's Shenandoah Valley Campaign, Spring 1862.* Mechanicsburg, Pa.: Stackpole Books, 1996.

Taylor, Richard. *Destruction and Reconstruction: Personal Experiences of the Late War.* New York: D.Appleton, 1879.

Thomas, Clarence. *General Turner Ashby: The Centaur of the South.* Winchester, Va.: Eddy Press Corporation, 1907.

U.S. War Department. *War of the Rebellion: A Compilation of the Official Records of the Union and Confederate Armies.* 128 vols. Washington, D.C.: 1880–1901.

Walker, Charles D. *Biographical Sketches of the Graduates and Eleves of the Virginia Military Institiute Who Fell during the War between the States.* Philadelphia: J.B. Lippincott and Co., 1875.

Warner, Ezra J. *Generals in Blue: Lives of the Union Commanders.* Baton Rouge: Louisiana State University Press, 1964.

——. *Generals in Gray: Lives of the Confederate Commanders.* Baton Rouge: Louisiana State University Press, 1959.

Wayland, John W. *Virginia Valley Records.* Strasburg, Va.: Shenandoah Publishing House, Inc., 1930.

Willard, W. *Three Years in the Federal Cavalry.* New York: R.H. Ferguson Co., 1874.

Wilson, William Lyne. *A Borderland Confederate.* Edited by Festus P. Summers. Pittsburgh: University of Pittsburgh Press, 1962.

Winchester-Frederick County Historical Society. "Captain George W. Kurtz's Account of the Valley Campaign of 1862." In *Diaries, Letters, and Recol-*

lections of the War between the States, 46–47. Winchester, Va.: Winchester-Frederick County Historical Society, 1955.

Wintz, William D., ed. *Civil War Memoirs of Two Rebel Sisters*. Charleston, W.Va.: Pictorial Histories Pub. Co., 1989.

Worsham, John H. *One of Jackson's Foot Cavalry*. New York: Neale Publishing Co., 1912.

Index